MW00830986

THEMATICS

SUNY Series, The Margins of Literature
Mihai I. Spariosu, Editor

THEMATICS

New Approaches

EDITED BY

Claude Bremond,
Joshua Landy,
and
Thomas Pavel

STATE UNIVERSITY OF NEW YORK PRESS

Published by
State University of New York Press, Albany

© 1995 State University of New York

© Published with the permission of Les Editions du Seuil.

All rights reserved.

Printed in the United States of America

No part of this book may be used or reproduced
in any manner whatsoever without written permission
except in the case of brief quotations embodied in
critical articles and reviews.

For information, address State University of New York
Press, State University Plaza, Albany, N.Y. 12246

Production by Diane Ganeles
Marketing by Theresa Abad Swierzowski

Library of Congress Cataloging-in-Publication Data

Thematics : new approaches / edited by Claude Bremond, Joshua Landy
    and Thomas Pavel.
        p.   cm. — (SUNY series, the margins of literature)
    Includes index.
    ISBN 0-7914-2167-8 (alk. paper). — ISBN 0-7914-2168-6 (pbk.   :
    alk. paper)
        1. Arts—Themes, motifs.   I. Bremond, Claude, 1929–   .
II. Landy, Joshua, 1965–   .   III. Pavel, Thomas G., 1941–   .
IV. Series.
NX60.T54   1994   94-72
700—dc20   CIP

10 9 8 7 6 5 4 3 2 1

CONTENTS

INTRODUCTION

Claude Bremond, Joshua Landy, and Thomas Pavel

The history of thematic criticism appears to fall into three distinct phases. In its early, free-flowing and relatively positivistic form, it held a prominent place in literary analysis for quite some time, before being swept away by the various formalisms of the sixties and seventies; now it is making a cautious return to a position of importance. Form, after all, is itself saturated with thematic implications; structures (one might think, with Françoise Escal, of certain *nouveaux romans*) can function as themes: behind an apparently exclusive devotion to design may lie an implicitly thematic reading, even if the theme concerned is merely that of themelessness. Contemporary critics have therefore felt justified in responding as Peter Cryle does to proponents of these methods: "you never stopped using themes, you just did so without knowing it."

Literary study cannot afford to ignore the theme. It is that through which we read and it is that around which one writes, the locus of artistic creation in its effort to balance tradition against originality, the point of intersection between fictional and nonfictional worlds. Nevertheless, thematics is a rather undisciplined discipline, beset with subjectivist strategies and terminological disputes; what is needed—given, as Shlomith Rimmon-Kenan points out, that traditional linguistics cannot be brought to bear here—is a methodological framework, a theory or set of theories to set against those which supplanted it. To this end, three symposia were held on the subject in France, in 1984, 1986 and 1988, with speakers at the first conference being given the following (non-exhaustive) pointers:

Thematic "relief": this term designates the procedures by which some of the statements and concepts in a work are made into themes, while others serve as background to these themes. This is a familiar problem in linguistics and in discourse studies where it is known as the articulation of *theme* and *rheme,*

1

or topic and comment. Thematic designation (the individualization of a theme), focalization (the emphasis on a specific theme) and resonance (the procedures by which rhemes or commentaries are articulated), as well as the relationships of theme to variation and theme to *topos*, all fall within the scope of this particular problematics. The historical dynamics and mutual demarcation of themes and rhemes would also be worth investigating.

The internal structure of thematics includes the constitutive elements of thematics and their syntax. Is a theme a concept (like love, death, the city or the double), a set of concepts (the prodigal son, death and the maiden), or a judgement ("life is a dream," "the course of true love never did run smooth")? What restrictions and what laws of attraction govern the combination of themes? What can be learned from the thematic syntaxes of music and the visual arts? How may manifest and implicit themes be told apart? Could there be a pathology of the theme, a study of thematic obsessions and of the connections between theme and fantasy? What about meta-themes, which thematize literary technique itself?

Textual organization and thematic groundwork. Do certain types of narrative structure impose specific restrictions on the distribution of themes? Or perhaps the other way around? What is the status of the motif, that provisional synthesis between narrative oversimplicity and thematic investment? May affinities be detected between thematic choices and the semantics of fictional worlds, between discursive categories (such as tense, mood, voice, person and perspective) and families of themes, between thematics and genre theory?

Thematics and the act of reading. In the light of recent studies on reading and reception, is there such a thing as thematic attention, or for that matter thematic readers, conditioned by the ambient culture and using, to find their way in the text, decoding strategies which remain to be codified?

Thematics and cultural history. Over and above thematic conventions, can relationships be drawn between themes and specific historical periods—given the fact that the former often seem to recur in more than one culture or period? How is one to describe the rise, expansion and fall of themes—whether they be prophetic, present or vestigial—or thematic cycles, or again the periodic return of manifest and implicit themes? Is there room for a sociology of themes, which would define their role in the social circulation of texts? How may the relationship between literary thematics and, say, moral, religious or scientific thought be articulated?

Empirical research. How do the recognition, retention and integration of themes operate? What is the role of these operations in the understanding of literary texts? Can we establish links with the technology of thematics, the analysis of content and documentary languages?

This manifesto, together with papers from the first symposium, was originally published in *Poétique* 64 (1985); some of these pieces, and others from the second and third symposia—printed, respectively, in *Communications* 47 (1988) and *Strumenti Critici* 60 (1989)—are reproduced here. All were delivered in French; those which were initially written in English we present in their original form, the rest in translation. Other English-language versions, including Claude Bremond's "Concept and Theme," may be found in Werner Sollors' 1993 collection, *The Return of Thematic Criticism*. We are happy to present an article by Sollors written especially for this volume.

The publication of Sollors' anthology attests to the resurgence of the theme, to its growing prestige as a critical concept; but its definition still remains elusive, its anarchic proliferation difficult to limit. While conceding the subjective nature of thematization, Menachem Brinker manages at least to determine its source: the theme we isolate depends on our particular aims and needs, whether we are in search of authorial intentions, readerly responses or our own pet subjects. Brinker defines theme as the principle of a possible grouping of texts, literary or non-literary, various such groupings being possible in each case. There are also limits to the arbitrariness involved, as to some extent reception is conditioned by a system of shared beliefs; Brinker appends the recommendation—although this carries its own share of subjectivity—that each theme should unify a substantial or significant set of components.

As if to illustrate this approach, Werner Sollors' analysis focuses upon a specific motif which allows several mid-nineteenth to mid-twentieth century texts to be gathered together. Sollors' diachronic examination of these texts, tracing the history of their common motif from emergence to disappearance, appears to confirm Brinker's suspicion that thematic material tends to come from without: the "bluish tinge in the half-moons" derives from non-literary texts and enters literature as the result of a shift in ideology. And his synchronic study, producing various families among the works according to which features they hold or lack, points toward Jean-Marie Schaeffer's claim (shared, incidentally, by Georges Roque) that no single variation can ever exhaust a theme.

In a formulation akin to that of Brinker, Schaeffer defines theme as a construct enabling links to be drawn between textual segments (though not whole texts) which exemplify a given theme in a similar (if not equivalent) way. Locating two major themes exemplified by the Faust subject—the damnation of an arrogant man and the salvation of a penitent—and focusing on the former, Schaeffer goes on to demonstrate the extent to which generic factors are involved in shaping textual segments, leading to disparities between two exemplifications of one and the same theme, and thus to difficulties in its isolation.

In a similar vein, Thomas Pavel describes how such generic considerations inflect the "thematic universe" of Racinian tragedy. Here, the progressive endeavor to separate the tragic mode from the epic leads to a certain quality of stasis, an emphasis on speech over movement. This also explains Racine's thematic focus: action having effectively been outlawed from the stage, his field of inquiry finds itself considerably constricted, and he innovates in narrating the birth of language.

If Pavel uses the term "thematic universe" it is because, as he and Claude Bremond argue in their concluding article, theme is extremely hard to pin down. Theme may be defined as the axis on which a *referential attention* meets the "aboutness" of a text; but how is one, from the meagre and misleading clues one is given, to determine this aboutness every time? And at what level does the referential attention operate? Does it focus upon material or design, on an age-old (possibly pre-literary) theme or on its treatment by a specific variant? Bremond and Pavel concede, with Brinker, that much depends on the goals and systems of the individual interpreter.

Refusing to be vanquished by the protean theme, Shlomith Rimmon-Kenan and Lubomír Doležel attempt to contain its endless multiplication, to diminish still further the element of subjectivity. For Doležel, each thematization may well be a construct, but each is also regulated by functional pragmatics; for both, there is a primary subject—though there may be minor themes as well (Rimmon-Kenan), and although different themes may present themselves at varying levels of a text (Doležel)—akin to the Jakobsonian *dominant*. Thematization, in this sense, means the selection of a single component around which to structure the work, or indeed the world: theme, for Doležel, is something that applies to all of human activity, a kind of experiential constant; and just as each action has its "mode," determined by the predominant type of motivation (instinct, passion, reason), so each text must have its theme. The theme is thus the top term in a hierarchy of thematic groupings, a "high-order label"—to use Rimmon-Kenan's terminology—possibly homologous to the principal formal aspect of the text. In Doležel's "structural thematics" (where thematics is defined as the extensional semantics of literary texts), themes—semantically invariant components of the structure as a whole—are formed from clusters of recurring motifs and, in turn, collect into *thematic fields*.

Not all thematicians seek such unity amid diversity, however: some prefer to valorize *dis*continuities. When Georges Roque and Cesare Segre do so, it is by affirming the primacy of *motif* over theme. For Segre, the motif (which, like the musical theme, is the smallest possible thematic unit) provides a royal road to the collective unconscious, indicating ways in which experience is conceptualized and subsequently verbalized. The most revealing analyses, then, rather than merely linking texts with features in common, are those which focus on *differences* in the way these features are arranged—the *plot*, as opposed to the *fabula*—privileging the syntagmatic over the paradigmatic. The exhaustiveness of a Thompson, argues Segre, is preferable to the universality of a Propp.

Roque's investigation centers on attempts by various modern movements, in part via a revalorization of the motif, to free the visual arts from their subservience to written forms. Avant-garde artists refuse to start from a theme or to let one dominate their work; theme becomes as much of a construct for the creator as it is for the viewer. The locus of aboutness—now frequently a self-referential aboutness, raising questions about the artistic process in its entirety—is henceforth the motif.

While visual art may seek to divest itself of meaning, however, music is often engaged in the quest for one. Typically, explains Françoise Escal, the theme of a musical piece has less in common with that of a literary text than with that of a linguistic utterance: explicit and immanent, it needs no interpretation, let alone construction. And quite unlike the literary theme, it is specific to a single work (or series); indeed, this fact is partly responsible for an event in music that might be termed the birth of the author. The language of music is not reducible to words, but the temptation remains, a temptation "to rival natural language," to describe, to tell, to endow the musical signifier with signifieds and even referents. This desire reaches its peak in the nineteenth century, as composers seek the status of apostles and music is thus *required* to communicate; the leitmotiv and musical anagram may be seen as symptoms of this general trend.

To a certain extent, this trend carries through to recent developments in composition, in particular to the "centripetal" attitude Jean-Yves Bosseur describes. Certain composers, like Kagel, Schnebel and Stockhausen, attempt to extend thematics beyond the relationships between sounds, so as to involve the musical operation in its entirety. Like the melodic theme, this new theme (or rather *thematics,* as what we have here is more of an inquiry than a concept) is a unifying and generative principle, ensuring coherence and engendering a specific process of play, a process with its own inner logic. Unlike the melodic theme, however, this "thematics of the acoustic act" changes in essence from one piece to the next. The "centrifugal" tendency, as instanced by the Fluxus group and John Cage, rejects even such a transitory form of control: all that remains is a "thematics of ambiguity and of paradox." Radically indeterminate and resiliently open-ended, this origin with no telos— not even the process is set up as a goal any more—takes music beyond aesthetics and turns it into an art of life.

This compositional style bears a close resemblance to Gaston Bachelard's phenomenological method-without-a-method, his structure which varies from one moment to the next, constantly requiring reinvention around particular images. Seeking a path beyond such nebulous individualism—one shared by

Georges Poulet, and denounced by Claude Bremond in "Concept and Theme"—and a way to introduce some continuity into the discontinuity, Peter Cryle proposes to set a Gadamerian philosophical hermeneutics against the theories of the semioticians and formalists who, when they displaced the phenomenologists, were able to do so without a fight. Gadamer replaces free play with a relatively controlled game, turning an indeterminate *I* into a somewhat stable *we;* theme is no longer a message for my reception, but now the object of our understanding.

Whether this can provide the method thematics so badly needs, one which acknowledges all the complexities of thematization without letting them tear it asunder, remains as yet to be seen. Meanwhile, such variations have at least had the merit of turning thematics back into a theme.

Contributions to the present volume were selected by Claude Bremond and edited by Thomas Pavel, the final preparation of the manuscripts being undertaken by Joshua Landy. Joshua Landy also translated all of the French pieces, with Thomas Pavel reviewing the translation.

The editors would like to thank Mihai Spariosu, editor of the Margins of Literature series, for his enthusiasm and unstinting encouragement; Carola Sautter, for her patience and helpful advice; Werner Sollors, for his insightful comments; Princeton University, for its welcome financial support; and Seuil, for their generous cooperation.

Part I

REASSESSING THEMATICS

WHAT IS THEME AND HOW DO WE GET AT IT?

Shlomith Rimmon-Kenan

Theme, as everyone knows, is what the literary work is about. But how far does this knowledge take us? What *is* a literary work about? And what do we mean by 'about?' Is *Madame Bovary* about Emma's relations with Charles, Léon, and Rodolphe—specific events and participants which Beardsley calls 'subjects' (402)? Or is it about, say, the fragility of love—a more general concept under which the specific elements can be unified, a concept which Beardsley calls 'theme' (403)? Or—yet another possibility—does *Madame Bovary* make a statement about the world, such as 'romantic ideas are inadequate for everyday life,' a statement which Beardsley labels 'thesis' (404)? Clearly, there is no need to accept Beardsley's terms—subject, theme, thesis—in order to see the different kinds of 'aboutness' emerging from them. But even within the same category, criteria for 'aboutness' are not forthcoming. Is *Madame Bovary* about the fragility of love, about enslavement to money, about the 'moeurs de province,' or about all these together?[1]—and if about all, how are the different themes related to each other? Is one 'major' and the others 'minor?' Does one subsume the others, or do they unite in a higher level of generality? It is to the question of what a theme is and how it can be identified that I intend to devote this preliminary study.

1. The linguistic connection: a limited contribution

In the naive hope of a 'scientific' answer, or at least a 'scientific' hypothesis, I have done what theorists of literature do all too often, i.e. turned to linguistics for help. The temptation in this case arises not only from the fact that the term 'theme' has been used in linguistics ever since the Prague school but also from its being one half of a pair—'theme' and 'rheme'—which, at least *prima facie*, seems similar to Beardsley's 'theme' and 'thesis.' So I plunged into linguistic texts, and I must admit that I have come away disappointed. The relevance of these studies to the formation of a systematic theory of theme in literature seems very limited to me. The enumeration of these limitations in the first part of the present paper is partly a sign of my longstanding jealousy of scientists who enjoy the privilege of reporting negative results, and partly an expression of hope that an understanding of the inapplicability may shed some light on the specific nature of theme in literature.

Of the two terms 'theme' and 'rheme' (Mathesius, Firbas) or their Anglo-American equivalents 'topic' and 'comment' (Keenan-Ochs and Schieffelin, Van Dijk, Reinhart), the first designates what the sentence or discourse is about, the second the information supplied about it. Thus in 'The boy went to school,' 'the boy' is theme or topic, i.e., the thing about which something is asserted, and 'went to school' is rheme or comment, denoting the thing said about the boy.

Most linguistic studies deal with sentence topics, but there have been some recent attempts to discuss discourse topics. Unfortunately, the study of sentence topics is well developed but not very relevant to literature, whereas the study of discourse topics may prove more relevant to literature but is as yet minimally developed. Let me start with the former.

A sentence topic must correspond to an expression in the sentence, and consequently linguists set themselves the task of formulating criteria for defining the topic expression. Reinhart (4–5) conveniently surveys the main approaches to this problem, and I shall reproduce her summary, ignoring the advantages and disadvantages of each approach within linguistics and commenting only on their shortcomings for the discussion of theme in literature.

I) Definitions in terms of linguistic structures

Linear order, syntactic function, and intonation have all been said to determine theme (topic). The topic, some argue, is the first expression or set of expressions in the sentence (Halliday); the topic, others suggest, is the subject of the sentence, generally agreed on as the unmarked case (see e.g., Susumu Kuno and the Prague School); the topic, a third group maintain, is the non-stressed expression in the sentence (Chomsky, Jackendoff, Taglicht).

Attempts to apply such definitions to theme in literature are likely to be hampered by a major difference between the uses of the term in linguistics and in literary studies. A topic in linguistics is conceived of as a component, an expression, within the larger unit of the sentence. A theme in literature is neither a component nor an expression, nor is it 'within,' and the larger unit to which it relates is not a sentence. A theme is not a component: there is no element in a literary work that can be called its theme, and no specific aspects are in charge of theme-formation. A theme is not an expression: although the theme is sometimes formulated explicitly, more usually it emerges implicitly, without corresponding to any specific expression in the text. An explicit formulation may, in fact, often serve as a cover-up for a more important but latent theme. Thus, the mention of 'cynicism' as a key word in Conrad's *Under Western Eyes* deliberately diverts the reader's attention from the uncanny element glimpsed through such recurrent motifs as phantoms, eyes, and black and white (Kermode). A theme is not within: it is not a segment within the text-continuum but a construct put together from discontinuous elements in the text. And lastly, the larger unit to which a theme in literature relates is not a sentence but the text as a whole, and the text is more than the sum total of its sentences.

If a theme is not a component within the text-continuum, it is clear why it cannot be defined in terms of linear order or of syntactic function. Intonation is in any case beside the point for non-spoken texts, and even a figurative use of the marked/unmarked distinction will not do, as the above example from Conrad shows.

II) Definitions in terms of the speaker's intentions and interests

For the supporters of this approach, the topic represents the center, or focus, of the speaker's attention (Schachter, Garcia)—although for others, confusingly enough, the same vague quality characterizes precisely the comment, or rheme, rather than the topic, or theme.

Definitions in these terms are difficult to apply to literature both because of the absence of criteria for 'center or focus of the speaker's attention' and because a literary work differs from a spoken utterance in encoding the *situation d'énonciation* within itself and rendering problematic any independent access to the speaker's intentions. For the most part, these intentions have to be inferred from the work, and if the definition of theme is made to depend on them, the procedure becomes circular.

III) Definitions in terms of information-status

The topic (or theme) is defined as 'old information' whereas the comment (or rheme) is 'new information.' Correlated with 'old information' are such terms as 'given,' 'assumed,' 'shared,' 'recoverable,' 'predictable,' 'background'—all relating the sentence under consideration to previous discourse (see Prince for a taxonomy of 'given-new' information). Since a literary work is, to some extent at least, its own context, it is hard to see what previous discourse it should be related to for the purpose of distinguishing 'theme' from 'rheme.' It is true that in a sense all themes can be labelled 'old information' because they depend on well-established codes—on the *déjà vu, lu, vécu*—for their formation, but the same is true of everything else in a literary work. If the status of 'old information' means being code-dependent and if this is taken as a sufficient definition of themehood, then everything in literature is a theme, and the definition fails to define. This is not to say that the given/new distinction is irrelevant to all literary analysis. On the contrary, it may be crucial to the discussion of the implicit reading-contract or of some aspects of style. It is only its relevance to the identification of theme that I am questioning here.

IV) Definitions in terms of 'aboutness'

The topic is conceived of as the expression whose referent the sentence is about (Kuno, Reinhart), and criteria for 'aboutness' are sought. The notion of 'semantic aboutness,' developed by philosophers like Goodman, seems problematic for the linguists, because it requires an independence of what the sentence is about from its various equivalent formulations, whereas according to the linguists different formulations may have different topics. This notion is therefore replaced by that of 'pragmatic aboutness' which Reinhart describes with the help of a library catalogue metaphor, topics corresponding to organization by subject (24). Although the specific formalization of the procedure as put forward by Reinhart would need modification if it were to apply to literature, the idea itself is highly suggestive. The main snag, however, is that a catalogue-like identification of themes in a literary text would tend to include elements which linguists relegate to the status of 'rheme' (or 'comment'). To take 'The boy went to school' again: while linguists unambiguously classify 'boy' as 'topic' (or 'theme'), students of literature might wish to open an entry 'going to school' which would constitute a part of the theme of education they expect to find in the text under consideration.

As we have seen, none of the above definitions is easily applicable to the way 'theme' is usually understood in literature. One could, perhaps, stipulate a narrower or more specific usage of the term, i.e. more in accordance with linguistic usage, but this would have the disadvantage of being counter-intuitive.

So far I have discussed only sentence topics. A few words should now be said on the notion of *discourse topic*, recently advocated by Keenan-Ochs, Van Dijk and Giora, among others. One advantage of this notion is that it designates topics with respect to units larger than the sentence and these can, by definition, be more abstract or more general than specific expressions figuring within a given sentence (Van Dijk 19, Reinhart 2).

Furthermore, some formulations of the differences between sentence topic and discourse topic sound promisingly akin to my own distinctions between 'theme' in linguistics and theme in literature. Using the notion of 'discourse topic' to define 'coherence,' Giora (1–2) sees the latter as supra-linear, in contradistinction to 'cohesion' which she considers a linear relation, relying on the notion of sentence topic. Without going into the details of her discussion, I would like to emphasize the similarity between what she says about discourse topic and my own claim that theme in literature is not a component within the text-continuum but a construct derived from discontinuous (i.e. non-linear) elements in the text. Later Giora argues that "In order for a text segment to be coherent it is not enough for it to be interpretable as being about a Noun Phrase as its discourse topic. Its range of predicates, too, has to be subsumable under the discourse topic" (20). This, I believe, is not a far cry from my own feeling that an attempt to model a definition of themes in literature on the concept of a metaphorical subject-catalogue will have to include not only those elements that linguists consider themes (or topics) but also those that they classify as rhemes (or comments).

One is led to hope that the study of discourse topics will eventually be able to contribute significantly to our understanding of the nature and formation of themes in literature, but this new field is not yet sufficiently developed for this purpose. One major drawback is the still widespread conception of discourse as a combination of sentences and the resultant attempt to anchor the discourse topic in the topics of the individual sentences—a requirement which (in my view) does not apply to the formation of theme in literature. Thus Van Dijk: "The obvious road to take is to make use of the formal criterion that for a sequence to have a topic, each sentence (or its underlying propositions) must 'satisfy' the topic directly or indirectly" (138). It is this limitation that Giora wishes to overcome, arguing that "the notion of discourse topic is independent of the notion of sentence topic" (20). Unfortunately, she finds herself incapable at this stage of proposing any formal procedures for deriving the discourse topic of a given textual segment (18).[2] While awaiting further developments in discourse analysis, the literary theoretician is free to explore other approaches to the subject.

2) Alternative suggestions

Turning from linguistics to literary criticism, I shall now examine the possibility of deriving some sort of theory from traditional discussions of theme. The suggestions hazarded in this section have the advantage of being close to the informal experience of reading and of talking about themes, but they are fraught with difficulties which I shall mention but cannot at this stage overcome.

a) Theme as a high-order label

I have said above that theme is a construct (a conceptual construct, to be precise), put together from discontinuous elements in the text. This 'putting together' or reconstruction is the (not necessarily conscious) work of the reader, and it consists of three closely related activities: linking, generalizing, and labelling. Items are first linked in an elementary pattern or low-order unifying category on the basis of some recurrence, similarity, contrast or implication discernible among them. The labels expressing the common denominator are similar to Reinhart's 'subject-catalogue,' but they integrate heterogeneous elements which also need not function as linguistic topics. The labelled categories are then linked to other categories of the same order, on the basis of the same cohesive principles, resulting in either a more generalized label or an increase in the integrative power of the original one. Themes are labels of the highest order, standing (as it were) at the top of a tree-like hierarchical structure. A similar tree-like construction can be used to describe the bringing together of various themes under one major or governing theme.

Let me illustrate this procedure by a partial analysis of the formation of a theme in Flaubert's *Éducation sentimentale*. Frédéric, who is in love with Madame Arnoux, is convinced that he has lost any chance he may have had with her when Arnoux designates him to his wife as Rosanette's lover. At the racetrack, Frédéric sees Madame Arnoux in her carriage and is again convinced that he has missed a crucial opportunity because of a trivial and lighthearted relationship. Meeting Madame Arnoux in the street, Frédéric finds only a few banal words to say to her, and she is no less taciturn. The first kiss between the two illicit lovers is interrupted by Rosannette who takes Frédéric back home; and the last opportunity of consummating their love is renounced by Frédéric out of the fear of desecrating his ideal—these and other similar events are likely to be linked by the reader and generalized under some such label as 'missed opportunities' or 'wasted potential' which is taken to characterize Frédéric's relationship with Madame Arnoux. Nor is the label limited to this single relationship. The wasted potential with Louise reaches an ironic climax when, repelled by his heartless relationship with Madame Dambreuse, Frédéric attempts to regain his long-lost purity by joining Louise—only to find her getting married to his friend and double, Deslauriers. Equally wasted is the relationship with Rosanette, as the death of their baby clearly symbolizes. 'Missed opportunities' thus becomes a label of a higher order of generality, unifying not only the various stages in Frédéric's relations with Madame Arnoux but also his relations with other women and probably with people in general.

But the process of integration does not stop here. 'Missed opportunities' characterizes not only the human relationships in this novel but also the political scene, the revolution of 1848 which aroused so many hopes only to shatter them subsequently. Various details about the revolution can be gathered together under a common label and this label's identity with or similarity to the one abstracted from the interpersonal relationships will then be discerned, endowing the label with an even greater integrative power. The two types of missed opportunity—the personal and the political—are conjoined not only in the process of reading and theme-formation but also in a specific scene in the novel itself. When, utterly devastated by Madame Arnoux's failure to come to the long-expected meeting, Frédéric desecrates his great love by sleeping with Rosanette in the hotel room he had religiously prepared for Madame Arnoux, the two inauthentic lovers watch from the window the revolution turned sour.

I should perhaps add, to complete this incomplete discussion, that the theme of missed opportunity emerges not only from the main nodes of the narrative but also from marginal or seemingly marginal scenes. In their youth, Frédéric and Deslauriers go to a brothel, dressed like gentlemen-lovers and holding flowers in their hands. The mixture of fear, guilt and pleasure upon seeing all the women at his disposal makes Frédéric turn pale with excitement. The girls laugh at his embarrassment and Frédéric runs away without experiencing any of the pleasures he anticipated. As in the relations with Madame Arnoux, as in the 1848 revolution, here too the immensity of the passion chokes the execution. This scene is hinted at in the beginning of the novel but only narrated at the end, thus framing the work and becoming a *mise en abyme* of the theme of missed opportunities.

The foregoing description of theme as a high-order label is not unproblematic. To begin with, linking, generalizing and labelling are by no means specific to theme-formation. Bremond shows them in operation in his analysis of the *histoire;* I myself have suggested their relevance to the discussion of character; and Hrushovski *(passim)* and Barthes, each in their own way, argue for their centrality to all reading and sense-making. Another problem is the generous dose of subjectivity which the process of labelling inevitably entails. There are many possibilities for grouping elements together and many ways of labelling the unifying categories. While this ensures the openness of theme-formation—which is all to the good—it also reduces the objectivity and uniformity which many require of a scientific (or quasi-scientific) theory.

b) Theme as a global signified homologous to various formal aspects

Like the previous suggestion, this tentative account conceives of theme as a unifying, integrative principle, only the direction of the integration is different. Instead of starting with low-order categories and following their inclusion under labels of higher generality, this approach starts with macrostructures and describes their integration with one another by means of some principle of correspondence or some recurrent feature. On this view, theme— or at least the governing theme—is the global signified, homologous to the common structural denominator emerging from all (or most) formal aspects of the literary work. Although I believe this to apply to both poetry and narrative fiction, my examples will be drawn from the latter.

In Tolstoy's "The Death of Ivan Illych," the three main categories of narrative discourse—time, focalization and narration—are structured in a similar way. Even a cursory perusal of the novella shows analepsis to be the most prominent feature of its temporal organization, in terms of order. With Ivan Illych's death opening and closing the narrative, the bulk of the novella is an analeptic account of his life. Further examination reveals that early in the text-continuum the analepses tend to be filtered through Ivan's friends, often triggered by some object in the dead man's apartment, but as the novella progresses they more and more take the form of Ivan's own memories. An analysis of duration yields an inverse proportion between story-time and its rendering in the text. While the account of Ivan Illych's healthy life is accelerated in the form of a summary (forty-five years in sixteen pages) interspersed with ellipses ("after seven years of service"), the narration of his illness and death is decelerated (a few months in thirty-six pages) and abounds in scenes.

Moving from time to narration and focalization, we notice that the narrative voice is extradiegetic-heterodiegetic throughout, but that the focalization changes. In the early stages the narrator is also the focalizer, preserving an ironic distance between himself and Ivan Illych. As the novella progresses, however, the dominant focalizer becomes Ivan Illych himself—a switch which corresponds to the increase in interior monologues and dialogues.

Framing a life-story by death and expanding the account of the illness by shifting from summaries to scenes are ways of granting death precedence over life. Moving from externally-triggered analepses to memories, shifting from external to internal focalization[3] and switching from dialogues to monologues (or to dialogues between two inner voices) are all ways of increasing our penetration into the character's consciousness. Only a slight reformulation is required to turn the combination of these formal aspects into a statement of the governing theme: "The Death of Ivan Illych" is about the life-giving, because insight-promoting, power of death. "Death is finished," says Ivan Illych paradoxically, at the end of his death-like life and the beginning of his life-like death.

To view theme in this way is to anchor it in structure—which I find appealing—but also to raise the problem of the inevitable leap between structural description and the formulation of its correlate in terms of meaning. Another problem, at least for some contemporary theoreticians, is the poetics of unity that such a view presupposes. Since deconstruction, unity has fallen into disrepute, and any discussion of theme as a unifying principle is likely to be seen as suspect. The situation is perhaps even more extreme: for deconstructionists, one might be tempted to say, any discussion of theme (whether in terms of unity or not) is suspect because logocentric. However, it seems to me that deconstructionist practice (as distinct from its theoretical tenets), especially in the United States, often falls into the 'trap' of suggesting a theme—be it only the theme of absence or of the impossibility of a stable meaning.

Even non-deconstructionists may find my concept of correspondence too demanding, and indeed it does bear attenuation. Instead of viewing theme as the homologue of the common structural denominator emerging from all (or most) aspects of the literary work—which it sometimes, but not always, is—one may think of it as homologous to the predominant structural aspect of the work under consideration. Thus, if the multiplication of analogous narrative levels is the predominant structural principle in Nabokov's *The Real Life of Sebastian Knight,* its corresponding theme may be the "unquenchable," "unattainable" nature of the "hell of mirrors" which we call reality (the expressions in quotes are from Nabokov's non-fiction); and if narrative ambiguity is the governing structural principle of Henry James's *The Turn of the Screw,* its thematic correlate may be the uncertainty of human knowledge. Note, however, the 'ifs' and 'maybes' in the previous sentence, for not only does the problem of the leap remain in this attenuated suggestion, but an additional problem arises, namely the absence of objective criteria for determining predominance.

It should be obvious from the foregoing discussion that work remains to be done on the question of what a theme is and how we get at it. Far from offering satisfactory answers, my contribution should be regarded as no more than a preliminary exploration, a tentative example of the theme of beginning.[4]

Works Cited

Barthes, Roland. *S/Z*. Paris: Seuil, 1970.

Beardsley, Monroe C. *Aesthetics*. New York: Harcourt, Brace and World, 1958.

Bremond, Claude. "La logique des possibles narratifs." *Communications* 8 (1966): 60–76.

——. *Logique du récit*. Paris: Seuil, 1972.

Chomsky, Noam. "Deep Structure, Surface Structure and Semantic Interpretation." *Semantics*. Ed. D. Steinberg and R. Jakobovits. London: Cambridge UP, 1971. 183–216.

Firbas, Jan. "Non-Thematic Subjects in Contemporary English." *Travaux Linguistiques de Prague* 2 (1966): 239–256.

——. "On the Concept of Communicative Dynamism in the Theory of Functional Sentence Perspective." *Sbornik Praci Filosoficke Fakulty, Brnenske University A* 19 (1971): 135–144.

——. "On Defining the Theme in Functional Sentence Analysis." *Travaux Linguistiques de Prague* 1 (1964): 367–380.

——. "On the Thematic and Non-Thematic Section of the Sentence." *Style and Text*. Ed. Hakan Ringbom. Stockholm: Skriptor, 1975. 314–334.

Garcia, Erica C. *The Role of Theory in Linguistic Analysis: The Spanish Pronoun System*. New York: American Elsevier, 1975.

Genette, Gérard. *Figures III*. Paris: Seuil, 1972.

Giora, Rachel. "Notes towards a Theory of Text Coherence." *Poetics Today* 6:4 (1985): 699–715.

Goodman, Nelson. "About." *Problems and Projects*. Indianapolis and New York: Bobbs-Merrill, 1972. 246–272.

Halliday, M. A. K. "Notes on Transitivity and Theme in English." *Journal of Linguistics* 3 (1967): 199–244.

Hrushovski, Benjamin. "Integrational Semantics: An Understander's Theory of Meaning in Context." *Contemporary Perceptions of Language: Interdisciplinary Dimensions*. Ed. Heidi Byrnes. Washington, DC: Georgetown University Press, 1982.

——. *Segmentation and Motivation in the Text Continuum of Literary Prose: The First Episode of War and Peace*. Tel Aviv: The Porter Institute for Poetics and Semiotics, 1976.

——. "The Structure of Semiotic Objects: A Three-Dimensional Model." *Poetics Today* 1 (1979): 363–376.

Jackendorff, Ray S. *Semantic Interpretation in Generative Grammar.* Cambridge, MA: MIT Press, 1972.

Keenan-Ochs, Elinor and B. Schieffelin. "Topics as a Discourse Notion." *Subject and Topic.* Ed. Charles N. Li. New York: Academic Press, 1976. 335–384.

Kermode, Frank. "Secrets and Narrative Sequence." *Critical Inquiry* 7 (1980): 83–101.

Kuno, Susumu. "Functional Sentence Perspective." *Linguistic Inquiry* 3 (1972): 269–320.

Mathesius, U. *A Functional Analysis of Present-Day English.* Prague: Academia, 1975.

Prince, Ellen F. "Toward a Taxonomy of Given-New Information." *Radical Pragmatics.* Ed. Peter Cole. New York: Academic Press, 1981. 223–255.

Reinhart, Tanya. "Pragmatics and Linguistics: An Analysis of Sentence Topics." *Philosophica* 27 (1981): 53–93.

Rimmon-Kenan, Shlomith. *Narrative Fiction: Contemporary Poetics.* London: Methuen, 1983.

Shachter, Paul. "Focus and Relativization." *Language* 49 (1973): 19–46.

Taglicht, Joseph. "Intonation and the Assessment of Information." *Journal of Linguistics* 18 (1982): 213–230.

Van Dijk, Teun A. *Text and Context: Explorations in the Semantics and Pragmatics of Discourse.* London and New York: Longman, 1977.

FROM MOTIF TO FUNCTION
AND BACK AGAIN

Cesare Segre

Once upon a time there was a motif, a theme and a subject. Then, at last, Vladimir Propp arrived.

What I would like to discuss here is a passage from his *Morphology of the Folk-Tale:*

> The functions of characters are those aspects which could replace Veselovsky's "motifs," or Bédier's "elements."[1]

Careful analysis reveals that when Propp says "replace," he does not mean "represent more adequately" but "substitute for," "take the place of." Indeed, whereas the terms *motif* and *subject* (i.e. plot) are often used in the first chapter, "On the History of the Problem," when one moves later on to the definition and inventory of functions, only *action* is employed. The word *suzhet* (plot) often reappears in chapter 9, "The Tale as a Whole":

> All predicates give the composition of tales; all subjects, objects, and other parts of the sentence define the subject.[2]

Hence the following schema:

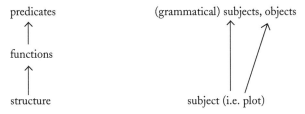

Veselovsky makes a distinction between plot and motif; Propp, in a way, could be said to have replaced this with an opposition between plot and structure. The reason for this is clear. "For Veselovsky," claims Propp, "motif is something primary, subject secondary";[3] Veselovsky further states that it is essential to "separate the question of motifs from the question of subjects," and in Propp's opinion, he is quite right to do so. Except that motifs (unlike functions) are not indivisible, as Propp has shown. Hence his rejection of *motif* both as term and concept.

It soon becomes apparent why Propp chose the structure-plot couple to work with. He sees each as a fundamental element: structure for his taxonomic purposes, plot for his history of narrative variants. In the latter, the motif (which turns out not to be an indivisible unit) merely serves as a subspecies of the subject (i.e. plot).

Veselovsky's definitions did not, in fact, allow the motif to be defined unambiguously. We only have to consider the most famous and most comprehensible one, later taken up by Shklovsky:

> A) By *motif* I mean the simplest narrative unit, corresponding imagistically to the diverse needs of a primitive mind and to the needs of ordinary perception. As a result of the similarity or, rather, unity of *material and psychological* conditions existing at the early stages of human development, such motifs could have arisen independently of each other and nonetheless could still have exhibited similar features at one and the same time. As examples, we may cite the following:
>
> 1) The so-called légendes des origines, the sun/eye simile, the sun (brother or husband)/moon (sister or wife) comparison, sunrise and sunset myths, myths about spots on the moon, eclipses, etc.
>
> 2) Everyday situations: abduction of a young woman (the folk wedding episode), abduction of "Rostan" (in fairy tales), etc.
>
> B) By *plot* I mean a theme, into which a variety of motif-situations have been woven. For example:
>
> 1) Tales of the sun and his mother (cf. the Greek and Malaysian legends of the cannibalistic sun).
>
> 2) Tales of abduction.[4]

Although Veselovsky clearly considers plot to be more complex, his definition of the motif actually appears more nebulous. And the various distinctions that have been drawn between *theme* and motif remain vaguer still, so much so that their definitions are often interchangeable.

Veselovsky's rationale, like Propp's, is taxonomic: tales or myths of different origin and separate areas of dissemination may be grouped together according to motifs they hold in common. This being so, the motif remains a useful instrument until the appearance of that imposing repertoire, Stith Thompson's *Motif-Index of Folk Literature* (which, though one might easily think it was much older, came out four years after Propp's study).

The Russian Formalists saw the motif as a tool for dividing the narrative text into segments; it is thanks to their influence that we still relate motif and function, even unconsciously, contrary to Propp's definition.

> After reducing a work to its thematic elements (writes Tomashevsky), we come to parts that are irreducible, the smallest particles of thematic material: "evening comes," "Raskolnikov kills the old woman," "the hero dies," "the letter is received," and so on. The theme of an irreducible part of a work is called the *motif*.[5]

This dissection will remain rather lifeless and uncommunicative unless we stop to consider the links between the isolated units. What brings them to light is the comparison of two other structures, *fabula* and *plot*.

> Mutually related motifs form the thematic bonds of the work (Tomashevsky continues). From this point of view, the story *[fabula]* is the aggregate of motifs in their logical, causal-chronological order; the plot is the aggregate of those same motifs but having the relevance and the order which they had in the original work.[6]

In the *fabula*, then, narrative content is paraphrased according to a causal and chronological order which is often fragmented in the text; when *plot* paraphrases the content, on the other hand, it respects the order of the units as they appear in the text. I apologise for these ultimately rather trite quotations, but it is important to emphasize the differences between the Formalists and such authors—otherwise very closely related—as Propp, since these differences may well prove thought-provoking. It should be noted, first of all, that Propp's analyses focus on the paradigmatic axis, whereas those of the Formalists are centered on the syntagmatic. In their analyses of narratives, the Formalists seek the discourse beneath the discourse, so as to highlight the way in which the narrated material is decomposed and recomposed: what mainly interests them in a given text is the relationship between the *fabula* and the *plot*. Propp's analyses, on the other hand, seek to reduce a corpus of tales to a single paradigm, of which each individual tale is just one instantiation. While the fabula/plot opposition refers to a single discourse on two different levels, the structure/plot distinction involves two opposite operations: the search for a common paradigm underlying different stories, and the search for common narrative elements in tales belonging to different paradigms.

As we know, when Propp and the Formalists opened up these two avenues of inquiry, they set off—quite unwittingly—a series of investigations, in two main areas: on the one hand, into the so-called deeper structures of the tale (a misnomer, by the way); on the other, into narrative models and their variants. But this is not the subject of my essay; I would prefer instead to return to the preliminary problems of classification and terminology. On this subject, I could perhaps suggest a few remarks, though nothing I say will be earth-shatteringly new.

Let us take terminology first. Using the term *motif* to designate "units of action content" is tantamount to paying homage to Veselovsky, Tomashevsky and the whole Formalist school. Words like *motifeme* and *mytheme* were subsequently adopted for the sake of a greater degree of generalization, albeit not the apex of abstraction attained by the *functions*. It is useful to remember that the use of terms like *motif* and *motifeme* is only warranted where motif is used to mean a minimal narrative unit, possibly relating to the fabula-plot pair. Research in this direction (by Lubomír Doležel in particular) has enabled considerable progress to be made in the areas of textual segmentation and of the immanent structures of discourse. Meletinski's theories tend the same way: using Fillmore's case-grammar to isolate the minimal cells of discourse, he surmises that the motif constitutes a mini-discourse, or better yet, a mini-plot.

Is it any wonder that a word like *motif* has had several semantic avatars? Right from the start, as far back as Darmesteter and Bréal, semantics has always concerned itself with such phenomena. Similarly, to turn to the *theme* for a moment, we should not be surprised by the amount of research and cognitive progress triggered by the Prague school's invention of the "theme and rheme," which American scholars thankfully turned into the more colloquial *topic* and *comment*. These semantic extensions and displacements can lend to confusion, particularly when the old meanings are still used (and still prove useful), and when there are not enough differences between them to avoid any misunderstanding. One should, for example, bear in mind that *motif* and *theme* formed yet another pair, with a considerable heuristic value of its own. By the turn of the seventeenth century, the word *motif* already stood for a "musical phrase which is repeated with variations in a piece and which gives it its character." The use in musicology of the word *theme*, borrowed from the Greek, to stand for the "characteristic melody forming the subject of a musical composition and providing the substance of its developments" or, as Grove would have it, "a piece of musical material in a complete, self-contained form, but used in composition for the purpose of development, elaboration or variation"[7] is much more recent—about 1835, in fact. According to these definitions, *theme* and *motif* are in a relationship of complex to simple, composite to unitary; or of idea to nucleus, organism to cell. The theory (still according to Grove) is that

> in subdividing musical works into their constituent portions, as separate movements, sections, periods, phrases, the units are the motifs, and any subdivision below them will leave only expressionless single notes, as un-meaning as the separate letters of a word;[8]

and that the theme is always larger than the motif, which is too short to possess a formally developed structure of its own.

This analogy with music allows us to put a certain amount of order into matters. *Theme* and *motif* are, of course, often used interchangeably: what is a theme for one writer is a motif for another. It is, in my opinion, beneficial to accept the musicologists' definitions—with which most literary critics would doubtless agree, in any case—according to which themes are elements that span an entire text or a considerable part thereof, while motifs—of which there may be many—are more localized elements. Very often, a theme is the product of several tenacious motifs. Motifs are easier to pick out on the level of linguistic discourse, in as much as they may, if repeated, acquire the status of a refrain; themes, in most cases, are meta-discursive in character. Typically, in fact, motifs function as discursive resonances of the meta-discursivity of the theme.

These suggestions are, of course, no full answer. What is left in abeyance is, above all, the antinomy between *mythos* and *dianoia* (content and inspirational idea) already aired in Aristotle—an antinomy I do not intend to address in this paper. I shall confine myself, for the moment, to Northrop Frye's reflections on this subject and to Panofsky's remarks, quite different but just as seminal, on the distinction between *subject* and *intrinsic meaning* or *content*. And I have no intention of getting lost in the forest where clichés and topoi merge with motifs and themes.

Mind you, motifs, themes, clichés and topoi *are* genetically similar. In the course of time, the commonplaces of collective memory become a store-house for blueprints of plot and situation, characteristic inventions of the imagination in stereotypical form. According to Knights,

> Our talk of themes . . . is simply a way of pointing to the centres of con-sciousness—*the collective consciousness, I would say*—that exert a kind of gravi-tational pull, to the dominant tones and emphases of a living mode of experience.[9]

We can take it for granted—without going back to the psychological assumptions behind our perceptions—that the verbalization of experience is a semiotic operation in which two moments may be distinguished: the connection of lived experience to schemata of representability (or stereotypes), and the linguistic realization of these schemata. Although the rules which govern this linguistic realization have not yet been described, we *do* know a little about schemata of representability pertaining to the set of possible plots and situations: they overlap with themes and motifs. The study of thematics thus puts us in touch with this erratic experiential material which humankind has developed over time, according to certain schemata. Writers have also contributed to this development, although all they have done is to formalize and consecrate the schemata drafted by collective experience.

Inquiries into the schemata of representability must, it seems, be conducted outside of literature—into all symbolic expressions of the imagination, in fact. Research performed by ethnologists and religious historians into symbols devised and modified over millenia, or by folklorists into the units of plot and situation recurring in the most far-flung and disparate narrations, must be compared to the symbolic activities of the unconscious and (if possible) their fluctuations. These observations should then be analyzed using a psychology of experiential schemata.

We should also avoid making excessively neat distinctions between the schemata of representability found in literature, whether popular or highbrow, and the ones brought to light by ethno-psychological observation. The way we schematize reality is partly determined by literary clichés, which easily spread to all levels of culture. If humankind lends characters, situations and events the status of more or less 'universal' themes, it is because it sees them as stereotypes according to which it interprets situations, events and characters in its everyday life. Themes are not just sublimations: they are also heuristic models. That is why the themes and motifs found in popular and literary texts constitute a well-defined category, with exchanges taking place between the literary and the popular. At one end of the scale there are fully stereotyped topoi; at the other, there are schemata which have not yet attained literary consecration, even if they are already recognizable as models of collective experience.

This explains why the theme-motif dialectic proves effective. Themes, more articulate and more easily recognizable, can act as "frames" *(types cadres)*, to use a term introduced by Paul Zumthor; but motifs may also acquire a personality, by being repeated in the text. Thanks to this process, the infinite mass of symbolic values inherent in a text's collected components may be driven into a process of self-selection. This selection by recursivity is then integrated with a selection by the convergence of motifs, creating areas of meaning which may be related to the theme. Thus the dialectic between themes and motifs contributes to the establishment of meaning.

As one might expect from the original meaning of the word *motif* and even more so from its Wagnerian derivative *leitmotif,* recursivity is a key factor in the formation of repertoires of motifs, themes, clichés and topoi. From a generic point of view, the recurrence of a motif within a single (usually literary) text is comparable to a recurrence over several different texts. It is, in fact, a single phenomenon that we are dealing with: as Lotman points out, a culture can be seen as a single text, the sum of the texts of which it is composed.

In the case of a literary text, the word *motif* comes to mind when a single thematic kernel is repeated several times; in the cultural text, on the other hand, it is the multiplicity of motifs, themes and the like that give them away. Collective memory (or the researcher's perception, running through this memory) is what gives the names "motif" and "topos" to these erratic materials, putting non-recursive plots and situations in the shade.

For this reason, it is inevitable that motifs (and they alone are concerned here) should be as heterogeneous as they are: sometimes minimal plots, sometimes types of relationship, sometimes even objects or operations. The opposition between synchrony and diachrony may be useful here, albeit provisional: motifs, being heterogeneous, are of course ideally suited to diachrony—to a diachrony, what is more, in which elements of variable duration are juxtaposed. Unlike their counterparts in language, however, these elements cannot be said to constitute a synchronic system. The synchrony in question is that of the individual story, in which the motifs are amalgamated into a coherent *fabula*. It would be better, then, to weigh the diachrony of thematic language against the synchrony of narrative discourse; though without making a hard and fast opposition between them.

This pair can only produce useable results when one turns to a third term, that of the narrative model. I am not referring to universal models, whose existence and nature have been insufficiently studied up to now, but models as identifiable historical products within certain clusters of myths, fantastic tales or short stories (setting aside the issues of which came first). A story is given form by the introduction of one or more motifs into a narrative structure developed, by necessity, from certain models. The two opposite meanings of the term *motif* are situated within this very general schema. The motif as micro-plot, *motifeme* and finally *function* falls within the domain of structure, with its universality; the motif as an unstructured or minimally-structured element permeating culture comes under the possibility of its cultural recognition, under characterization and sometimes even meaning. These few remarks could perhaps be taken as the starting-point for research into the ending and its potentially privileged status, or into the relationships between tale and meaning and between plot twist and character motivation, or into all these relationships in their chronological development.

As may now seem a little clearer, systems of nomenclature are bound to go in one of two directions. The path opened up by Propp allows tales in a given corpus to be classified by relating the diversity of narrated actions to the permanence of the paradigm, via the identification of functions. This system preserves the universality of individual tales; it can, however, only be applied to a homogeneous corpus. One could even say that it abandons the individual and the characteristic—necessarily so—in favor of the greatest generality.

The extremely empirical methodology of Stith Thompson and the Finnish school does not conflict at all with that of Propp, given that their aims and objectives have nothing in common. Instead of tackling a finite corpus, it aims at an exhaustive inventory; it does not confine itself to homogeneous tales but considers the old together with the new, the literary as well as the popular. A survey of such scope does not allow all of the texts to be reduced to homologous structures; the only landmarks are the distinguishing features I have just mentioned. And it is natural that a tale should often be definable as a combination of several such elements (which could only be called motifs). While Propp's morphological research gave rise to modern-day "story analysis," Thompson's *Motif-Index* and its derivatives remain invaluable for research of a comparative or historical nature.

As is only too obvious, Thompson's categories and definitions are often debatable. What should be emphasized, in my opinion, is quite simply the fact that no adjustment, however desirable, can ever purge motifs of their heterogeneity. I therefore propose, using the following few examples, to demonstrate the existence and even the necessity of motifs which do not consist of actions and which may consequently not be represented in the form of a minimal set of sentences. To this end, I shall analyze two widespread fables with ancient or even archaic origins. What I am anxious to show is that the horizontal sequence of their constitutive actions could not by itself guarantee their survival: their unity and meaning consist in motifs of a non-narrative nature.

Here, first of all, is Fable 1; I shall give it in summary form, leaving out, for the time being, the motifs on which it is based. I shall analyze these later.

> A pupil promises great gifts to his teacher if his lessons permit him a brilliant career. When this comes to pass, the pupil gives presents to everyone, especially the members of his family, but not to his teacher.

The tale would not be viable in this form, in its flat self-evidence, because the teacher's reactions and the potential punishment or humiliation of the pupil are missing. In short, it needs an exemplary quality which is absent from the fable, in the form in which I just presented it.

Following Vincent de Beauvais' *Speculum Morale*, Étienne de Bourbon (mid-thirteenth century) imagines the teacher presenting himself before his pupil, now a bishop, with two lighted torches in broad daylight. When questioned, the teacher replies that these torches are to warn him of the blindness that has prevented him, ever since he has been rich, from seeing in his master those merits he used to see when poor.

This reproach, at first symbolic and then explicitly stated, expresses the equation "poor=seeing, rich=blind" which, most likely, already existed independently in the archives of paroemiology. At any rate, Étienne's *exemplum* breathes new life into it. We are witnessing the amalgamation of a tale and a proverb; bringing the proverb to life completes and fills out the tale. We have located a motif of a paroemial order.

A far more sophisticated treatment is to be found in the *Tabula Exemplorum*. After that, the motif passes to the *Scala Coeli*, to Bromyart, to Herolt and especially to Juan Manuel, who makes a masterpiece out of it. These writers hit upon a doubling of time frames, situating the pupil's ingratitude in an imaginary time zone—by way of a magic spell—and then, when he finds himself back where he started, removing the advantages he acquired in real time.

Thus, in the *Tabula Exemplorum,* the master uses magic to make his pupil emperor. When the latter, as usual, declines to give him any reward, he removes the spell, saying "I am the one who gave you all this, and now I am taking it away again." From time A, the time of promises, the pupil moves into time B, the time of success and ingratitude, only to fall back into time A. The exemplum's entire moral and narrative value derives from this temporal reduplication.

Juan Manuel adopts and adapts this *fabula,* introducing an even shrewder innovation: it is only when the pupil falls from the peak of his highest position—the papacy—that the reader finally learns of the existence of the spell. The transitions from time A to time B and back again are marked by a simple everyday detail—the partridges for dinner, which are about to be put on the fire at the time of the first transition and which the cook really does put on at the time of the second—a detail which becomes symbolic. In short, the partridges form the *switch* between time A and time B.

So the tale of a case of ingratitude is either crowned by a symbolic scene that ends in a proverb or inserted into a system of dual time, sometimes through the use of a switch. Now the content of the proverb, the temporal redoubling and the switch are all motifs; most importantly, they have an autonomous existence, one which links them to other *fabulae.*

For the first motif, I might mention Abstemius' *Hecatomythium Primum,* in which the issue is not ingratitude but the arrogance of a newly-appointed cardinal who disowns his friends. For the second, innumerable examples could

be cited, especially from visions and journeys to the beyond. The reduplication of time frames is usually accompanied by a disparity in chronological
duration: the mystical experience, or the crossing of infernal or heavenly
regions, sometimes takes an exceedingly long time—centuries, even—while
being experienced as if it were only a few days; conversely, what is instanta-
neous in real time sometimes lasts for years in the hero's imagination.

Examples for the third can be found in very varied contexts. Mohammed's
journey to Heaven and Hell begins, according to the Koran, with the water in
a pot about to boil; it ends just in time for him to stop it tipping over by
removing it from the fire. Arguably the most interesting case is found in tale
XXI of the *Novellino,* which describes the career of the Count of San Bonifazio.
He wins a war, gets married and has several children—all of which would be
completely devoid of interest were it not for the fact that these events, which
occupy more than forty years in the mind of the hero, really occur at Federigo's
court while his guests wash their hands. This hand-washing is a switch analogous to Juan Manuel's partridges. And the magicians who work this kind of
magic have only their own skill to prove.

Let us leave aside the paroemial motif, however, and go a little deeper
into the other two, the temporal reduplication and the switch. As I see it,
these motifs could already be said

(1) to be theoretically detachable from their *fabulae,* and sufficiently
distinctive to connect all of the tales which contain them;

(2) to be essentially formal in nature: although they can be put into
narrative form, in themselves they are neither narratives nor narrative segments, but merely conceptual models;

(3) to form fundamental constitutive elements of the *fabulae,* which
would lose their effectiveness and even their meaning without them.

Now we should consider whether it is possible to categorize these
motifs, and if so, how. To this end, let us proceed to Fable 2, popularized
by La Fontaine with his pretty Perrette (*Fables* III: 10) and hence better
known than Fable 1. First seen in the *Pañcatantra,* this fable next appears
in the *Hitopadesa* and, through the intermediary of Arabic, Greek and
Latin translations (Giovanni da Capua's *Directorium Humanae Vitae,* for
example), ends up in the Castilian version, *Calila e Digna.* In the form of
an *exemplum,* and with considerable modifications, it is found again
in Jacques de Vitry, in Étienne de Bourbon, in the *Dialogus Creaturarum*
and in Juan Manuel. There is no need to mention all of its subsequent
versions.

I intend once again to summarize the *fabula* without paying attention to
its motif; we shall analyze the latter soon enough. The *fabula* could be presented as follows:

A poor person acquires an object of little worth. She dreams of selling this object and growing rich by investing the proceeds ever more shrewdly. With one sudden movement she loses the object, and will consequently never be rich.

It is not just the abridgement of this tale, the elimination of all its picturesque detail, which tarnishes its beauty; it is also the omission of what, by all accounts, represents its key motif. The charm of this fable consists in the activity of the character's imagination as she builds herself a brighter and brighter future in her mind, thanks to the commercial transactions she sees herself performing with the only little object she possesses. But the key to the fable, its crucial trigger, consists of a movement made in the course of the dream of riches, a movement that deprives the character of the very object which was to make her fortune. She might cuff or affectionately kick her child (as yet unborn), or clap and spur her horse (as yet unowned), or slap her own forehead, or dance about.

We have, in short, the passage of a character from time A (real) to time B (imaginary); the movement she makes in time B, in relation to the events of time B; and her return to time A, accompanied by a downfall. Before the swift transition into time B, time A contains a potential for riches (the object), destroyed by the movement made in time B. So the movement is a switch, like the one we found in the other fable.

Another important element the two fables hold in common is the way in which time B presents the hero in an apparent process of advancement, one which is subsequently neutralized by the return to time A.

There are also considerable differences, however. In the first fable, the switch belongs to time A; in the second, it is a movement made in time B whose consequences affect time A. And what triggers time B in the first fable is a magic spell cast by another character; in the second, the imagination of the hero herself is responsible.

It would not be hard to come up with a new definition of the motif, broad enough to fit both *fabulae:* "a switch between imaginary time and real time" would do perfectly. From a taxonomic point of view, this would allow the two fables to be grouped together—along, perhaps, with other tales, examples of which I have just given. The fact that the imaginary time is the site of a process of advancement, a process which is neutralized in real time, is something the *Novellino* story has in common with both of our fables. Still, the discrepancies between the latter bring us back to the particular requirements of two different types of thematics. Fable 1, of the bilateral class (it has to contain two characters), serves to test the enchanted character in his relations to the other man—revealing, for example, his ingratitude (as in the above-mentioned stories); it can also (as in the *Novellino*) involve nothing more than the surprise caused by the two transitions, time A → time B → time A. Fable 2, of the subjective species (one character is sufficient), can serve, as in the example mentioned, to warn against flights of the imagination. That the same motif should be used in two quite different themes is not at all surprising. What *is* worth pausing over is the fact that it provides the key to the treatment of both. One would be tempted to conclude that a formal taxonomy can prove more powerful than a conceptual one, whether it be semantic or thematic. This becomes even clearer when the eschatological tales I mentioned are also taken into account. Here the function of the switch is no longer narrative but theological: it stresses the thoroughly human character of the chronology we perceive, compared to eternity and its symbolic approximations.

The existence of formal-type motifs is, it seems to me, indisputable. In the field of discourse, they could be labelled with the formalist term "procedure"; but in fact they affect the narrative content itself (I am thinking here of the temporal reduplication), to such an extent that no summary can ever afford to ignore them. It is pointless to object that the techniques in question are literary techniques, when we consider the dissemination of the second fable, its diffusion into the popular domain. A reexamination of the storehouse of fables in search of such formal-type motifs could, I believe, produce considerable results and highlight the value of the method Propp applied to the taxonomy of structures for empirical and characteristic repertoires. Let us not imagine that this suggestion will renew the inventory of motifs from top to bottom; but its results will not, perhaps, be entirely devoid of interest.

THEME AND INTERPRETATION

Menachem Brinker

Asked what *Anna Karenina* is *about*, we could answer that it is about Anna's love for Vronsky, Levin's love for Kitty, Karenin's oversized ears, Stiva Oblonsky's favorite dishes, and many other things. We could go on at length and enumerate all of the events taking place in the "world" of the novel. Yet we could also reply, "Anna Karenina is about a series of successive causally related events bringing about crucial changes in the lives or destinies of several human beings."

Though nothing is logically or factually wrong with these two answers we would not find them satisfactory formulations of the novel's theme (or themes). They would both be disappointing, as the second is true of too many novels while the first sticks too closely to the specific poetic world of Anna Karenina and is true of this novel only.

Though we may and do speak of theme *in* a novel in terms completely analogous to that of a musical theme, that is, pertaining to a specific representational component that recurs several times in the novel, in different variations—our quest for the theme or themes *of* a story is always a quest for something that is not unique to this specific work. The theme is understood as potentially uniting different texts. Various stories and poems are written on one and the same theme, and most often so are various additional texts other than poems and stories. A theme is, therefore, the principle (or locus) of a possible grouping of texts. It is one principle among many since we often group together texts considered to have a common theme, which are importantly and significantly different in many other respects.

We do, however, classify texts according to their themes with different aims in mind. It is this difference in aims which decides the varying degree of generality or particularity involved in the theme's formulation. Theme's most common function for critics is the aid it affords in the description and interpretation of a work or a group of works. Accordingly, changes tend to occur in degree of generality vs. particularity or of abstractness vs. concreteness as scrutiny shifts from the individual work to a group of works (for example, a collection of short stories), to the whole corpus of an author's work, to the work of a literary group, generation, or school.

A reader who knows the appropriate language will very rarely come up with a totally wrong answer when asked what a story is about. Yet the answer may easily be a useless one, being overly detailed or too abstract relative to our specific needs. As we search for "the theme," we constantly have these specific aims in mind, which is precisely why we're not interested in everything that the work may be about. What we're getting at, rather, are the things which it is significantly or importantly about. Significance and importance may vary from one interpretive context to another, even within the same work.

Given alternative identifications of theme, it is sometimes suggested that we should prefer the one unifying the largest number of linguistic and representational components. L. M. O'Toole argues to this effect when defending his identification of the deep theme of Conan Doyle's stories as the Reason/ Irrationality opposition, which he prefers to the Safety/Adventure opposition suggested by Shcheglov.[1] In his admirable analysis of *The Sussex Vampire*[2] he points out that this opposition is represented in the fable, and in various aspects of the poetic world (from the spatial division of the setting to characterization). Furthermore, it is also suggested by the language, which is rich with oxymorons and paradoxical formulations (of which the title itself is one instance). He points out quite convincingly, in my opinion, that all other significant oppositions (British/Foreign; Familiar/Exotic; Healthy/Sick), including the one identified by Shcheglov (Safety/Adventure), can be regarded as manifestations of the more basic opposition of Reason/Irrationality.

Despite the significance of O'Toole's work and of that of Zholkovsky and of Shcheglov,[3] it is my view that this generative-transformational model creates expectations that will prove unfulfillable, as regards more complex stories or less uniform collections. Theme as the infrastructure of a story, controlling and generating all elements of fable, poetic world, and language is, perhaps, just one possible configuration of the literary theme.

In recognizing theme as an interesting meeting point of texts, which proves fruitful in creating the context in which to interpret a work (at least partially), we have no need of the postulate according to which theme should unify all the linguistic and representational components of a work. We can definitely make do with the fact that it unifies a large or conspicuous or important portion of these components, relative to a specific descriptive interpretation of the work's "world" and language.

At least one of the usual pretheoretical uses of the term "theme" does not supply grounds for assigning the theme a fixed place in the metaphoric space of "surface structures" vs. "deep structures" within which we place other elements of the work. Nor does it assign theme a fixed role in connection with the metaphoric political relations of dominance and subjugation. This is the standard use of the term employed in discussions admitting a plurality of themes as opposed to the activity of searching for "the" (singular) theme of a work. My interest here is in the common ground shared by these two uses.

Even in purely fictional works we often identify themes on the most explicit surface of the text. These themes may actually be named by the narrator, and they may tie up with the work's more implicit and "deeper" meanings in many disparate ways. St. Petersburg, for instance, is widely recognized as a theme in Dostoyevsky's work and should be considered as such even when it fails to unify all of the meanings of each specific work. At a certain level of abstractness and schematization, we may describe the story of *Crime and Punishment* without mentioning the specific atmosphere of the Russian megalopolis. Yet the theme of St. Petersburg and its unique atmosphere is so conspicuous throughout the poetic world of this novel (and in Dostoyevsky's work in general) that we cannot consider it to be derived or generated from another, "deeper" theme. The real grounds for critics' widespread recognition of this as a central theme is the fact that Dostoyevsky presents a unique poetic vision of St. Petersburg.[4] This vision is implicitly related not only to former poetic visions of the city in Russian literature but also to various depictions of St. Petersburg in nonfictional and nonartistic texts.

While, of course, St. Petersburg is much more than the local "setting" for Dostoyevsky's stories, other fictional works may motivate the development of theme from local or historical "settings." Themes may be constructed or suggested by shorter segments of text. Their relations with the fable may be far looser. Our use of such a minimally defined concept of theme enables us to identify a variety of themes which neither generate the fable nor derive from it. Aristotle, the original propounder of organic unity, recognized the legitimacy of combinations of free motifs in the epic and saw very clearly that an "organically unified" literary artwork might include any elements that were possibly juxtaposable and not just those that were necessarily so. Thus the relationships between many themes and "their" fables may well be none other than indifferent coexistence. Nineteenth-century novels tended to construct satirical themes from combinations of free motifs. We should avoid reducing these to mere manifestations of deeper more encompassing themes, even when this is possible. The opera in *War and Peace*, for example, should be regarded as an independent theme, and not only a reflection of the Natural/Artificial opposition so basic to the novel as a whole.

The liberal pretheoretical use of the term "theme" described (and implicitly defended) by me so far is not the only one contrasting sharply with the
generative model. Theorists such as Tomashevsky[5] and Frye[6] systematically
identify theme with something nearer the surface than the "deepest" layers of
narrative which are exclusively composed of motifs or archetypical images (respectively), the ultimate and irreducible conventional units of literature. Far
from generating these ultimate units, "themes" are, rather, generated by their
various combinations. Themes serve to displace mythical patterns and disguise
the composition's purely literary ends by fostering realistic or referential illu-
sions. Yet such a concept also bypasses our ordinary use of the term. We
recognize themes that emerge from various combinations of free motifs (in
Tomashevsky's terms), serving realistic motivation and existing on this or that
"wrapping," as it were, of the fable's deeper compositional motivation. We
recognize "themes" that tie themselves to the local or historical setting of the
fable. We recognize yet other themes that are identified with traditional and
conventional fables or with more abstract formulas generating types of fables,
such as the "fall of a prince" formula instrumental in generating tragedy, or that
of the young lovers overcoming all obstacles, instrumental in generating comedy. These traditional thematic "deep" formulas leave ample space for the emergence of other themes, such as that of obsessive mania in Molière. Even this
may in turn be looked upon as too abstract or too "deep" in relation to the more
concrete theme of a specific comedy, such as the specific obsession which is the
obstacle facing the lovers. Though these are respectively the formula of romantic comedy from Plautus to Molière, the formula of Molière's comedy, and the
formula of each specific comedy of Molière, we call all three of them "themes,"
despite the fact that each is situated differently in relation to genre and to the
naturalization of its conventions.

In terms of the spatial and political metaphors standardly employed to
describe narrative structures, the position of the theme vis-à-vis other narrative elements is allowed to vary. And yet, for both readers and critics, it has a
minimal invariable identity: it is a semantic point of contact between the
individual text and other texts. It is a meeting place of texts of various kinds:
artistic and nonartistic, fictional and non-fictional, and, quite often, narra-
tional and nonnarrational. "Themes" are loci where artistic literary texts encounter other texts: texts of philosophy or the social and human sciences,
texts of religion and social ideologies, journalistic texts, including gossip columns, and personal texts such as diaries and letters. The various degrees to
which a specific theme obviously dominates and generates other elements of
an individual work indicate the various degrees to which the work allows,
seeks, or resists consideration as an artistic equivalent of nonartistic texts.

When emphasizing that theme is, potentially at least, the meeting point
of various texts, we may overlook the fact that themes are not limited to

linguistic texts. Pictures and pantomimes also have themes and, as happens with linguistic texts, these may be only partially identified with their referents. In a fictional work the most significant theme is not necessarily mentioned explicitly in the text. When it isn't we identify it as represented implicitly in (or by or through) the poetic world of the work. We connect aspects of the poetic world with what is signified by other texts or nonlinguistic (mental or pictorial) representations. In these cases we recognize the distinction—formalized by Beardsley—between the *subject* of the story and its *theme.*[7] We anticipate two possible answers to the question, What is this story *about?* For instance, the tenth Aesopian fable, the first without an explicit moral, is about a fox, a crow, and a piece of meat.[8] But it is also about cunning people, simpletons, and how the former may exploit the latter by flattering their vanity. Since the theme is not explicitly formulated in the text it is difficult to see what kind of help we might get from linguistic attempts to identify the theme by sorting parts of speech and calling only some of them "themes." In some important sense the construal of theme in this case is closer to its construal in the case of a painting or a pantomime than to the construal according to which a linguistic theme is located by underlining certain types of words or phrases in the text. The Aesopian narrative, clearly, could have been presented in the form of a pantomime with no resulting shift in theme.

On the level of the story itself there seems to be nothing wrong or problematic in considering everything mentioned to be part of what the story is about: "the cat is on the mat" can be taken to be about the cat, about the mat, and about the fact that the cat is on the mat. Yet very often in the case of a fictional text none of the things mentioned will present us with its hidden or implicit theme.

However, the philosophical model of aboutness, the alternative to the linguistic model, also has its catch when applied to fiction. Gilbert Ryle distinguished between what a discourse is *linguistically about* and what it is *referentially about;*[9] Nelson Goodman rephrased this distinction as that between what a discourse is *rhetorically about* and that which it may be taken to be *referentially about* when read *metaphorically.*[10] John Searle had a similar distinction in mind when he set the fictional text as *pretended speech act* (with its pretended reference) apart from the *serious,* that is, *referential speech act* possibly conveyed by it.[11] All of these distinctions are made in terms of references and not in terms of signifieds. The kind of aboutness ascribed by philosophers to texts which are not purely rhetorically, linguistically, or pretendingly about something is unfailingly referential. In other words, a statement is contained in them, separated from its rhetorical or fictional cover, which is actually, though indirectly, asserted and may be true or false.

In recognizing a theme in a fictional work, we often mean much less. Though themes are usually formulated in referential terms and do indeed suggest models for relations in the real world (as in the case of the themes of family, adultery, and the quest for a meaningful life in *Anna Karenina*), we reserve the full-fledged referential reading of a fictional work for specific genres of works: allegorical and satirical works, parodies, the *roman à thèse* or in general the exemplum (or apologue). It is only in these cases that missing an implicit referent will be counted as misunderstanding the work itself.

The potential reference of fictional texts is fully recognized in today's analytical philosophy. Earlier denials of the possibility of deriving veritable statements from pseudo-statements were abandoned as soon as it was recognized that pseudo-statements could construct a poetic world which could, in turn, be interpreted as a representation in the strong referential sense. The parallelism is still intact; the opposition of fictional vs. referential speech still has metaphorical vs. literal speech as its counterpart. Yet, instead of denying the referential potentiality of fiction, we now turn our attention to the fact that a metaphor may be true or false, despite its metaphorical nature. Recognizing an "implied truth" in a fictional text[12] is no longer seen as tantamount to the derivation of the (literal) phrase "John has a specific kind of tail" from the metaphorical "John is a lion" as soon as "John is a lion" is recognized as a judgment that may be true or false despite its metaphorical nature.[13]

However, to consider a fictional work a unit of metaphorical speech (to consider *Anna Karenina* a statement on the relations among adultery, the family, class, and meaningful life either in general or in nineteenth-century Russia) is to treat the poetic world of the novel in a very special way. Quite naturally applicable to some fictional works, this mode of treatment is still possible with regard to many others, but becomes very unnatural and "forced" (if not actually impossible) in the case of a great many fictional texts. A theme's recognition is the recognition of a *virtual reference,* but by no means is this virtuality necessarily actualized. Identification of a theme in a fictional text does not automatically entail the existence of an "implicit predication," or an "implied truth," in the work. We would not claim, for example, that the theme of Romantic Comedy really refers to love in the real everyday world, suggesting its power to overcome all obstacles. This theme may be tied to our dreams and desires in much the same way as other themes are related to our nightmares and fears. Though there is indirect reference even here, this kind of referentiality is not part of our *thematic* understanding of the work.

Identification of themes is a necessary condition for an emotional response to a literary work and its poetic world. But a referential reading of fiction implies more than that. It implies seeing some conspicuous elements of its poetic world as models of structures of the real world, and this must divert our attention from the poetic world itself toward a poetic vision of some nonpoetic reality. We ascribe different teleologies to different fictional works and there are different motives for our reading them. Therefore we are interested in actualizing the virtual references to the real world contained in the theme only when we have in mind a specific cognitive teleology of the work or of our reading of it. But we do not go to see a good production of, say, *Othello* in order to learn something new or intellectually exciting about human behavior. Therefore we would not see its poetic world as a model of some real structure of the human world (erotic jealousy, for instance).

Aristotle saw the need of setting explicit and detailed thematic constraints upon the tragic plot so as to maximize pity and fear. The audience needed to understand numerous things in connection with the theme of the tragic fall in order to respond imaginatively to its reversals and recognitions. Yet they accepted its apparent plausibility as grounds enough to do so. Of course canons of plausibility and verisimilitude refer indirectly to the real world or at least to the reader's beliefs about the real world. There are certainly many cases where fictional plots and poetic worlds aspire to convince us that as potential, imaginary continuations of the world they may also be used as models for its understanding. However, not every illusionistic or "realistic" work is so directed.[14] The fictional work cuts its referential ties to the world on its linguistic level. In order to resume them on its representational level we require an interpretive motive. This motive may be supplied by the work itself or by a chosen interpretative context. But neither verisimilitude nor the mere recognition of a familiar theme is a necessary or sufficient condition for such a motive. As Susan R. Suleiman remarks, we can always ascribe some practical lesson or proverb or "truth" to a fictional tale.[15] Yet we are not always urged to do so.

On the other hand, as the thematic (in distinction from the referential) understanding and organization of what we read is a necessary servant of *all* kinds of teleologies (or narrative desires) inherent in literary texts, themes are universals of literary works. Existing and comprehended in the intertextual space created by the partial overlapping of artistic fictional texts and other cultural texts, they are rightly suspected of extraliterary origins or at least of impure (literary) blood. Yet literature is always inescapably contaminated with their existence.

The extraliterary origin of "themes" is one reason why some theorists show such a reluctance to discuss thematics. A second reason has to do with the fact that the themes of fictional stories or novels tend to depend more heavily upon interpretation than the other components of the works. They depend upon our familiarity with texts that are neither necessarily artistic nor fictional and upon various beliefs held by the reader or the interpreter concerning general cultural and human issues.

Such dependence of a given text's thematization upon the reader's acquaintance with other texts is by no means peculiar to the fictional text. In the essay cited earlier, Nelson Goodman distinguishes that which a given discourse is *absolutely about* from that which it may be only *relatively about*. The sentence "the book is on the table" is absolutely about the book, the table, and the fact that the book is on the table. Yet relative to the information received this morning, according to which "if Peter buys the book he will leave it on the table," the first sentence ("the book is on the table") is also about Peter and about the fact that he bought the book and left it on the table. By implication it may also be about the fact that Peter keeps his promises, that the book has arrived in Israel, and so on and so forth. In stressing that the literary referent is a construct, created by different segments of the work's text-continuum and by other texts outside the work in question, Benjamin Hrushovski has made very similar points about aboutness, though these are limited to the referents within the literary work.[16] We may conclude that whatever a specific text is absolutely about is ascertained by what the specific text states. Yet that which it is only relatively about is ascertained by the juxtaposition of this text with other, relevant texts (or with beliefs derived from them).

Adding these distinctions to the ones mentioned earlier, with regard to fictional texts, we may now say that a purely fictional text is only absolutely about those fictional events and people, that is, only about that which it is rhetorically or linguistically about. It may be about nonfictional events or people only relatively, relative to the other texts which we bring to bear upon the work's interpretation. Thus those adhering to this or that brand of psychoanalysis, Marxism, Existentialism, or any other concept of Man, Society, God, or Culture, will identify different themes in the same fictional work. Is the implicit theme of *Crime and Punishment* that of the fatal results of the isolation of modern man who has been led by pride to shut his eyes to the "Christian truth of the brotherhood of all in sin and in redemption?" This is the claim put forward by Viacheslav Ivanov.[17] Does it have as its underlying theme the extreme polarities and inner contradictions of the Russian soul, as Nikolai Berdiaev suggests?[18] Is its theme the blind revolt of man in the capitalist era expressed by his attempt to transgress the moral conventions mocked by the parties in power, as Georg Lukács claims?[19] If there are criteria for deciding issues such as these they must be found, at least to some extent, outside Dostoyevsky's novel. One would need, first, to decide whether or not to believe in the existence and the explanatory power of entities such as the capitalist era, the solidarity of men in sin, or the Russian soul.

It is always possible, I believe, to make the effort of reading a novel as it was read, or meant to be read, by its author, while identifying in it the themes recognized by its contemporary (the work's empirical) addressees. In this way the dubious epistemological status of the words of the dead was made a central theme of *Hamlet*. Yet clearly this is not the only possible way nor even the only natural way of reading fiction. We do indeed call upon models of description and explanation undreamt of by the author of a work in constructing our thematic interpretations, and sometimes even our referential ones. In the interest of sidestepping the ongoing dispute in modern hermeneutics (between Gadamer's following and that of Hirsch) as to whether or not it is possible to read a work originating in a different epoch or culture as it was read by the author, we limit ourselves to remarking that this is not the only way of reading fiction.

Yet this process of shifts in the thematic perception of a fictional work need not lead us to the conclusion that anything may represent everything as long as we frame it with a suitable interpretive context. We are capable, up to a certain point, of describing the language of a text and its projected poetical world, while leaving aside and deeming problematic any global hypotheses about its hidden themes or the range of its potential implicit reference. The determinate components of the poetic world limit the freedom of the interpreter. For instance, we should not accept a reading of the biblical narrative of the sacrificing of Isaac which explains Abraham's behavior on the grounds that he is jealous of Sarah's love for their son. Though for some modern readers this may be the only plausible explanation left for his behavior, we should still not accept it as a possible "reading" of the biblical narrative, as such an introduction of a Freudian theme necessarily ignores determinate elements of the story, besides several other things implied by them. Poetic worlds and fictional narratives may always be open to different and incompatible thematic readings. Nonetheless, they are possessed of determinacy enough to reject some thematic interpretations as unconvincing, forced, or, at least, unnatural.

The scope and subject of my discussion here are not suited to a full account of what this strange concept involves (the opposite of a natural reading is not a conventional, but an artificial reading). I believe, however, that several sections of Wittgenstein's *Philosophical Investigations,* especially those that deal with "seeing as," describe a reasonable approach to the question of the thematic reading of fictional works.[20]

The group of phenomena discussed in the *Philosophical Investigations* under the label "seeing as" is heterogeneous. Yet members of this group interest Wittgenstein for what they share and not for the "fine shades of behavior" separating them from one another. They are all examples of a *category,* and therefore there is more than just a family resemblance tying them all together. They all have common features and form a class: (1) They are all perceptual phenomena (usually drawings) that may be "seen" (or "heard") in more than one way. (2) In all of them we may be given to, or taken by, one way of perceiving them; consequently we shall not be aware that our viewing is really a kind of interpretation, a case of "seeing as," and we shall consider it an ordinary case of seeing. (3) Nevertheless, all of them can in principle be perceived successively in different and exclusive ways, and, perceiving them in multiple ways, one becomes aware that more than ordinary seeing is involved. One tends to account for this additional element by using the word "image" or "thought." Consequently one tends to describe this experience as a mixture either of perception and imagination or of perception and thought. (4) Shifts from a familiar or entrenched way of seeing toward a new one may occur instantaneously: "the dawning of an image" or "a concept forcing itself on us." (5) This sudden occurrence of the image or the thought guiding our perception and responsible for our interpretation reveals itself as an aspect of the perceptual phenomenon itself and not just as an element of our "mental experience." In suddenly recognizing a drawing as a representation of A or as a representation of A rather than a representation of B, we become aware simultaneously of the new aspect of the seen object and of the interpretative character of our viewing.

To avoid two symmetrical yet opposite misunderstandings of Wittgenstein's point in discussing "seeing as" as a peculiar phenomenon, we should keep in mind that he uses the expression "seeing as" as a technical term. There is, of course, a sense in which every seeing—being an identification of an object—is "seeing as." Yet Wittgenstein sets "seeing as" in opposition to ordinary seeing. This is not done so as to make the interpretative element, implicit in ordinary seeing, an explicit one. For shaking our metaphysical belief in "the pure given" and insisting that our ordinary perceptions are category-bound, previous-experience-bound, or forms-of-life-bound, Wittgenstein has no need of "seeing as." Perceptual identification of X as a fork is a simple case of ordinary seeing, not because it is noninterpretative but because, given a certain form of life, one is necessarily pushed into seeing X in this one (and only one) way. Yet pertaining to the group of phenomena allowing "seeing as," no form of life can supply us with rules or criteria for deciding the "correct" way of seeing. Lacking such rules or criteria we may see a certain drawing as a duck or as a rabbit. None of these ways of seeing the drawing could count as the one (and only one) correct way. Yet this does not entail sheer anarchy. It must be shown that different ways of seeing the drawing are possible, that the drawing *can* invoke this particular "image" or this particular "thought." In other words, it must be shown that under a particular interpretation, organized around a certain image or thought, the drawing may assume a new aspect. Thus the different ways of seeing X are partially rooted or inscribed, so to speak, in X itself. This explains the fact that though we lack a grammar for distinguishing acceptable from unacceptable moves in the game of "seeing as" it is not the case that we have to accept *every* seeing ("reading" or "understanding").

There are two subgroups in the class of phenomena included in Wittgenstein's descriptions: (1) those in which there is no way of seeing, identifying, or describing the drawing without interpreting it in some way (the duck-rabbit drawing is an example of this subgroup). (2) Those in which you can step, as it were, away, not committing yourself to one of the representational readings, and offer a neutral account of the drawing. (The triangle that may be taken as the representation of seven different objects is the most obvious example, as it can always be described in purely geometrical terms.) The claim, or suggestion, I make in this paper is that if we allow ourselves to disregard the perceptual character of most of Wittgenstein's examples, "seeing as" may be construed as a model for a whole territory of cognitive acts. In all of them there are neither rules nor criteria nor interpretative anarchy. The thematic reading of fiction will then belong to this second subgroup of "seeing as."

As we have seen, Dostoyevsky's *Crime and Punishment* is actually read not only as a novel which is about Raskolnikov, the murderer of the pawnbroker Aliona Ivanovna and the Marmaladovs, but also as a novel about the extreme contradictions within the Russian soul, about the fatal results of atheism, and about the spiritual situation of the individual in capitalist society. All of these "abouts" are relative "abouts." They are relative to certain teleological, philosophical, or sociological texts and beliefs. In Wittgenstein's terms they are due to the dawning of a certain image or thought on the reader.

The merits of "seeing as" are that it shows in an absolutely lucid way the intertextual character of thematic interpretation and the kind of "game" (or the kind of rationality) we may expect in critical disputes of this kind: (1) A thematic or referential reading of fictional works of the contemplative, nondidactic, and nonallegorical kind cannot be imposed by an appeal to a rule or a convention as there is more than just one (natural) way of reading them. (2) At the same time such a reading is not assigned by a merely private and arbitrary association of ideas. The referential reader is guided by a certain image or thought which he may convey to other readers. (3) This image or thought relates a group of conspicuous elements in the poetic world to an event, process, or structure of any kind in the "external" world. (4) Such an act of relating entails *(a)* a certain thematic organization (or processing) of the fictional text, and *(b)* a certain view of a represented reality. As none of these are part of private experience, in principle it is possible, even when *a* depends on *b*, to invoke the same image or thought concerning both *a* and *b* in another reader. (5) Through referential reading, the fictional work assumes "an aspect" it did not have before, yet it is possible to describe and identify the work in a neutral way. The linguistic and representational qualities of a literary fictional work (here, representational in the weak sense of the term) may be described prior to, and outside of, any thematic interpretation of the work. (6) By agreeing on such a description critics may narrow the sphere of their disagreement. Such a minimal "structure of identity" will reveal the impact of images and thoughts in the reading process and will also delineate both the interpreter's freedom and its limits.

Implicit in these claims is the view that a theory of literature, in and of itself, cannot—and need not—supply such tools for interpretations. A theory of literature cannot be expected to yield criteria for the identification of themes. The criteria according to which a given fictional work is about, let us say, the Oedipus complex, are located, at least in part, in theories of the Oedipus complex, just as the criterion according to which a given novel is a fictional autobiography of its author is located in a knowledge of the author's biography, assimilated from other sources. Expecting a theory of literature or a narratology to supply us with theme-identification criteria is analogous to expecting a theory of painting to supply us with criteria for determining that a given figurative painting is a depiction of a cow while its neighbor is a depiction of a horse. A theory of literature, then, should not be expected to generate a description of all the themes that are possible candidates for discovery, under all the reading types that might possibly be assigned to works of literature. However, it can and should be expected to clarify the compounded and richly intertextual nature of the literary theme and its interpretation.

THEMATIC CRITICISM

Peter Cryle

The history of criticism, it is worth remembering, intersects to some degree with the career of certain researchers; or rather with their *names,* in the discourses and institutions which convey and sustain them.[1] There was a moment in the history of modern French criticism when the *nouvelle critique*[2] was predominantly concerned with issues of a thematic order. I am thinking of the sixties: of Gaston Bachelard, of Charles Mauron and his *psycho-critique,* of Georges Poulet and the Geneva school's phenomenological criticism. As we all know, this critical approach was quickly displaced by Semiotics and Formalism, so that it was already possible in the mid-sixties to speak of a *nouvelle nouvelle critique.*[3]

Such, will say the wise, is the fate of any fashion; this is the lot of the modish and the modern. But instead of allowing ourselves to be swept away by progress and the eternal impatience of scientists, it may be about time we asked ourselves what forms this displacement or abandonment has taken. How semiotics, in its obsession with methodology, has managed so often to dismiss thematic issues is not the issue here: I imagine the explanation, or explanations, are fairly well known. Instead I would like to follow the trail of events in the field of general debate, the field of polemics. After what battles was thematics forced to cede to semiotics? What is the history of this defeat?

Let me say straight away, in answer to these questions, that few signs of battle remain to be seen. It seems, indeed, as if no collision ever took place, as if there was practically no feud between these two "schools." The big names in thematic criticism are not usually associated with polemics. True, there was one remarkable exchange between Roland Barthes and Raymond Picard, when the latter, having appointed himself a defender of the old criticism, went to war against the "new imposture" (his word for the *nouvelle critique*).[4] There again, it was not the masters but the neophytes of thematic criticism,

Serge Doubrovsky and Jean-Paul Weber, who replied.[5] One might wonder
what the veterans' silence betokened, whether calm, disdain or maybe both
together; but a psychological explanation would not get us very far. In an
introduction to *The Poetics of Space,* Bachelard writes: "Merely with a view to
summarizing this discussion, I should like to make a polemical remark, although indulging in polemics is not one of my habits."[6] And "habits" mean
more than mere character traits: these are methodological habits, deep-seated
dispositions, as it were. In people like Bachelard and Poulet, the refusal of
polemics is utterly *systematic,* to such an extent that they will publicly pro-
claim it. Strictly speaking, in fact, thematics and semiotics are not two opposing camps, or even schools which define themselves in opposition to each
other, but two types of knowledge which neither ground nor articulate themselves in the same way.

If the Thematics War did not take place, this is ultimately because there
was no thematic theory to defend.[7] Not that thematicians simply fail to
speculate, or lack a system. If Bachelard and Poulet have no theory, this is
because theory is inappropriate to the kind of literary criticism they seek to
pursue—or rather, to the criticism which they think they are already practis-
ing. And if they do not engage in a debate with the "nouvelle nouvelle
critique," it is doubtless because they find it inauthentic, not to say absurd.

Nowhere is this refusal better seen than in the later Bachelard, the
Bachelard of *The Poetics of Space* and *The Poetics of Reverie.* The same writer
who elsewhere indulged in epistemological and metatheoretical speculation
now strives to make the study of the "poetic image" a theory-free zone,
perhaps *the* theory-free zone. This is possible and even necessary because the
image is a "psychic event"[8] which takes place "in an individual consciousness."[9] What attracts his attention, what he would like to highlight in his
"poetics" is the *newness* of every image. As if the point were not only to
understand innately distinct consciousnesses but also *events* which are unique
every time.

There is a kind of second-degree individualism at work here: in an
individual space, experiences take place which are themselves individual.
And the image is not a unit of meaning cut out of meaningful cloth; it is an
entity—one might almost say an *organism,* for there is no such thing as a
partial image in Bachelard—which starts life alone but which, as if by a
miracle, rejoins the universal. In the experience of the image, he says, there
is a focalization of the mind: "how can an image, at times very unusual,
appear to be a concentration of the entire psyche?"[10] What allows it to
commune with the whole of the reader's being is doubtless its uniqueness
and its organicity.

But let us not launch at this point into an individualistic lyricism which
is very unlikely to elicit contemporary enthusiasm. In order to avoid any risk

of misunderstanding, it is sufficient to remember that the individualist dimension exists, without expecting anything special from it. As I shall try to
show later on, of the few attempts made by formalists and poeticians like
Ricardou to polemicize against thematics, not one ever foregrounded this
difference in ideology.

Besides, as is quite clear, Bachelard does not intend merely to *sing* the
image, so to speak: he wants to study it. To this end, he adopts what he calls a
phenomenological approach. What does he mean by this exactly? Above all, I
would say, a method with no prefabricated model, a method without theory.
To engage in phenomenology, for him, is above all to *forget*, to adopt a
methodological amnesia. He has to "forget his learning and break with all his
habits of philosophical research."[11] This is presumably how he understands
Husserl's *épochè:* only by marginalizing the "long . . . effort of putting together
and constructing [one's] thoughts"[12] can one experience the image directly.

Bachelard is obviously not concerned with *integrating* the image into any
given structure. Integration is typical of scientific epistemology, and that is
precisely what he is trying to avoid.[13] If a theoretical model were already in
place, something "general and co-ordinated" to "serve as a basis,"[14] a new
phenomenon could come along to challenge it. This could even give rise to
polemics; for the polemic, in theory at least, indicates a desire for integration.
But Bachelard insists that the image is not a concept: "the image comes *before*
thought."[15] What captivates criticism and what criticism wants to capture is
the image which, in its unpredictability, seems not to be connected to a
whole.

Bachelard thus assigns phenomenology a paradoxical task. As a method,
it is to be reinvented every time, in the act of reading: the image, he says, is
not an object;[16] in the phenomenology of the poetic image, what is at stake is
the ability to understand the act of reading without making it the fixed object
of a theoretical description. Henceforward, it becomes difficult to pin down *a*
Bachelardian thematics. For this to be possible, thematics would have to
create and perpetuate itself, whereas the "philosophy of poetry" envisioned by
Bachelard "must appear and re-appear through a significant verse, in total
adherence to an isolated image; to be exact, in the very ecstasy of the newness
of the image."[17]

Significantly, Bachelard's metaphors in the text I cite here are highly
coherent. This was doubtless to be expected from someone who formulated
the concept of authentic imagination, but this very coherence could also be
seen as an indication of a refusal of theory. It is as though Bachelard were
inviting us into a poetic reverie; the image we are supposed to grasp is, in a
way, the image of imagery. This reverie chiefly consists in a temporal imagination: the image reveals itself in the moment, or rather it is only thanks to
its power and novelty that there *are* moments at all in the reading experience.

So, faced with the experience of novelty, what we should *not* do is to measure
the distance between the image and a pre-established norm: this would be a
way of situating and thus integrating it. What really matters is novelty *per se:*
it breaks with routine duration, with the "day-in, day-out effort."[18] It makes
time into a space,[19] a self-sufficient moment. It is, in short, the time of the
individual.

True to the richest paradoxes of individualism, the image-moment still
connects to the universal. What is (provisionally) abolished is recent time, the
time of causality and of history: "the poetic act has no past, at least no recent
past, in which its preparation and appearance could be followed."[20] What
remains is the distant past, the time and space of archetypes.[21] This felicitous
suspension of duration allows for a complete rearrangement of space; it controls the comprehension and the interpretation of the moment-image. Instead of entering into a context, the image surrounds itself with resonances.
This, as Bachelard says, is the opposite of causality.[22]

This control of interpretation may provide an indication of what, for
Bachelard, the function of a semiotic or structuralist thematics might be.
There are, he says, two axes, that of resonances *[résonances]* and that of reper-
cussion *[retentissement]:* "The resonances are dispersed on the different planes
of our life in the world, while the repercussions invite us to give greater depth
to our own existence."[23] By all accounts, the vertical axis—as almost always in
our culture—is the one that counts: it represents the dimension of depth, of
roots, of everything original or archetypal. This is the axis which links the
present moment to the distant past, the individual to the universal. The
horizontal axis, on the other hand, is the axis of "multiplicity":[24] we speak of
retentissement in the singular, *résonances* in the plural. Bachelard does not go
into resonances in great detail: he feels drawn to unity and singularity. Yet
this axis might at last provide a space in which the individual image could
meet the *collective* (as opposed to the universal). Culture, as we have seen, is
not the main object of this thematics-without-a-thematics; but it could, so to
speak, be its residue. Not, again, that the image simply ends up finding its
place in the horizontal world: rather, as it dissipates, it sets off a multitude of
associations. By pursuing this path, we might end up with a phenomenology
of culture—of culture in the process of self-creation—instead of the
encyclopaedia so dear to semioticians.

So as to avoid confining ourselves to Bachelard's idiosyncrasies, and lest
this reading of a book of his degenerate into a mere description of its distinctiveness, I should like to turn to a text by Georges Poulet: *La conscience
critique.* In his "phenomenology of critical consciousness," Poulet discusses the
act of reading, the experience of a person in the process of reading.[25] This, as
is instantly apparent, is not the attitude of someone preparing to read a text
and wanting to adopt a method. On the contrary, everything is accompanied

by surprise; it is the attitude of someone who literally "doesn't see things coming." Surprise, like the feeling of novelty in Bachelard, points to a certain causal and temporal discontinuity. The experience of understanding is never really *predictable*.

What is so surprising in the reading experience? A certain fusion, a meeting of two minds, making one wonder: "How did this happen? by what procedure, through what mediation? How did I manage to open my mind to things which are normally kept out? This usually impenetrable thought process—how did I manage to enter it with such ease? I just don't know."[26]

The background which brings out this fusion and which thus produces surprise is a way of understanding consciousness which can be described in spatial terms, as is evident from the passage I have just cited. *A priori*, everyone is trapped within their own consciousness. A subject defines itself in terms of its objects; these objects are the intentional objects of this subject. How can one step outside oneself and enter another? It seems impossible, indeed inconceivable, to move toward the other's heart or mind in a long hermeneutical struggle. But these apparent problems disappear at a stroke. As if by a miracle, we find ourselves in the position of one who understands the objects of the other.

It is, then, the drama of intersubjectivity which is being acted out: "what happens when I read a book? Am I the subject of a series of verbs which are not *my* verbs?"[27] This is no Bachelardian drama of individualism or of understanding through the universal: the phrase "my verbs" does not refer to personal property, but to that which defines the subject, that which allows one to say "I." To be precise, what interests Poulet is not the image in isolation, but a certain *set* of objects. We might even talk in terms of a "structure," as long as we understand one another, for objects have a subjective unifying principle: only a consciousness can make them into a set. It guarantees a certain uniformity, whatever the rifts or contradictions between them. Jean-Pierre Richard would presumably say that this is structure in its subjective sense, form shaped by intention;[28] one might just as easily call it structure without Structuralism, without the demand for a purely internal form of coherence.

In any case, the fact that sets of intentional objects are absolutely autonomous can only add to the surprise. For Poulet's conception of the norm is presumably not so far removed from that of Sartre: any given subject-subject relationship may merely be a subject-object relationship. Reading (literature), perhaps the sole exception, allows subjects to change places, or rather to coexist on equal terms, without either party becoming the object of the other's consciousness. To avoid any possible confusion, we should point out that Poulet sees reading as a *general*, quasi-miraculous exception to the rule of intersubjective relations. His approach to literature does not involve measuring its *divergence*, by studying it from the vantage point of a phenomenological or existential norm, any more than does Bachelard's.

The following could thus be said of the phenomenology of critical consciousness: just when it proves to be laden with philosophical consequences, it shrinks from any actual theoretical project. Poulet's text continually implies this, at least, though without ever defining itself polemically. I am thinking of the play of metaphors, so conspicuous in this section of *La conscience critique*. Not the spatial metaphors (inside/outside), which are perfectly "serious," but that whole series of religious terms (intercessions, miracles, Grace—all without God, of course) and especially those little sentimental metaphors, such as the dogs awaiting their master. Perhaps it is the scope and variety of these metaphoric choices which are largely responsible for the gentle irony, the almost British whimsy which is rarely found in the great theoreticians.[29] Similarly, a doubt suffuses Poulet's text which has nothing particularly methodical or Cartesian about it, and whose function therefore seems vaguely ironic. Are the caged dogs in the shop really waiting to be bought? Are the library books really waiting impatiently to be pulled down from the shelf? Georges Poulet doesn't seem to know.

What he does know, and what ultimately allows us to correlate his approach with that of Bachelard, in spite of their major differences, is that there is a *joy* of reading. In Bachelard, joy is psychologized, so to speak: it is all about the subjective nature of the reverie, a sort of pleasure grounded in the impossibility of maintaining a substructure. It is not, as in Barthes, the pleasure of contradiction, of provocation.[30] It is a joy which never ceases to affirm and to confirm the recognizable, the understandable and the old, even while encountering the new. In Poulet, pleasure is more abstract: the experience of understanding is a happy chance. The apparently innocuous pun which connects good luck with euphoria, in French and German as well as English, regains its full power here. Bachelard and Poulet both seem to be saying that it is lucky we can understand, and that they are happy to have understood. And when one is speaking out of happiness, why bother with polemics?

Assuming that people noticed it, this attitude must have helped to defuse criticism: if the semiotic and structuralist wave managed to bypass the positions of thematics so quickly, rather than taking them by storm, the reason must simply be that few theoreticians felt compelled to take up arms against the pacifists. Jean-Pierre Roy, a rare exception, wrote a whole book[31] against the image/concept dualism as it is found in Bachelard, challenging the latter's treatment of the image in the name of a would-be scientific semiotics whose scientific side is, in fact, an epistemology like Bachelard's own. But Roy's work dates from 1977, and this rather belated attack can only be seen as a revival of Bachelard, an attempt to take him seriously: one exception in a history of neglect.

Confining ourselves, then, to France in the nineteen-sixties, we need a very active polemicist like Jean Ricardou to articulate, more or less systematically, a critique of phenomenological thematism. This comes through most strongly in *Les chemins actuels de la critique*. It is surely no coincidence that there are two editions of this text—the first, "edited by Georges Poulet," only containing the papers; the other, "completed by Jean Ricardou," also containing the debates.[32] In the complete edition, then, following a letter from Poulet on "identification criticism," there is a definition of criticism as an "awareness [*prise de conscience*] of the other's consciousness":

> When I consider this definition, I notice that it could easily fit some quite different activities, such as friendship and love: these, too, involve the awareness of another's consciousness. This definition, then, is a little vague. What is most to be feared, however, is that it should manage to make literature utterly irrelevant. Literature in this definition is, it seems, an accessory; merely a means to move toward the other, something to be transcended if one is to reach another mind.[33]

This criticism, it must be said, is at once perceptive and irrelevant. To say that Poulet's theory sounds like friendship or love seems a totally accurate assessment; Poulet himself agrees, in a statement which ends the polemics right there: "I accept that the awareness of consciousness means more or less the same thing as a relationship of friendship or of love. For me, no other relationship is possible in the field of literary criticism."[34] Where Poulet is concerned, we are indeed talking about friendship rather than universality.

Other questions in Ricardou's attack remain unanswered, however—the reason doubtless being that they would require a polemical reply from Poulet, one which would reveal his basic premises. Ricardou accuses his opponent of side-stepping literature; for Poulet, literature was never "there." Between, say, a vase as an aesthetic object and a book as subject/object he sees all the difference in the world.[35] Not for nothing does he speak of the *book* rather than of the *text*—the text, I take it, being that which the (hermeneutic and/or semiotic) method sets up as an object for study. In Poulet, there is no approach to the text and therefore no text, and hence no side-stepping, strictly speaking: it is neither a matter of dodging the hermeneutical problems (which do not interest Ricardou anyway) nor of dismissing the formal properties of the work (which interest him greatly). The happy reading does not recognize hermeneutical problems as such; the phenomenology of critical consciousness sees no positivity in literary forms. Ricardou and Poulet were really at cross purposes, and this is what terminated the exchange. Poulet, it seems, will only agree to argue where there is a basis of mutual understanding, to confirm and elaborate upon an initial agreement.

Ricardou's attack on Bachelard is more specific and more elaborate. He dedicates his Cerisy paper to it, in fact: "Let me say here that I and several of my *Tel Quel* friends, each in our own way, would challenge the importance with which some people still seem to want to credit Bachelard."[36] Apart from the rhetoric of progress (the word "still"), what stands out is the collective nature of Ricardou's position—albeit with one or two concessions to individualistic ideas. It is as if Bachelard were being targeted as the spiritual father of the old *nouvelle critique*. Unlike Poulet (who always says "I") and Bachelard (who, when he says "we," really means all readers), Ricardou uses the "we" of politics. But at no point in the discussion is he confronted with the "we" of the other side.

He accuses Bachelard of reading frivolously, and sets out to find the reason for this lack of seriousness. The fact, he says, is that Bachelard "constantly avoids the page with its cornered quarry."[37] In other words, Bachelard is not faithful to the text in its entirety: "Why do some writers with ingenious minds and often prolific imaginations abandon the text so quickly, before having cleared the territory?"[38] Here again, there was a reply to be made: that Bachelard's attention was only caught by individual images, that his dynamic imagination liked to stray beyond the narrative logic of the text, and that the "entirety" of the text was, in any case, far from being a fact, a positive reality. But such a reply would have demanded a completely different rhetoric from that of Jean-Pierre Richard, the most brilliant of Bachelard's heirs.

In a sense, Richard found a better reply anyway: it is a triumph, as well as an evasion. He evokes the imaginary universe of Ricardou, which he contrasts with that of Bachelard, translating the polemical "we" into a subjective "I" and setting up this subjective difference as a sort of absolute. In a sweeping gesture, the desire to polemicize is thus explained, Ricardou's attitude is *understood:* "here the opposition is an opposition of universes . . . ; Bachelard's substantialist and dynamist bias makes him opaque to a world perfectly defined by a static, formalist bias like Ricardou's."[39] Richard's procedure is true to a certain subjectivist custom, rhetoric and tradition; but no one within this debate, not even Ricardou himself, seems to have recognized this. Ricardou thinks he has exposed a mistake, and Richard thinks he has understood Ricardou on his own terms; but the formalist-structuralist polemics has not *engaged* with thematic interpretation.

This is a story with a rather sad ending, a 'story' which isn't one, strictly speaking. But isn't this what makes us return to the scene of the debate? Perhaps it is only by doing so that we may move beyond the fiasco without forgetting it entirely. For on the one hand—and this is what I have been driving at right from the start—it might help us grasp what might be called the law of communicational deafness. On the other hand—and this is what still remains to be covered before I conclude—we should bear in mind that some valid questions have been neglected, in the absence of any real debate.

Certain (latent) conflicts can always be revealing. Without aiming for an ultimate resolution of these conflicts, a sort of "der des ders" of polemics, I wonder whether the issues cannot be re-animated, or rather re-articulated, if we shelve certain assumptions which are liable to hinder our progress.

Besides the charges of positivism and philosophical naiveté, Ricardou's one-way polemics contains at least two criticisms which *are* worth considering when one is pondering the place of thematics. First there is the question of the paradigmatic and its status. Gérard Genette, speaking at the same colloquium, formulates this the most precisely:

> [Bachelard] may certainly be taken to task for this kind of paradigmatic ecumenicism which, when he is faced with an image, makes him think of a whole series of alternative images drawn from the entire field of literature. This paradigmatic bias,[40] as Jean Ricardou has shown, prevents him from perceiving the equally important relations which provide a work's unity and continuity, the ones the linguists call syntagmatic.[41]

As we have said, to formulate this criticism is to have other aims in mind than does Bachelard. We might still wonder, however, whether *his* thematics lends itself to transposition or translation into paradigmatic terms. As to whether every case is one of a translation of terms, a metaphorical usage and not a more direct appropriation, there should be no doubt, for the paradigmatic and the syntagmatic, strictly speaking, must be defined in relation to one another. How can one speak of a paradigm where there is really neither segmentation nor substitution? For resonances and repercussions do not count as functional equivalences in the strict sense of the word. How then to account for the coherence of this pseudo-paradigm? How is this unit, which Bachelard sees as quasi-organic, to be *reconstructed* theoretically?

Ricardou's second criticism doubtless aims to anticipate this series of questions, by deploring a vague theory of coherence which he thinks he detects in Bachelard. He calls this an "ideological" assumption: the text, he says, is only there to "express an antecedent."[42] Once again, this criticism does not "hit the mark" in the Cerisy debate, largely because it doesn't fit Bachelard very well, especially the phenomenological Bachelard who seems to be interested in *reception* without positing a corresponding "expression." It can still serve as a warning, however. The literary theme often tends to be viewed as a message—what Ricardou would call the "something-to-say." This certainly goes for the original champion of the theme, Jean-Paul Weber, a scholar we had such difficulty taking seriously, perhaps because he wanted his theory to be thoroughly scientific. His "monothematism"[43] literally consisted in using one central theme to explain, account for and condense an author's entire corpus. From this angle, the text or set of texts signed by a single author was a single problem to be solved, and thematics culminated in a sort of hermeneutical triumphalism.

This leads me to reformulate Ricardou's questions in the following way. Firstly, how can one address paradigmatic problems without first having established syntagmatic equivalences in the text? Secondly, doesn't thematics come down to a hermeneutics of the message, a reductive and, in short, primitive hermeneutics?

By thus imagining (in a generous conjecture) a positivism-free Ricardou, we may picture a thematics which is not such a sideline of individualism. Besides, thanks to Gadamer's philosophical hermeneutics,[44] this field may be about to open up. Like Bachelard and Poulet, though much more explicitly, Gadamer starts from a philosophy of understanding. But for him, the subject of the understanding is always plural. He challenges the supremacy of the *I:Thou* nexus, and he would most certainly also dispute that of Poulet's *I:I* relationship. Understanding, for Gadamer, always starts with the *we:* for the *I* and *Thou* positions to define themselves in relation to one another, there must first be an agreement, an *Einverständnis*.[45] And if there is such a thing as understanding, says Gadamer, it must be an understanding *of* something. There is an object *(Sache)* which is not the Saussurian referent but the essential target of understanding.[46]

Out of this comes the following, still relevant question: isn't the theme precisely this *Sache*—not the referent of the textual sign (in the singular), but that which allows the act of understanding to take place, as well as forming its target? If this were so, a Gadamerian thematics would have made the following answer possible: "at the end of the day, what is interesting is not that inauthentic object, the *something-to-say*, but what one might call *the understood*[47]—the thing without which the act of reading could never have been entered into. Even if an already-articulated message cannot always be expressed exactly as it is, one always ends up in the knowledge that one was dealing with *something* in the hermeneutical process: this is what Formalist criticism failed to realize."

As one might gather, I can almost see thematics making a counterattack, using a rhetoric almost diametrically opposed to that of the Formalists. Where the latter might say "you forgot the syntagm," thematics would retort: "you never stopped using themes, you just did so without knowing it." Thematics would have this to say to the modern Formalist: "now you have found the fold, the hole, the blank, the rupture everywhere; but you've been dealing with a theme all along, the rather special theme of themelessness. And if you found it just about everywhere, that's because it had to meet an expectation within *you*." This thematics would also point out that the Formalist poetics exists within a cultural context, and that, in terms of understanding, forms themselves function more or less like themes.

If thematics wished to take on Formalism in this way, however, it would have to hold a different ground. It would have to abandon that vision of discontinuity which crops up constantly in Bachelard and Poulet: there could be no more talk of the image-moment or of consciousness-within. Here again, Gadamer shows the way in speaking of *wirkungsgeschichtliches Bewusstsein:* the effects of history, that is, and also the history of effects.[48] For him, consciousness has a place within tradition; it is inscribed in language, a continuity transcending the individual. No longer is the subject a radically different being every time it appears, but a position defined by a game—by a type of open structure, in other words. With this in mind it would be hard to speak, as Ricardou does, of a textual object set against a vague and unstable subjectivity, or to invoke, as Bachelard does, a universal subjective depth transcending cultural scope and dissipation at a stroke. Gadamer is also not afraid to speak of depth; but for him it is the anticipation of understanding, deeply rooted in tradition. This depth is culture itself.

Finally, I would like to point out that my own paper's methodology has, I feel, been in keeping with the Gadamerian (and structuralist) thematics I have just discussed. My procedure has been reflexive and retrospective: this is not the heroic manifesto of an as yet unimagined and unimaginable theory. What I have tried to construct, in a short space of time, is a *thematics* of theoretical and quasi-theoretical discourses in their problematic plurality. What we have here is a reformist inquiry, not a revolutionary project. Still, modesty does not exclude optimism here, for by striving to pursue the various traditions of critical thought, even in the study of a historical failure, we can ultimately claim to understand misunderstanding.

A THEMATICS OF MOTIVATION AND ACTION

Lubomír Doležel

1. The idea of a general thematics

At this advanced stage of our endeavors, we should consider the possibility of a general thematics, a universal theory which would encompass both actuality and fiction. The view that thematics is a bridge between fiction and reality is not new. It has already been stated in general terms by the Prague school scholar Felix Vodička:

> *"Thematics is precisely that layer of literary structure through whose mediation the contents of the practical interests and period problems of a community exercise the most powerful influence on the immanent evolution of the literary structure"* (1948, 168; Vodička's italics).

In the specific domain of narrative thematics, Bremond clearly perceived the same connection:

> "Aux types narratifs élémentaires correspondent . . . les formes les plus générales du comportement humain. . . . Technique de l'analyse littéraire, la sémiologie du récit tire sa possibilité et sa fécondité de son enracinement dans une anthropologie" (1966, 76).

It is encouraging to see that hands have also been stretched out from the other side, from the "anthropology" of human acting. The best known outline of a non-literary thematics, Gerald Holton's thematic analysis of scientific activity (Holton *passim*), takes its inspiration from art criticism, musicology and folkloristics. Holton believes that thematic analysis reveals "a link between scientific activity and humanistic studies." Scientific themata, like the themes of the folklorist, are not explicit in texts; they are categories of an "underlying thematic structure and recurrence" (Holton 1978, 9). Despite their "hidden" character, themata are powerful forces in the development of scientific thought: "The imagination of a scientist may be guided by his, perhaps implicit, fidelity to one or more *themata*" (Holton 1978, viii). Holton arranges his themata, just as the binarizing ethnographers and mythographers do, into "antithetical couples," such as evolution–devolution, constancy–simplicity, holism–reductionism, hierarchy–unity, efficacy of mathematics–efficacy of mechanistic models, etc. He believes (imitating Propp, one is tempted to say) that themata of science are limited in number and suggests that "the total of singlets, doublets, and occasional triplets will turn out to be less than 100" (1978, 10).

If we go back several decades, to the research project of Henry A. Murray and his Harvard team, we come across the concept of "thema" applied to a much broader domain: human acting in general, Murray finds the concept useful for setting up a dynamic theory of human personality, a theory of the acting man. He frames human action by need—"a hypothetical force . . . within the organism"—and press: "a tendency or 'potency' in the environment" which obstructs or facilitates satisfaction (1938, 42, 40). The thema is the "dynamical structure" of a simple or complex episode of behavior in a "particular press-need combination" (1938, 42).[1] The number of Murray's themas is, again, restricted. The personality structure is dominated by a 'unity-thema,' "an underlying reaction system" which is the "key" to an individual's unique nature. The unity-thema is formed in early childhood and "repeats itself in many forms during later life" (1938, 604–05).[2] Because an individual is a set of "the most recurrent themas," he or she "displays a tendency to react in a similar way to similar situations. . . . Thus there is sameness (consistency) as well as change (variability)." The biography of a human being is "an historic route of themas" (1938, 43–44).

Murray's and Holton's works are typical of the epistemology of general thematics, in their shortcomings and foresight both. On the negative side, we search in vain for a sharp definition of the concept and for a logically well-founded taxonomy. The concept remains vague and a consistent taxonomy elusive primarily because the themes' logical form remains indefinite. Holton reveals this weakness when he speaks of three different "uses" of the term—the thematic concept, the methodological thema and the thematic proposition (hypothesis)—without dealing with the troubling consequences of this logical hodgepodge.

On the positive side, general thematics asserts three important theoretical tenets: 1. Thematic analysis is part and parcel of a structural (holistic) epistemic strategy. This principle can clearly be seen at work in Murray's enquiry: his thematic psychology issues from a "molar" view of the acting man; it is a macrostructural theory of personality.[3] 2. Themes are *invariant* universal features of human acting underlying *variable* particular occurrences. Human acting in all its variety is subject to the constraints of thematic patterns. 3. Themes are generated on various levels of the action structure, depending on the purpose of thematization.

The last point seems to me to be very important for further theoretical development: it invites us to focus on the activity of thematization. Thematization is a necessary, initial stage of representation. A world or domain is thematized in the process of being represented. Thematization consists in choosing from the world (domain) a constituent or a set of constituents which will serve as the dominant feature of or starting point for the particular representation. Around the theme all the world's (domain's) constituents are arranged in a network of levels and relations; in other words, the theme operates as a macro-instruction, as a global command according to which the representative organizes the world (domain). It serves our initial purpose well that this conception of thematization can be applied to both referential and fictional discourse. But a fundamental difference has to be emphasized in realist ontology: referential themes are macro-instructions for world-description (for the formulation of cognitive models), while fictional themes serve as macro-instructions for world-construction (for the creation of fictional images).

The most important gain to be made in taking the general thematics perspective is the recognition that each world (domain) can be thematized in many different ways, depending on the purpose of its representation.[4] Thus, for example, in representing human acting, psychology will choose other themes than will philosophy or sociology or political science. Fictional representation generates the richest and most varied set of themes because it strives to perform all possible thematizations on all possible worlds.

The complexity of the procedure of thematization and the breadth of its scope explains the theoretical difficulties of general thematics. The immensity (some would say, impossibility) of its task has deflected thematics onto an empirical route: themes have simply been identified with *recurrent* representations. In other words, historical endurance rather than operational force has been taken as the defining feature of the concept. Is there any conceivable way out of the empiricism and historicism of thematics? I believe there is, but at this stage we have to follow Horton and attempt to develop general thematics for restricted, specific domains. I intend to indicate how we could proceed towards a general thematics of human action. The selection of this domain is a result of my interest in narrative themes to which my contributions to Thématique I and Thématique II were devoted (see Doležel 1985 and 1988). This paper, then, is an attempt to integrate the thematics of fictional narrative into the general thematics of acting.

2. Basics of a theory of motivation

In contemporary philosophy of action as well as in post-behavioristic psychology (for a survey, see Brand 1984, 6-23) the idea that human acting is crucially linked to, or caused by, mental factors has prevailed. The "proximate" mental event, the event which initiates or triggers acting, is called *intention*. Intention is a necessary condition, a defining feature of acting. The presence of intention differentiates actions from other events (in particular, those caused by forces of nature). Owing to its necessary character, intention is taken for granted and as a result usually goes unnoticed. This circumstance explains a curious discrepancy: while in philosophical theories of acting the concept of intention is the center of attention, in representations of acting it is almost always deleted. As a rule, intention (in terms of desire or wanting) is only mentioned in the case of failed or forfeited actions. Empirical action theories find little use for the concept of intention for yet another reason: being invariable (undifferentiated, non-graded), intention cannot serve as a criterion for distinguishing and classifying varieties of acting.

The difficulties with intention disappear if we recognize that it is a necessary *but not sufficient* determinant of human acting. Action in context, in its link to the person-agent and its societal embedding, is conditioned by other, more powerful and more obvious mental factors, designated by the general term 'motivation.' Motivational factors determine the "the choice, the intensity and the persistence of activities" (Birch and Veroff 1966, 10). As more or less stable constituents of personality structure, motivational factors generate ways of acting characteristic of individuals or of personality types. On a more general level, they constitute the regularities and specificities of *action modes.*[5] For all these reasons, the concept of motivation is crucial to a theory of action in general, and to a thematics of acting in particular.

I have emphasized that the role of motivation becomes apparent when action is considered in its connection to the acting person. Not surprisingly, we need to turn to psychology rather than to philosophy if we want to learn about motivation. I propose to begin our brief excursion into motivational psychology by getting acquainted with a neobehavioristic taxonomy of motivations. Summarizing many years of observations and experimental research, Birch and Veroff (1966) enumerate seven motivational systems: 1) the sensory system stimulates bodily responses which aim at releasing pressure or tension in the organism; 2) the system of curiosity makes the organism react to new stimuli; 3) the affiliative system motivates a person's contact with others; 4) the aggressive system provokes reactions to frustration by others; 5) the achievement system stimulates goal-oriented performance; 6) the power system provides a person with the ability to withstand influence by others; 7) the independence system motivates persons to act on their own.

Birch and Veroff claim that these motivational systems taken together "account for most of man's significant recurrent behaviors" (1966, 41). Today, their taxonomy appears to mean the end of those theories of human acting which restricted motivation to drives (instincts). Contemporary developments in motivational psychology are remarkable for two main reasons. First, it has been recognized that human drives acquire specific features through cultural conditioning. As Vernon points out, "even simple homeostatically motivated behavior may in human beings become complicated, diversified and modified through interaction with tastes and habits of eating and food seeking which are to a considerable extent acquired and maintained through social pressures" (1969, 39).[6] Of still greater import is the second moment of the recent development: gradually, models of human mental life have become more and more complex and, correspondingly, the set of motivational systems has been expanded. It is especially significant for our purpose that the newly legitimized (or rather restored) mental domains and motivational factors include the emotional and cognitive capacities of humankind.

Behaviorism treated emotions as adjuncts of drives; contemporary motivational psychology thematizes them as autonomous mental and motivational forces. Thus, for example, Averill 'unpacks' the aggression system to separate from it a motivating emotion—anger. He argues convincingly that "aggression . . . may take many forms, of which anger is only one. Conversely, anger may be expressed in a great variety of ways, nonaggressive as well as aggressive" (1979, 11). Averill is especially helpful to us in pointing out that legal systems acknowledge the motivational force of emotions by recognizing "crimes of passion" (1979, 35). Another motivational psychologist goes so far as to claim that "the emotion system is the primary motivational system for human beings over the life span" (Izard 1979, 167).

Cognitive factors were already deemed decisive for human acting in Greek philosophy. In Aristotle's theory of action they were formalized in the syllogism of 'practical reasoning.' Contemporary cognitive psychology and artificial intelligence research have re-thematized these factors by postulating that cognitive operations guide human acting at all stages—goal-setting, selection of alternatives, monitoring, evaluation of results, etc. Artificial intelligence research has been particularly influential in foregrounding global designs—"plans" or "scripts"—which are followed in more complex actions and activities (for a survey, see Brand 1984, 204–21). Let me emphasize that cognitive factors of acting include not only universally shared knowledge but also, and primarily, personal beliefs and opinions, group ideologies, communal conventions, etc.

Contemporary motivational psychology should provide a new taxonomy of motivational factors but I know of no systematization comparable to Birch-Veroff's. It therefore seems reasonable to me to restrict our thematics to the minimum set of determinants which we have specified: *drive—emotion—cognition*. The thematic role of these systems lies in determining the degree of control that the agent exercises (or is capable of exercising) over his or her actions. Drives have the power to compel agents to act against their will; emotions affect them as "passions," i.e. inflicted forces which, overwhelming the agents, escape their direct control;[7] only cognition gives them control over their acting to the degree that they are able to set a goal and weigh deliberately the range of alternative actions which would lead to its attainment.

Motivational factors are differentiated in theoretical discourse, but in human acting they operate jointly, in clusters. Erotic activity provides a remarkable example of such a cluster: all of the factors which we have established—drive, emotion and cognition—are mobilized in its pursuit. But the clusters are arranged hierarchically, with a particular *master* factor dominating the acting and thus determining its mode. The second thematic role of motivation thus becomes apparent: the mode of acting which a particular agent pursues on a particular occasion depends on the master factor of his or her motivational cluster. We thus come to the conclusion that acting can be thematized on the basis of motivational factors. The final part of this paper will indicate the kind of action thematics that can be derived within this frame. In the spirit of Vodička and Bremond, we will move easily from the thematization of motivation in the actual world to the themes of fictional acting.

3. Motivational themes of acting

Traditional thematics of fictional acting derived from the physical moment of action; narrative themes were configurations of physical actions. Thus, for example, the core of Propp's popular thematics is a set of functions—generalized physical acts (travel, abduction, pursuit, fight, transfiguration, the building of a palace, etc.). Barthes's haphazard list of descriptions of actions *(proaïrétismes)* and action sequences (1970, 259–63) is dominated by physical actions *(sortir, toucher, entrer)* and speech acts *(narrer, poser une question, déclaration d'amour);* they are interspersed with mental states *(jouissance, tristesse, peur)* and intentions *(vouloir sortir)*. This mélange reflects a dualism typical of traditional narratology: action is in the physical domain, character is a set of mental properties (traits, dispositions). In other words, narrative structure is split into physical story and psychological personage.

A thematization of acting on the basis of motivation transcends this dualism. It brings about a radical psychologization of the story and, at the same time, makes the personage an acting entity, a mind in action. This direction is already pointed to in Bremond's "logique du récit" (1973). According to Bremond, a person is led to acting (or to abstention from acting) by three kinds of binary "mobiles": hedonic (desire/aversion), pragmatic (favorable/unfavorable calculation) and ethical (awareness of obligation/of interdiction). But as far as the control and the mode of acting is concerned, the Bremondian agent remains an Aristotelian agent par excellence. He or she is a voluntary agent when "ayant conçu le projet de modifier l'état des choses existant, [il] passe à l'acte pour réaliser ce changement"; he/she becomes an involuntary agent only by ignorance or by error (176, 235).

Our set of motivational systems enables us to produce a richer narrative thematics. Let me survey rapidly some of the possible procedures for thematizing the domain of fictional acting:

3.1. Reflecting the pressure of the master factor, acting is thematized into an instinctual, a passional and a rational mode

One and the same physical action will be thematized ('interpreted') differently depending on its motivational background. Thus, for example, the murder committed by Raskolnikov (in Dostoevsky's *Crime and Punishment*) is a rational (ideologically motivated) action, the murder committed by Rogozhin (in Dostoevsky's *The Idiot*) is a passional action (crime of passion), and the killing of the Arab by Meursault (in Camus's *L'Étranger*) is instinctual.[8] In each case, the thematic character of the key action (murder) is determined by its master motivation—by perverse ideology in *Crime and Punishment*, by desperate passion in *The Idiot*, by subconscious drives in *L'Étranger*.[9]

3.2. Actions are thematized by being engendered in a conflict of motivations

This procedure is probably the most popular generator of narrative themes, yielding dramatic thematic structures in which agents act or interact in the dynamics of tension, instability, sudden reversals and insuperable torments.[10] Let me indicate how this vast thematic field could be mapped:

3.2.1. THEMES OF *INTERNAL CONFLICT* ARE LOCALIZED WITHIN THE MIND OF THE ACTING PERSON. They can be further subdivided into intrasystemic and intersystemic conflicts. Intrasystemic conflicts arise when constituents of one and the same motivational system, a negative and a positive factor of the same kind, compete for control of acting. Within the drive system, tension between the affiliation and independence drives generates a typical maturation theme (often represented in the *bildungsroman*). A well-known if not notorious theme emerges within the achievement drive: the incompatibility of a woman's achievement goals, i.e. her family's well-being and her career (see Birch and Veroff 1966, 64). The theme of jealousy arises from a conflict within the emotional system, from the tension between possessive love and fear of loss or withdrawal. Themes of internal intersystemic conflict are produced when different motivational systems vie for the control of a person's acting. The core of this thematic field is constituted by a conflict between the instinctual and the rational mode of acting—a conflict which exhausts the energy of Prince Myshkin, hero of *The Idiot*. No less popular is the clash between passion and ideology—the theme of Mme. de Rênal's behavior in *Le Rouge et le noir*, from the moment she realizes that Julien is one of "ces jeunes gens des basses classes, trop bien élévés" who could make possible the return of Robespierre (ch. XVII).

3.2.2. THEMES OF *INTERPERSONAL CONFLICT* ARISE IN INTERACTION, WHERE THE MOTIVATIONS OF ONE AGENT ARE NECESSARILY LINKED TO THE MOTIVATIONS OF HIS OR HER CO-AGENTS. While the agents are in conflict, feedback may, paradoxically, reinforce each individual's personal motivations. The Dostoevskian "scandal," the "hideous scenes" in which the most intimate private issues are aired in public, is a fascinating instance of this thematic structure. Mutually reinforcing their passions, the antagonists gradually lose control over their acting and scandal rises to a furious climax of screams, insults and physical blows. A sudden de-escalation occurs when one of the participants escapes from the deterministic chain of conflictive reinforcement. This is what happens in the *The Idiot* (ch. I, 8) when the innocent bystander Prince Myshkin fails to retaliate in response to a displaced physical assault.[11] His reaction is totally incongruous with the motivational energy of the scandal and brings about its collapse.

3.3. Mme de Rênal's story proceeds within the theme of inner motivational conflict until she is forcefully made aware that she loves a man "qui n'est point son mari."

At this moment, another theme—adultery—takes over. Mme de Rênal's theme is a very popular one, but it is just a single instance within an extensive thematic field, generated in the opposition between personal motivation and suprapersonal modal restrictions. Persons are endowed with more or less limited action capabilities, trapped in predetermined roles, faced with societal prescriptions and prohibitions, surrounded by values and dysvalues, manipulated by powerful ideologies. Individuals cope with the modally circumscribed world in many different ways. Themes of misfits, aliens, rebels, etc. are generated in the conflict between personal motivation and societal restrictions, while themes of acquiescence, repentance, punishment, etc. are engendered in the submission of personal motivation to suprapersonal powers.

The thematization of the relationship between individual existence and its supraindividual environment transcends the real theme of this paper, i.e. the motivational thematics of action. It requires, obviously, the introduction of societal (codexal) conditions, conventions and norms. We shall not enter this thematic field here, leaving it for a more detailed study (see Doležel forthcoming). Let me just conclude with a few words in defence of my own motivation for presenting this work in progress. Actional thematics derived from motivational factors is fraught with theoretical dangers. We have to enter the human mind, a realm which even its greatest explorers recognized as a construct of tentative representations, working hypotheses and provisional conceptualizations. On the other hand, progress in actional and narrative thematics requires the clear recognition that human acting is intextricably bound up with it. For this reason, it is worth making the attempt.

References

Atkinson, John W., and David Birch. 1978. *An Introduction to Motivation*. 2nd ed. New York: van Nostrand.

Averill, James R. 1979. "Anger." In Dienstbier, ed. 1979. 1–80.

Barthes, Roland. 1970. *S/Z: Essai*. Paris: Seuil.

Birch, David, and Joseph Veroff. 1956. *Motivation: A Study of Action*. Belmont, CA: Brooks/Cole.

Bloom, H. 1986. "Freud, the Greatest Modern Writer." *New York Times Book Review*, March 23, 1, 26–27.

Brand, Myles. 1984. *Intending and Acting: Toward a Naturalized Action Theory*. Cambridge, MA: MIT Press.

Bremond, Claude. 1966. "La logique des possibles narratifs." *Communications* 8: 60–76.

———. 1973. *Logique du récit*. Paris: Seuil.

Brooks, Peter. 1984. *Reading for the Plot: Design and Intention in Narrative*. New York: Knopf.

Danto, Arthur. 1973. *Analytical Philosophy of Action*. Cambridge: Cambridge University Press.

Dienstbier, Richard A., ed. 1979. *Nebraska Symposium on Motivation 1978: Human Emotion*. Lincoln: University of Nebraska Press.

Doležel, Lubomír. 1985. "Un champ thématique: Le triangle du double." *Poétique* 64: 463–72.

———. 1988. "Thématique de la solitude: Robinson Crusoe et Des Esseintes" *Communications* 47: 187–97.

———. forthcoming. *Possible Worlds and Literary Fictions*.

Geha, Richard E. 1988. "Freud as Fictionalist: The Imaginary World of Psychoanalysis." In Paul E. Stepansky, ed. *Freud: Appraisals and Reappraisals* (Contributions to Freud Studies, vol. 2). Ed. Paul E. Stepansky. Hillsdale, NJ: The Analytic Press, 103–60.

Holton, Gerald. 1973. *Thematic Origins of Scientific Thought: Kepler to Einstein.* Cambridge, MA: Harvard University Press.

———. 1978. *The Scientific Imagination: Case Studies.* Cambridge: Cambridge University Press.

Izard, C. E. 1979. "Emotions as Motivations: An Evolutionary-Developmental Perspective." In Dienstbier, ed. 1979. 163–200.

Mahony, P. 1982. *Freud as Writer.* New York: International Universities Press.

Murray, Henry A. et al. 1938. *Explorations in Personality: A Clinical and Experimental Study of Fifty Men of College Age.* New York: Oxford University Press.

Prince, Gerald. 1985. "Thématiser." *Poétique* 64: 425–33.

Vernon, M. D. 1969. *Human Motivation.* Cambridge: Cambridge University Press.

Vodička, Felix. 1948. *Počátky krásné prózy novočeské*/The Beginnings of Modern Czech Fictional Prose/. Prague: Melantrich.

Part II

THEMATICS IN LITERATURE

THE BLUISH TINGE IN THE HALFMOONS; OR, FINGERNAILS AS A RACIAL SIGN: THE STUDY OF A MOTIF

Werner Sollors

Les métisses ne diffèrent des blanches que par quelques signes imperceptibles.

—Eugène Sue, *Les Mystères de Paris*

Die größten Dinge der Welt werden durch andere zuwege gebracht, die wir nicht achten, kleine Ursachen, die wir übersehen, und die sich endlich häufen.

—Georg Christoph Lichtenberg, *Sudelbücher* (1765–1770)

The Sign

In a great variety of French, American, German, and English literary texts that were published from the mid-nineteenth to the mid-twentieth century and that have as one of their subjects black-white romances and families, a small but startling detail recurs with some frequency.

Sir Walter Murph comments, in Eugène Sue's immensely popular novel *Les Mystères de Paris* (1843ff), on the American Mulatto woman Cecily's charm:

> Il faudrait l'oeil impitoyable d'un créole pour découvrir le *sang mêlé* dans l'imperceptible nuance bistrée qui colore légèrement la couronne des ongles roses de cette métisse; nos fraîches beautés du Nord n'ont pas un teint plus transparent, une peau plus blanche.

(It would require a Creole's pitiless eye to detect the *sang-mêlé* [person of "mixed blood"] in the imperceptible dark shade which lightly colors the crowns of that Mulatto woman's rosy fingernails; our fairest Northern beauties do not own a more transparent complexion, nor a whiter skin.)[1]

The Irish-American melodramatist Dion Boucicault wrote the play *The Octoroon* (1859), which is set on the Louisiana plantation *Terrebonne*. The fairskinned title heroine Zoe describes herself as ineligible for matrimony with her white cousin George Peyton because she feels separated from him by a gulf which she explains to him in the following way:

> *Zoe.* . . . George, do you see that hand you hold? look at these fingers; do you see the nails are of a bluish tinge?
>
> *George.* Yes, near the quick there is a faint blue mark.

Boucicault's Zoe interprets this and other signs as "dark, fatal" marks which point to her slave descent and cause her to feel racial shame. She has thus accepted a racial hierarchy within her own constitution:

> Of the blood that feeds my heart, one drop in eight is black—bright red as the rest may be, that one drop poisons all the flood; those seven bright drops give me love like yours—hope like yours—ambition like yours—life hung with passions like dew-drops on the morning-flowers; but the one black drop gives me despair, for I'm an unclean thing—forbidden by the laws— I'm an Octoroon.[2]

In Theodor Storm's North German novella "Von jenseit des Meeres" ("From Across the Sea") (1865), the architect Alfred describes Jenni, his beloved cousin from overseas, with a particularly detailed account of the mark:

> Als ich dabei unwillkürlich auf die schlanken weißen Fingerchen blickte, welche die meinen gefangen hielten, erschien mir daran, ich wußte nicht was, anders, als ich es sonst gesehen hatte. Und plötzlich, während ich darüber nachsann, sah ich es auch. Die kleinen Halbmonde an den Wurzeln der Nägel waren nicht wie bei uns Andern heller, sondern bläulich und dunkler als der übrige Teil derselben. Ich hatte damals noch nicht gelesen, daß dies als Kennzeichen jener oft so schönen Parias der amerikanischen Staaten gilt, in deren Adern auch nur ein Tropfen schwarzen Sklavenbluts läuft; aber es befremdete mich und ich konnte die Augen nicht davon wenden.

> (Then, when I inadvertently looked upon her slender little white fingers which held mine captive, something about them, I don't know what, seemed different from the way I had perceived it before. And suddenly, while pon-

dering upon it, I saw what it was. The small half moons at the roots of her nails were not, as ours are, lighter than the rest of the nails, but darker and bluish. I had not yet read then that this is considered the identifying sign of America's frequently very beautiful pariahs in whose veins even a mere drop of slave blood is coursing; but it was a strange sight, and I could not take my eyes off it.)[3]

In Rudyard Kipling's short story "Kidnapped" (1887), set in India, young Peythroppe is prevented by his friends from marrying the "Spanish"-complexioned Miss Castries whose "little opal-tinted onyx at the base of her finger-nails" reveals her racial identity "as plainly as print."[4]

Around 1884 Mark Twain composed a sketch in which a nameless character decides to pass for white: "At last, seeing even the best educated negro is at a disadvantage, beside being always insulted, clips his wiry hair, wears gloves always (to conceal his telltale nails), & passes for a white man, in a Northern city." In Mark Twain's novel *Pudd'nhead Wilson* (1894) Roxana (who is one-sixteenth black) is upset that her son "Tom" Driscoll has refused a duel; she berates him and then mutters to herself: "Ain't nigger enough in him to show in his finger-nails, en dat takes mighty little—yit dey's enough to paint his soul."[5]

In Gertrude Atherton's novel *Senator North* (1900) the white heroine Betty Madison encourages her illegitimate Mulatto half-sister Harriet Walker to pass for white; looking at Harriet's fingernails, however, Betty notices something: "There was a faint bluish stain at the base of the nails; and she remembered. It was the outward and indelible print of the hidden vein within. The nails are the last stronghold of negro blood."[6]

Dorothy Canfield writes in her novel *The Bent Twig* (1915) that the segregated black Washington Street school in the midwestern town of La Chance

> was filled with laughing, shouting children, ranging from shoe-black through coffee-color to those occasional tragic ones with white skin and blue eyes, but with the telltale kink in the fair hair and the bluish half-moon at the base of the finger-nails.[7]

In his short story "Elly," written in 1929 and published in 1934, William Faulkner focuses on the title heroine's rebellion against the restrictions imposed upon her life by her cold grandmother. Elly is provocatively flirtatious and necks with numerous men until she finds herself drawn to Paul de Montigny whom the inhabitants of Jefferson suspect to be a Negro. Elly is partly attracted to Paul because a relationship with him would signal her defiance of the ultimate Southern taboo; yet while she obviously assumes Paul is a Negro in her dealings with him, she denies it when speaking with her grandmother—whereupon the grandmother tells Elly: "Look at his hair, his fingernails, if you need proof."[8]

In Fannie Hurst's bestselling novel *Imitation of Life* (1933) the black woman Delilah Johnston explains why her daughter Peola is so light:

> Her pap jes' had style mixed in, I guess, wid a teaspoonful of white blood back somewheres, an' it got him through life an' three wives widout ever turnin' them lily-pink palms of his. Style, but not a half-moon to his finger nails, and doan' you forget it.[9]

The Foxes of Harrow (1946), a novel by the popular African-American writer Frank Yerby, includes a dialogue between Stephen and his son Etienne that takes the following turn: "All I do know is that Aupre Hippolyte has a touch of the tarbrush about him. Ye should have studied his nails."[10]

Such descriptions of fingernails appear in texts set in India, Germany, France, Britain, and—most frequently—the United States; they can be found in short stories, novellas, novels, autobiographies, plays, and nonfiction, and are particularly prevalent in popular literature. Many more examples could undoubtedly be found, and some will be cited later.

Specialized studies of individual texts have mentioned in passing the puzzling occurrence of this small descriptive detail in a few particular works. What, however, are we to do when we confront the evidence culled from numerous different texts? What are we to make of the recurrence of such a small element? We might think of details, however small, as *motifs*, though this particular example is probably even more minute than the ones usually regarded as motifs. Speaking of motifs and themes often means, and here I am following Menachem Brinker's useful suggestion, setting up a potential relationship among various texts; in this fashion we might try to search for the recurrence of motifs in several texts in order to raise certain questions.[11] This, however, constitutes a "thematic approach" to literature—an approach that seems to have gone out of fashion under heavy attack from various camps. For example, René Wellek called thematic history the "least literary of histories."[12] More recently, Barbara Herrnstein Smith questioned the very *existence* of a "thematic plane" in texts, citing as evidence that there are a thousand variants of *Cinderella* tales and concluding:

> All of these stories are in some respects similar and in some respects dissimilar. The incidence, nature, and degrees of resemblance and disparity are so diverse, however, that they allow just about every conceivable type of causal relation among the stories, including none at all.[13]

Are we therefore moving into the realm of methodological illegitimacy when trying to explore "versions" of a theme or a motif? Or when attempting to link a single detail in one text with similar such details in other works? Are we merely making up a relationship between texts? Should we just discard such cumulative evidence as inconsequential and demand that recurrent elements in literature ('constants') be ignored in favor of the uniqueness of individual texts?[14] Does assembling such a series of instances create the illusion that texts are only derived from each other and not, for example, from experience or observation?[15] Are these "instances," in fact, at all "versions" (a concept Herrnstein Smith would seem to question) of what one could call "the fingernail motif," or do they contain more variables than can be generalized under such a motif? Does the fingernail motif, in fact, refer to "observation," and if not, how and why did the motif originate and how was it disseminated and transformed? What ideological and cultural meanings can be located in such an element?

Two broad approaches most readily offer themselves for this endeavor. One is a systematic-structural-synchronic method that searches for constants and variants (and their patterns), and the other a historical-genealogical-diachronic procedure that investigates changes—origins, transformations, substitutions, and disappearances—in the context of cultural history.[16] I shall here attempt to develop both approaches in order to provoke more thinking about the many questions and problems this essay will attempt to address and answer only in part.

Patterns of a Motif

Surveying the instances of a motif one notices shared features as well as differences among the texts; this invites the construction of certain groupings of the motif. In the case of the fingernail motif, in all instances the inspection of the nails is expected to yield clues to a character's nonwhite racial ancestry, however remote it may be and how white in appearance the person in question is. Yet the variations are considerable.

The fingernail sign may need description and explanation. This is the case in Storm's story where the visual recognition is presented as taking place before Alfred had read anything about the sign, and in Boucicault's dialogue where Zoe's lengthy explanation retards dramatic action. In Atherton the narrator intercedes with the explanatory description even though the argument is made in the text that the sign is instinctually recognizable. The description of the sign varies, too, from a dark shade to a bluish tinge and from an opal-tinted onyx to a half-moon.

Upon other occasions the reader's familiarity with the motif seems to be taken for granted, hence requiring no description beyond the quickest reference to "telltale nails" (Mark Twain, Hurst, or Yerby). In some borderline cases, the mark may be assumed to be known to readers even when it is *not* explicitly mentioned in the text. For example, in Kate Chopin's short story, originally entitled "The Father of Désirée's Baby" (1893), the rapid growth of the child's fingernails is explicitly commented upon by Désirée: "Look at his legs, mamma, and his hands and finger-nails,—real finger-nails. Zandrine had to cut them this morning." Though it is not made a more explicit "sign" in the story, Kate Chopin may have counted on her readers' knowledge of the fingernail as a racial clue. After all, Désirée seems to be the last to find out that her baby is "not white," whereas her foster mother, everyone in the household, and her husband have been able to read the signs, perhaps at the baby's birth.[17] Similarly, in Ross Lockridge's epic novel *Raintree County* (1948) the disturbed Susanna Shawnessy spends a long time looking at her newborn child's "little hands and feet and its blue eyes," inquiring whether there was, perhaps, another child, a twin that had been thrown away. Such cases constitute a thematics of *absence*—according to which we look at a given text in a certain way by drawing on details that are present only in other works.[18]

Some texts presuppose that there really is such a mark in nature (for example, Sue, Boucicault, Storm, Atherton, Kipling) and that it is proof of racial identity. Others (fewer in number) imply or state that there is no such sign in reality and that looking for it yields unreliable results. Thus the very lightskinned African American Walter White told Claude McKay stories of his experiences passing for white, and McKay reports in his autobiography *A Long Way From Home* (1937):

> To me the most delectable was one illustrating the finger-nail theory of telling a near-white from a pure-white. White was traveling on a train on his way to investigate a lynching in the South. The cracker said, "There are many yaller niggers who look white, but I can tell them every time."
>
> "Can you really?" Walter White asked.
>
> "Oh sure, just by looking at their finger nails." And taking White's hand, he said, "Now if you had nigger blood, it would show here on your half-moons."

McKay concludes:

> That story excited me by its paradox as much as had the name and complexion of Walter White. It seemed altogether fantastic that whites in the South should call him a "nigger" and whites in the North, a Negro. It violates my feeling of words as conveying color and meaning. . . .
>
> For me a type like Walter White is Negroid simply because he closely identifies himself with the Negro group—just as a Teuton becomes a Mos-

lem if he embraces Islam. White is whiter than many Europeans—even biologically. I cannot see the difference in the way that most of the whites and most of the blacks seem to see it. Perhaps what is reality for them is fantasy for me.[19]

The sign may also be believed to be generally reliable, but not in specific cases. The generational novel *Crescent Carnival* (1942) by Frances Parkinson Keyes, for example, has a subplot involving the dark strain in the family. When Laure first appears, the Southerner Breck explains to his New England wife Anna: "That girl you saw is one-sixteenth colored. It won't ever show in her hair or her skin or her eyes—not even in her fingernails, and they're the greatest giveaway."[20] For Keyes, the fingernail mark—while expected to work in principle—fails to identify fourth-generation descendants. Put another way, in such works as *Crescent Carnival* (as in *Pudd'nhead Wilson* or *Imitation of Life*) the absence of the fingernail mark is no proof of "whiteness."

For some authors the sign is permanent, indelible, ineffaceable. According to others, it can be covered, erased, deleted, or otherwise effaced; thus Mark Twain lets his character always wear gloves. In Edith Pope's *Colcorton* (1944) the white writer Clement Johnson has fingernails that are "the whitened colour of their moons"; Johnson instinctively suspects that the heroine Abby Clanghearne is partly black. Abby, who has been living in the Florida family homestead Colcorton yet passing for white all her life, recalls how she reacted after finding out her true ancestry:

> She remembered the frights she had had when she thought folks looked at her kind of queer. Many's the day she had nearly scrubbed her skin off fancying it was getting black; and the times she had studied her fingernails, and that once—she was young then and right foolish—she had bruised them with a stone to make white marks come that she could play like they was moons; and how she had baked her brains to a frazzle going bareheaded so as to bleach her hair.

In order to let her nephew Jad—who was born prematurely and "without fingernails hardly"—escape from the disadvantages of a public discovery of his racial identity and a family history of passing, Abby encourages her sister-in-law Beth to go North with him and change their names.[21]

Such camouflage may not always be successful since other characters may be able to see through it. For example, Atherton has Betty's friend Sally explain how she knew about Harriet's true racial identity: "I *felt* it. So vaguely that I scarcely put it in words until lately. And I never saw such an amount of pink on finger-nails in my life" (166). Atherton thus suggests that the use of nail-polish may be a possible cover for the racial mark of the fingernails; it is a useless effort, however, since the suspicious Sally finds out about Harriet anyway. When Robert Jones, the narrator of Chester Himes's _If He Hollers Let Him Go_ (1945), looks at his lightskinned girlfriend Alice Harrison, he comments on her fingers:

> I watched the fluid motion of her long slender fingers as she absently fiddled with the steering wheel and thought wonderingly that I'd never noticed before how beautiful they were. Then I thought of what they said about being able to tell a Negro by the half-moons in their finger-nails, and reflected half laughingly on what they'd have to do if the nails were painted.[22]

In some texts the sign is readable "as plainly as print" (Kipling). In others it is ambiguous. In Sinclair Lewis's social satire _Kingsblood Royal_ (1947), for example, the bigoted royal-ancestry-hunting Minnesotan banker Neil Kingsblood discovers that Xavier Pic, his great-great-grandfather, was not, as he had hoped, a white French aristocrat, but a black man born in Martinique. Neil immediately looks for clues of this ancestry in his body:

> he wanted to stop and look at his hands. He remembered hearing that a Negro of any degree, though pale of face as Narcissus, is betrayed by the blue halfmoons of his fingernails. He wildly wanted to examine them. But he kept his arms rigorously down beside him (so that people did wonder at his angry stiffness and did stare at him) and marched into the elevator. He managed, with what he felt to be the most ingenious casualness, to prop himself with his hand against the side of the cage, and so to look at his nails.
>
> No! The halfmoons were as clear as [his daughter] Biddy's.

Lewis's Neil keeps investigating his nails nervously, "tapping his teeth with his fingernail, occasionally looking suddenly at that nail again" or dropping his hand in his lap, studying his nails and wondering: "Was it this mercury vapor light, or was there really a blue tinge in the halfmoons?"[23] Neil's nails have acquired an indeterminable quality. This is also the case in Robert Penn Warren's novel _Band of Angels_ (1955), in which the lightskinned narrator Amantha Starr, who grew up as if she were white, is sold down the river upon her father's death. As she is going from Kentucky to Louisiana on a steamboat, she ponders her new condition and the history of her identity:

> I remembered how my father, back when he held me on his lap and played pattycake, had looked at my hands and then kissed each finger. Had he been secretly looking all the time for the tell-tale blue half-moons on my fingernails— the sure mark, they said, of black blood, even if only a spoonful?

Now in the cabin, I looked at my fingers. They told me nothing I could be sure of.[24]

The mark on the fingernail may be noticed in a character's self-examination that Sinclair Lewis, for example, represents with an allusion to Narcissus. Pope's and Warren's heroines, too, inspect themselves for the mark. The sign may also be detected by another character (Kipling) or a trained observer (Sue).

It may be recognized by a narrator or character in order to classify the person who carries it (Storm, Kipling). However, looking at the sign can also identify the observer who does not carry it but whose gaze is directed at it on another character: in Sue the description of the nail is combined with a critique of the pitiless gaze of a Creole observer (rendered by an English translator as "a slave-driver's practiced eye"). To cite some further examples, Mary E. Braddon's *The Octoroon* (ca. 1862), a derivative though not unsuspenseful novel written in the wake of Mayne Reid and Dion Boucicault, introduces the fingernail motif in the very first chapter when Mortimer Percy discusses the beautiful woman who turns out to be the Octoroon Cora Leslie with the British artist, Gilbert Margrave, who is destined to marry her. Percy says:

> Had you been a planter, Gilbert, you would have been able to discover, as I did, when just now I stood close to that lovely girl, the fatal signs of her birth. At the extreme corner of the eye, and at the root of the finger nails, the South American can always discover the trace of slavery, though but one drop of the blood of the despised race tainted the object upon whom he looked.[25]

Percy both identifies the woman's racial background and ascribes the ability to detect the sign to a special group of Southern planters. (By "South Americans" the hurried pulp novelist Braddon apparently meant U.S. Southerners). Paul Bourget's *Cosmopolis* (1893) contains an episode on the racially mixed descendants of Napoléon Chapron in which the habit of inspecting fingernails for racial clues is considered peculiarly *American*. The twelve-year-old Florent Chapron is being educated in an English country college where he is simply known as the grandchild of a great French officer (that he truly is); his fellow students are unaware of any difference between them and Florent. The narrator adds, quite in Sue's manner, and in a possibly clichéd phrasing which resembles Storm's:

> Il fallait le coup d'oeil d'un Yankee pour discerner sous les ongles de ce bel adolescent un peu bruni la toute petite goutte de ce sang noir déjà si lointain.

(It would have taken a Yankee's glance to notice that very small drop of black blood, already so far removed, under the fingernails of this beautiful and slightly tanned youth).

For this reason, Florent is apprehensive when an American who has come to the college seems to give him the disdainful glance to which he had often been subjected in the United States. It turns out, however, that this American student, Lincoln Maitland, was raised by his English mother in an environment as little American as possible and lived outside the United States since he was five, so that he has no difficulties in becoming Florent Chapron's close friend.[26] Once again, rather than the mark on the nails itself, the *gaze* that is directed at them serves as a sign of group membership, here within the category "Yankee." This is also the case, though for the category of the Anglo-Indian, in George Aberigh-Mackay's *Twenty-One Days in India* (1881; 6th ed. 1898). In the chapter "The Eurasian; a Study in Chiaro-Oscuro" he writes that the "Anglo-Indian has a very fine eye for colour":

> He will tell you how he can detect an adulterated European by his knuckles, his nails, his eyebrows, his pronunciation of the vowels, and his conception of propriety in dress, manner, and conduct.[27]

The fingernail motif is intricately linked to race and gender. The characters concerned are more likely to be women, but there are also some male figures who bear the mark (in the texts by Bourget, Mark Twain, Faulkner, White, and Lewis); they are often young and in a situation of courtship (Sue, Boucicault, Braddon, Kipling, Atherton, or Faulkner), but they may also be babies (Chopin), children (Bourget), in midlife (Lewis), or in advancing years (Pope). They may be entering a crisis because of the death of a father (Warren), because they have attempted to "pass" racially (Pope), or because their aristocratic pretensions make them search for ancestors (Lewis). The sign may work as a marriage impediment (in Kipling, one version of Boucicault's play, or Faulkner) or not (in another version of Boucicault's *Octoroon*, in Braddon, or in Storm—who, however, also contemplated an alternative, "tragic" resolution to his story). While the belief in the sign may cause antiracist amusement (Himes) or criticism of an American "fantasy" (McKay), the mark's recognition in texts which presuppose its real existence may cause romantic fascination (in Storm's Alfred, who could not take his eyes off it) or racist revulsion (in Atherton's Betty Madison who, upon looking at her stepsister Harriet's fingernails, "dropped the hand and covered her face with her muff").[28]

As a motif, the fingernail as a racial sign is sometimes linked with other signs which both transform the body into a text and are presumed to be racial indicators—such as hair, skin, or eyes; the sign is very strongly determined racially, and the instances where even its absence functions as a racial marker suggest that some of the texts imply a reader who shares certain ideas about race. The motif is intimately connected with the theme of passing; there are also clusters in which "fingernails" are linked to such diverse other motifs as Narcissus, twins, the gaze, and the rhetoric of reading (or "studying") print language. The contexts of the motif are very varied, indeed.

No single instance contains all elements of the motif, and some instances share only very few or no elements with some others.[29] As a conclusion to this structural approach to the fingernail motif one could attempt to present at least a crude and simplified model that distinguishes some actualized and nonactualized elements in the various occurrences.[30]

Mark	Seen By	Reaction
VISIBLE		laughter
		anxiety
	character with sign	camouflage
	another character	neutral observation
	narrator	attraction
	a hypothetical figure	rejection
	of a certain category	revulsion
MARK INVISIBLE	NOT SEEN	
NO MARK		

As Joachim Schulze has stressed, such models generate groupings that are indifferent to chronology: it does not matter whether an example originated earlier or later than another one. This changes when we approach the motif historically.[31]

The History of a Motif

A historical procedure might start with the observation that all the evidence presented so far comes from the century or so between Eugène Sue and Robert Penn Warren. It is in the period from the 1840s to the 1950s that the fingernail motif seems to have been conventionalized and stabilized as a peculiarly racial sign. Yet how did stabilization set in? What could have caused the theme's emergence? What functions could it have fulfilled? What may have led to its disappearance?

In order to pursue this line of questioning we must be prepared to relate the literary series with more nonliterary texts, yet this raises the possible problem of proceeding randomly. How is literary discourse connected with

other discourses? Can we avoid the randomness of association that Thomas
Pavel criticizes, and try to establish a legitimate and convincing form of
intertextual lineage?[32] The fingernail motif, in contrast with such timeless and
universal motifs as the full moon or the parting of lovers, seems eminently
historical, culturally specific and constructed; hence it invites such a procedure all the more.

One point of departure might be the exploration of literary texts from
the time before the motif had become conventionalized. In 1839, just four
years before Sue's *Mystères de Paris* began to be serialized, a little-known
historical novella of the *Revue de Paris* of 1838 was placed into a new collection of the author's novellas with a frame narration;[33] and it is the discussion
in the frame narrative of this collection by Mme. Charles [Henriette Etienne
Fanny] Reybaud, entitled *Valdepeiras*, that illustrates the status of the fingernail
motif *before* stabilization set in. Mme. Reybaud's novella "Les épaves" ("The
wrecks") is set in Martinique in the 1720s. The story ends with a marriage
between the white French heiress Cécile de Kerbran and the beautiful Mulatto genius Donatien, which the vindictive and cold-hearted Belgian M. de
la Rebelière, Cécile's guardian, and his spirited white Creole wife Éléonore
(who has also—despite her prejudices—fallen in love with Donatien) are re-
signed to accept. At this point the storyteller, the Creole woman Zoe, com-
mences a conversation with the audience of the frame narrative. In response to
the listeners' question she authenticates the story with the statement: "c'est
vrai, . . . ma mère était l'arrière-petite-fille de Donatien, et il y a du sang mulâtre
dans mes veines. . . . " ("it is true, . . . my mother was Donatien's greatgrandchild,
and there is Mulatto blood in my veins"). Since she is white-looking, she puts
forth her little hands; and the frame narrator comments: "elles étaient fines,
déliées, charmantes; mais autour de ses ongles il y avait une légère nuance
brune" ("they were refined, delicate, and charming, but around her fingernails
there was a light brownish tinge"). Mme. Reybaud uses the revelation of Zoe's
fingernails not only as proof of the narrator's "Mulatto blood" but also as the
sign of her own individual identity and hence of the authenticity and veracity of
her tale. The mark that serves as evidence of her descent from the genius
Donatien is, of course, a sign of honor; and racial identification was not the
absolute, freestanding, self-important, and all-determining matter that it was to
become, say, in Atherton, but served primarily as a device calculated to support
the authenticity of a tale.[34]

Zoe's gesture of stretching forth her hands as proof of her racial background as well as of her truthfulness may go back to Victor Hugo's early
historical novel *Bug-Jargal* (2nd ed. 1826), set at the time of the Haitian
Revolution. It is also a text which suggests the moment before motif-stabili-
zation had set in and which, as it turns out, takes a pivotal place in the textual
interaction between scientific and literary discourses.

In Hugo's novel, an unnamed Haitian planter—often presumed to be of mixed descent by his peers but so resentful of such suspicions that he once challenges the narrator Leopold d'Auverny when he voices them—falls into the hands of black rebels. Ever an opportunist, he tries to convince Biassou, the leader of his captors, that they have seized not a white but a man of mixed blood:

'Monsieur le général en chef, la preuve que je suis sang-mêlé, c'est ce cercle noir que vous pouvez voir autour de mes ongles*).' Biassou repoussa cette main suppliante" (307).

('General, the proof that I am a *sang-mêlé* [mixed blood] is this black circle that you can see around my nails.' Biassou repulsed the suppliant hand.)

The gesture of stretching forth one's hand in order to demonstrate truthfulness and racial identity (that Reybaud's Zoe performs more convincingly) is here made by a parvenu for whom the narrator has few sympathies.

Hugo's is the earliest literary text I have found in which the fingernail motif is used. But did Hugo invent the fingernail sign? He does seem unsure of his readers' knowledge of the matter and—perhaps in the service of verisimilitude—adds a clarifying footnote:

Plusieurs sang-mêlés présentent en effet à l'origine des ongles ce signe, qui s'efface avec l'âge, mais renaît chez leurs enfants.

(Many *sang-mêlés* bear this mark at the root of the nails; it is effaced by age, but reappears in their children.)[35]

Hugo thus explicates the mark as something that reveals—though not with absolute certainty, since only "many" *sang-mêlés* are said to bear it—what language may obscure. This makes nails what one might call "ascriptive clues"; they have the status of "evidence" that can support, or be held against, a person's claim in order to classify and define that person—in the way Ernst Bloch has outlined in his "Philosophical View of the Detective Novel."[36] In the context of a modern political revolution during which a semiotic "proof" of whose side characters are on may seal their fates, the offering of the fingernails as evidence goes together with the planter's politically unwise choice of the word "Mulatto" to describe himself.

From where did Hugo get this notion? Hugo's footnote suggests that this sign of mixed racial identity wanes with the subject's age, though Hugo did not hesitate to use it in a fully grown character (rather than a newborn baby). This contradiction between text and authenticating footnote directs the reader toward other footnotes in the novel. And it is in these notes that Hugo's text positions itself in such a way as to make an intertextual approach plausible even to the most exacting demands made by scholars who require *textual* evidence for an author's putative knowledge of other discourses.

In one of his notes, Hugo explicitly states that he adheres to Moreau de Saint-Méry's system of classification of 1797, revised from Benjamin Franklin's, as Hugo claims. According to Moreau de Saint-Méry's startling text, which looks at times like a parody of Enlightenment mathematics, all human beings are divided into the 128 parts that constitute their seven-generation ancestry. Adding the possible racial variables of African, Indian, and European, Moreau de Saint-Méry arrives at an unusually elaborate racial nomenclature that includes, for example, twelve possibilities of being a Mulatto. In Moreau de Saint-Méry's system, a sang-mêlé has between 125/128th and 127/128th parts of white blood (and is, correspondingly, only 3/128th to 1/128th black). In other words, a sang-mêlé may be seven generations removed from any black ancestry, and yet there is the claim in *Bug-Jargal:* "Le sang-mêlé, en continuant son union avec le blanc, finit en quelque sorte par se confondre avec cette couleur. On assure pourtant qu'il conserve toujours sur une certaine partie du corps la trace ineffaçable de son origine" (172n) ("The sang-mêlé, continuing its amalgamation with the white blood, is finally lost in it. We are assured, however, that there is always perceptible on a particular part of the body the ineffaceable trace of its origin") (27n). Hugo's "always" stands in a contradictory relation to his statement, cited earlier, that "many *sang-mêlés*" bear the mark. This suggests that fictions of racial difference may express a yearning for *permanence,* especially in Creole societies, while a text that expresses such yearning may at the same time recognize the absence of any such permanence. What reconciles the contradiction between the reader's wish for verisimilitude and the text's ambivalence are such phrases as "we are assured" or "it is said" that were also noticeable in several of the later texts cited and that invoke scholarly, scientific discourse as an authenticating device.

Hugo's text thus contains several contradictions: the sign is present in all *sang-mêlés* / in many *sang-mêlés*. It is present in infants and is effaced later in life / it is ineffaceable and may be present on an adult planter. As we have already seen, later writers followed those different possibilities, with some choosing newborn characters (Chopin and Lockridge) and most others writing about adults; with some writers believing in the absolute permanence of the sign, and many others representing various degrees of impermanence or even unreality of the sign.

The contradictoriness of the descriptive detail is reconciled by Hugo's footnotes that refer the ignorant or skeptical reader to scientific discourse. Moreau de St. Méry also offers the observation, by now familiar to us, of the nails as a racial sign:

Les enfans nègres ont, à l'époque de leur naissance, une peau dont la teinte rougeâtre laisserait indécis sur leur couleur, si un léger bord noirâtre ne se faisait pas remarquer autour des points que la pudeur veut qu'on cache, et à la naissance des ongles.

(From the time of birth black children have a skin in which a reddish tinge would leave their color undecided, were it not for a small blackish rim which one can observe around the areas which shame wants covered, as well as along the roots of the nails.)[37]

Moreau's observations were similar to those made by many other writers of learned and travel literature of the eighteenth century. Ultimately all instances seem to go back to an anatomical report to the French Royal Academy of 1702.[38] This report describes Alexis Littré's efforts to test the assumption advanced by Marcello Malpighi that black skin coloration was caused by an internal liquid.[39] Finding Malpighi's theory untenable and connecting blackness instead to exposure to air, Littré is said to have noticed—according to the Academy report—that children of Moors were born white, and that

quand les enfants mâles des Mores viennent au monde, ils ont au bout de la verge une petite tache noire, qui s'étend ensuite sur le bout du gland découvert, & même sur tout le corps, & s'étend, si l'on veut, par l'action de l'air. . . . Nous remarquerons en passant qu'outre cette petite tache qui n'appertient qu'aux mâles, tous les enfans Mores ont en naissant l'extremité des ongles noire.

(when male children of Moors are born, they have, at the tip of the penis, a small black sign which then extends on the top of the uncovered gland, and even to the whole body, and extends, if one wishes, through the action of air. . . . We note in passing that, apart from that little sign which only appears in boys, all Moorish infants have at birth nails which are black at the extremity.)[40]

The anatomist's gaze is here focused on the symbolic source of blackness and on the borderline between covered and uncovered skin. In these parts male "Moors" are defined at birth, and *all* black children are believed to carry a sign in another borderline area. While the general association of fingernails and sexuality was frequently made, such an explicit description of the male sexual organ was, of course, to remain rare in nonanatomic writing. Some eighteenth-century writers believed that it was only the boys' genitals (Le Cat focused on the scrotum rather than the penis) that carried the racial signs, others (Bernard Romans, for example) thought that boys and girls had the sign in the area that shame wants covered; but all saw the fingernails as an analogous but more easily accessible indicator of a newborn child's racial identity. The Jesuit Father Joseph Gumilla also found, in addition to the black fingernail sign, a round mark on the back of the spine that he believed to be the equivalent identifier of Indians.[41] Different writers approached this detail with different questions in mind. Littré and the anatomists were interested in the development of all babies' skins during the first days and weeks of life. Count Georges Louis Leclerc de Buffon, who was curious about the relation of heredity and climatic environment in the case of skin pigmentation, notes:

> on remarque que les enfants des Nègres ont, dans le moment même de leur naissance, du noir à la racine des ongles et aux parties génitales: l'action de l'air et la jaunisse serviront, si l'on veut, à étendre cette couleur, mais il est certain que le germe de la noirceur est communiqué aux enfants par les pères et mères, qu'en quelque pays qu'un Nègre vienne au monde il sera noir comme s'il était né dans son propre pays.

> (it has been observed, that the children of Negroes, as soon as they come into the world, have black genitals, and a black spot at the roots of their nails. The action of the air, and the jaundice, may, perhaps, help to expand this colour; but it is certain that the rudiments of blackness are communicated by their parents; that in whatever part of the world a Negro is brought forth, he will be equally black as if he had been born in his own country.)

Buffon ends his observations with the thought that this does not imply that color will always continue the same: he speculates that, if transported to a northern province, the descendants of blacks in the eighth, tenth, or twelfth generation "seraient beaucoup moins noirs que leurs ancêtres, et peut-être aussi blancs que les peuples originaires du climat froid où ils habiteraient" ("would be much fairer [than their ancestors] and perhaps as white as the natives of that [cold] climate [in which they lived]").[42]

Jean-Baptiste Labat, who was interested in children of mixed couples as proof that both father and mother have a decisive influence on progeny, looked at the fingernail sign as a way of telling black children from Mulatto children at birth. In a chapter on Mulattoes for his *Nouveau Voyage aux Isles de l'Amérique* (1722), he takes his point of departure from the observation that all children are universally born light and that black skin pigmentation emerges only eight to ten days after birth. In order to predict blackness one can look at the color of the babies' genitals (for him, apparently of both boys *and* girls), which are, Labat writes, black in Negro children but white or nearly white in Mulatto children. He also recommends the simpler method of ascertaining race by observing, immediately upon delivery, the baby's nails at the point where they grow out of the flesh:

> if they are black in this area, the child will also become black, according to this infallible mark; should this spot, however, be white or nearly white, one

may say with certainty that the child is a Mulatto, whether descended from
a white man and a Negro woman or a a white woman and a Negro man.[43]

From such sources variants of this notion proliferated in historical, philosophical, and numerous other works of the eighteenth century.[44] Fingernails—whether their extremities or their roots—are thus established in the
eighteenth-century texts not just as a general "sexual symbol" of sorts, but
expressly as a substitute for, and even a more legible improvement over,
genitals—whether the French Academy's "penis" or Le Cat's "scrotum." Sexual
organs are, of course, symbolically associated with the realms of ancestry and
descent; yet fingernails, too, seem to extend beyond the individual's lifespan,
as they grow before birth and continue growing even after death.

The Royal Academy's, Gumilla's, Le Cat's, de Pauw's, and Buffon's mark
("tache," "seña," "marque," or "signe") of the fingernails served mainly to make
distinctions at birth, not between Mulattoes and whites but between Negroes
and all others; Labat looked explicitly for a method of distinguishing newly
born Mulattoes and blacks. Though Le Cat insisted on the universal reddish
birth, some of the repeated descriptions and their variations also served the
purpose of representing nonwhite skin as if it were the result of the "loss" of
"original whiteness." The eighteenth-century authors often made attempts at
offering systematic classifications of racial mixture with an appropriately scientific terminology, though most classify as white a person who is three, four,
or at most five generations away from a black ancestor. Such was not the case,
however, for Moreau de St. Méry who was Hugo's central source and who
believed that the sign was "always" there in babies.

As we have seen, Hugo made the fingernails the mark that distinguishes
racially mixed people who are very lightskinned, not from darker-skinned
blacks but from *whites;* and, despite the claim in his footnote that the sign "is
effaced by age," he makes fictional use of the motif in a grown man. Perhaps
because of the background of the Haitian revolution, the distinction between
white and Mulatto nonwhite appears to have become more relevant than any
other differentiation; and it was more useful in fiction if it could apply to
adults. It is also this distinction that was to become crucial in biracial societies
like the United States where the difference between only two categories—
"white" and "nonwhite"—came to be drawn more sharply than in societies
which recognized many gradations of difference.[45]

With this development it became possible to imagine a definition of
"whites" as "people without marks on their fingernails" and to believe in the
possibility of a lifelong detection of even distant non-white ancestry in others. Such an identification may also have been desirable because it helped to
define who was slave and who was free in societies that made the status of the
mother alone the touchstone of her descendants' enslavement or liberty. The

motif of the fingernail is thus an ideological one that helped to fix racial categories against "appearance"—and give away to the trained observer what Atherton would call "the indelible proof of the hidden vein within."

Hugo's choice was all the more momentous in that his text may have acted like a funnel gathering forms from other discourses and utilizing them, however contradictorily, in fiction; his work, through the dissemination of *Revue de Paris* novellas (like "Les épaves") and feuilleton fiction (like *Les Mystères de Paris*) may thus have been the literary *Urtext* of the motif under scrutiny. A vast number of nineteenth-century readers (and writers) may have come across the sentence in a footnote by Sue that serves as an epigraph to this essay and that, again, contains the contradiction between the statement that *métisses* differ from whites only in certain signs and the qualification that these signs are imperceptible.

Conclusion

In the course of the nineteenth century, the use of the motif generally developed from the belief in a method of distinguishing at birth who—male or female—was to become darker-skinned or lighter-skinned within days or weeks, into a supposedly lifelong, essential difference between people with black ancestry and people without, no matter how white they may be in appearance. (It was, incidentally, exactly his hope of finding a permanent mark "indicating Race and Temperament" that made Francis Galton develop the finger print technique.)[46] What was initially the result of a predominantly classificatory interest in a sign which—however differently it appeared to various observers—was presumed to be universally readable turned into an element that could evoke first a romantic shiver of fascination and then a racist shudder of disgust, as it also began to require a specially trained eye to be decoded. Like the much less frequently represented physical signs for which it substituted, the fingernail mark was viewed as a symbol of attraction and repulsion. Especially prominent in plot situations involving courtship, the motif also became part of the arsenal of ideological strategies that helped legitimate and make natural the feeling of a racial hierarchy with white superiority. The mark of the fingernails was occasionally used to authenticate a character or a tale; it was inverted to identify the person who *stares* at fingernails as white Creole or American; it appeared in stories of "passing" in connection with various possibilities of camouflaging the mark that might otherwise give away a "suspicious looking brunette" (Atherton) or a "tanned" young man (Bourget); and, finally, it receded into uninterpretability or into the dimension of folkloric hearsay knowledge of a by now largely forgotten white superstition. The story of the fingernail motif may thus also be a *pars pro toto* of the story of changing notions about race, about reading, and about specialization; its tellings include romantic, realistic, and modern versions.

Once universally readable—and in the case of Moreau de St.-Méry, the very means of deciding what would otherwise remain undecidable—and then telling to the specialist, or identifying the viewer as Creole, American, Southern, Anglo-Indian, or biased, the fingernails (like other signs in the twentieth century) have become enmeshed in indeterminacy. By the mid-twentieth century they had become telltale nails that tell nothing. They no longer yield any certainties, they merely symbolize the problematic way in which a daughter reads her father's relationship to her; or the strange reflection of neon light.

Taking seriously the substitution for sexuality which is involved in the fingernail sign also means reading some of the passages anew. The area "shame wants covered" extends to Harriet's fingernails in the case of Atherton's heroine who is tellingly described as "Southern to her fingertips." In Pope's *Colcorton* Abby Clanghearne who once tried to efface her fingernails also has no progeny. The "hand," so often the symbol of a possible matrimonial connection in fictions thematizing the racialized fingernail, also becomes the image of a taboo, suggestive of the dialectic of attraction and repulsion, or of looking while not daring to look. To introduce somewhat different examples, Elizabeth Madox Roberts writes in *My Heart and My Flesh* (1927) about the heroine Theodosia Bell who was to find out about her father's dark past and her unsuspected relatives in the course of the novel:

> Theodosia would watch the long brown hand with its yellow shadowed nails when Lucas passed a plate of some food at her side. While she helped herself to a serving her eyes would cling to the hand where it folded at the edge of the plate, the thumb near the food, and she would remember the baby on the quilt in Aunt Deesie's yard. An exquisite disgust of the hand would make the food taste doubly sweet in her mouth when the hand was withdrawn.[47]

And, in a quite different context, Gustave Flaubert describes the first encounter between Charles and Emma in *Madame Bovary* (1857) when the shy Charles sees Emma sewing and does not dare to look directly at her face:

> Charles fut surpris de la blancheur de ses ongles. Ils étaient brillants, fins du bout, plus nettoyés que les ivoires de Dieppe, et taillés en amande.

> (Charles was much surprised at the whiteness of her nails. They were shiny, delicate at the tips, more polished than the ivory of Dieppe, and almond-shaped.)[48]

Seeing the fingernails again functions as a substitute for seeing more hidden and intimate parts of the body. Though Roberts racializes and Flaubert does not, it is interesting to note that the description of Emma's fingernails is quite emphatic about their polished-ivory whiteness.

Such examples (as well as those of Chopin and Lockridge) illustrate the possibility that one can encounter instances, in the course of such a sweeping survey of a detail, which throw light on the whole development without actually constituting an explicit part of it. This raises the question of whether it is in the nature of such motif line-ups to incorporate everything, if not as a variant then as an absence.

Even though it was early propagated by scientists, Jesuits, travelers, and scholars and adopted as factual and conventionalized by many writers, the literary motif of the tell-tale "dark moons" on the fingernails does not seem to be based upon any anatomical facts. It may be the elite equivalent to the kind of folk superstitions recorded by Newbell Niles Puckett in 1926:

> [Some] Negroes say that the number of white spots under your finger nails betokens the number of friends you have. In England yellow spots on the nails of fingers indicate coming death. They are sometimes called "death-mould"; the Negro calls them "death-moles" or "death-mules," and sometimes says they are blue spots instead of yellow ones, but always the sign is death.[49]

There is also a superstition that the growth of fingernails is the result of original sin.[50]

In 1932, Samuel Monash, who deplored the absence of any "systematic study of pigmentation of the nails of the Negro," published an illustrated essay in which he noted "longitudinal stripes running the length of the nails" which are not usually present at birth, but may appear at any age, so that, contrary to Victor Hugo's assumption (derived from eighteenth-century scholarship), their frequency *increases* during the span of a life. Monash also emphasized that there "is no deeper pigmentation of the nail bed under these pigmented stripes" and that among "the lighter Negroes such pigmentation is uncommon."[51] When asked by a literary critic whether the motif of the dark moons in characters of mixed blood referred to a real phenomenon, Dr. Monash replied in a letter: "I can assure you that there is no truth in the statement that Negro blood shows in the moons of any person."[52]

A SEMANTICS FOR THEMATICS:
THE CASE OF THE DOUBLE

Lubomír Doležel

Thematics seems to have a problem all of its own: it cannot find its proper place in the ensemble of literary disciplines. This uncertainty is revealed most clearly in the fact that there exist absolutely contradictory opinions regarding the significance of thematics for the study of literature. In an oft-quoted statement (cf. Weisstein 1973, 134f.; Jost 1974, 40; Trousson 1980, 4), Wellek is said to have delivered a "mortal blow" to literary thematics, evicting it, for all practical purposes, from literary criticism and history: "*Stoffgeschichte* [Wellek uses the traditional German term] is the least literary of histories." A theme in a historical tragedy, to take one example, could be of interest "for the history of political sentiment" and "incidentally illustrate changes in the history of taste," but it presents "no *critical* problem" (Wellek and Warren 1956, 250; italics mine).

In his dismissal of thematics, Wellek completely ignores the work of the Prague school (to which, incidentally, he himself belongs by virtue of his scholarly origins). Inspired primarily by Tomashevski, Mukařovský and Vodička not only developed an impressive system of literary thematics (see Doležel 1982), but also assigned it a pivotal position in the history and theory of literature. Its centrality was derived from the observation that the literary structure is linked to its "extraliterary" foundations in and through thematics. On the one hand, thematics links literature to language: after all, "every thematic constituent is introduced into the work by linguistic means" (Vodička 1942, 353; cf. Mukařovský 1928, 11). On the other, thematics connects literature with life, society and history:

> "Thematics is precisely that layer of literary structure which mediates the powerful influence exercised on the immanent evolution of the literary structure by the life interests and historical problems of a community" (Vodička 1948, 168).

89

How should we explain such a fundamental contrast in opinions, coming as it does from scholars of a common cultural background? Are these, in fact, opinions on the same issue? The answer is: yes and no. Wellek and Vodička are both referring to literary thematics, but they have in mind two entirely different modes thereof, two traditions which have ignored each other, developing without mutual contact or exchange. Let us briefly characterize these two modes.

1. Selective thematics

I will use the label 'selective thematics' to designate those trends which share a conception of theme as a striking, prominent, in some way characteristic feature of literary content.[1] The best known representatives of selective thematics are two branches of historical thematics *(Stoffgeschichte)*, one in folklore studies, the other in comparative literature. In spite of their long tradition and impressive research results, there has been surprisingly little crossover between the two branches.[2] It is, however, readily apparent that their aims and bases are practically identical: they study the preservation, mutation and migration of perennial themes through ages and cultures. The migrating themes of folk literature are the domain of folkloristic *Stoffgeschichte*, while its comparative counterpart follows the transmission of themes in written literatures. *Stoffgeschichte* does have a theoretical side, but its main accomplishment lies in catalogues and dictionaries of themes (see esp. Thompson 1955–58; Thompson 1964; Frenzel *passim*). The folkloristic *Stoffgeschichte* achieved prominence in the works of the so-called Finnish school (Christensen, Thompson), while the comparative branch has often been claimed as a German monopoly. More recently, Jost has announced an "internationalization" of the field (op. cit., 15) and Weisstein (op. cit., 24f.) has credited its resurrection to comparatists from Belgium (Trousson), Germany (Frenzel) and America (Levin).[3]

Selective thematics exists in a third, more recent version: thematic criticism (Todorov's term), practiced especially in France (by Bachelard and Richard, among others). Thematic criticism takes theme in its broadest sense, to include "verbal" themes. It is not interested in major historical and cross-cultural migrations; rather, it searches for themes characteristic of particular writers or of individual literary works. Studying themes as recurrent, typical, but at the same time highly variable features of literary texts, thematic criticism could be characterized as a kind of literary stylistics.

There is no need to offer a critique of selective thematics; it would largely be redundant as it would do no more than confirm Bremond's recent assessment. Bremond's critical analysis applies, I feel, to all modes of selective thematics, although he only deals specifically with the folkloristic branch.[4] Focusing on the vagueness of its basic concept—'motif'—Bremond points out three general epistemological deficiencies: "(1) arbitrariness in the identification of textual occurrences elevated to the status of motif; (2) slackness in the conceptualization and formulation of motifs extracted from these textual occurrences; (3) anarchy in the categorization and classification of motifs" (Bremond 1982, 129). Let me just add that these and other deficiencies of selective thematics have, in my view, a common denominator: a dependence on the dated and sterile dichotomy of form and content.[5] The theme in selective thematics is a content element separated from its form. The concept of structured content or of thematic structure is alien to selective thematics.

2. Structural thematics

For structural thematics—in contrast to selective thematics—structuralization of content is axiomatic; content in literature is structured and cannot be studied independently of its structuring. Structural thematics may be as old as Aristotelian poetics, but its present paradigm, within which we work, has been established relatively recently by a truly international pleïade of scholars including Bédier, Barthes and Greimas in France, Dibelius in Germany, Tomashevski and Propp in Russia, and Mukařovský and Vodička in Czechoslovakia.[6]

Two epistemological postulates derived from the axiom of structured content are fundamental to the project of structural thematics: a) themes must be identified as integral constituents of the literary structure as a whole; b) themes must be formulated as semantic invariants; at the same time, the range of their hypothetical variability needs to be determined. On these epistemological principles, thematics is established as a subdivision of literary semantics. Since I am interested in narrative thematics only, I will specify its place within a model of narrative semantics.

The narratological model outlined in Schema 1 is an attempt to synthetize the concepts and conceptual levels which are characteristic of the contemporary narratological paradigm. It appears that such a synthesis can be achieved on the basis of Fregean semantics in which two dimensions of meaning are distinguished: intension *(Sinn)* and extension *(Bedeutung)*. Intension is the meaning carried by the original wording of a literary text, by its texture; extension is the referential invariant of equivalent intensions, expressed in a semantic representation (paraphrase) of the texture. Two main features of the model deserve a brief commentary:

a) While the basic strata of the model—intensional and extensional semantics—reflect the Fregean base, the separation of extensional semantics into a first-order, *representational* thematics and a second-order, *interpretational* thematics is necessitated by modern narratology's need to account not only for thematic structures but also for their narrative functions. On each level, the model defines its units of analysis and the rules of their combination and integration. Intensional narrative semantics is, as a rule, identical with an appropriate general text semantics; in a most primitive version, its units can be identified as morphemes, words, phrases, sentences and suprasential structures; their combinatorial rules will correspond to a text grammar. Representational thematics is the semantics of motifs with their necessary constituents (actions, states, agents, objects, etc.). The last level of our model, interpretational thematics, is constituted by semantic terms of a specific interpretive system. In narratology, the Proppian system (motifemes, functions, actants) is most popular; however, any other version of interpretational thematics (archetypal, Freudian) will be placed on this level of narrative semantics.

b) The levels of the model are linked by transformational procedures; the levels of extensional semantics are reached by transforming texture into its semantic representations. In my view, the most suitable form of semantic representation is proposition or propositional function, i.e. a semantic structure consisting of a predicate and one or more arguments (cf. Doležel 1976). Motifs are propositions instantiated by terms which express the appropriate extensional categories. The vocabulary of second-order representations is provided by the interpretive system—for example, by a list of actants and functions in a motifemic interpretation. Each step in the transformational procedure results in a reduction of variety: motifs are invariants of variable textures, motifemes invariants of variable motifs. One of the basic tasks of thematics, the assignment of invariants to variables (and *vice versa*), is thus formulated as a translational, paraphrastic procedure. At every level of analysis, meaning is bound to its appropriate form of expression. Studying meaning in a well-defined form, literary semantics in general and literary thematics in particular satisfy their theoretical axiom: no meaning without structure.

The Fregean model of narrative semantics is presented here in its barest outline; we have no other aspiration than to suggest a solution to the embarrassment of thematics, i.e. to find it a proper place in the framework of literary study. Thematics is the extensional semantics of literary texts; on its representational level it identifies, defines and formulates themes by expressing them in terms of motif representations; on the interpretational level, it proposes functions of themes in terms of interpretive systems.

I will not proceed further with the development of this narrative semantics model. My aim in this paper is to demonstrate the method of structural thematics by studying a particular theme, that of the double. The analysis will be concerned with the identification of the theme and with an outline of its variability, which means that it will be confined to first-order thematics; possible second-order interpretations of the theme will not be considered. This restriction is not imposed solely by time limitations; rather, I feel that first-level thematics is the weakest point of narrative semantics and that we have to concentrate on its elaboration. All too often the 'method' of literary interpretation has been nothing more than an intuitive leap from unanalyzed texture to terms of a borrowed interpretive system. What results is a set of fancy but purely arbitrary interpretations, which cannot be evaluated because a solid identification of the first-order thematic structures is lacking.

3. The double and its family

Selective thematics identifies themes by their permanence, their capacity for historical survival. In structural thematics, theme can be conceived of as a cluster of recurrent motifs; it will be constituted in relationships to other, similar or contrasting themes. Every theme is a member of a mini-system of kindred themes, a *thematic field,* and its structure is primarily determined by the oppositions existing within this field.

My selection of the theme of the double is not fortuitous: this theme has been extremely popular in oral and written literature from antiquity to surrealism. Because of its permanence, the theme is well established in selective thematics (cf. Thompson 1955–58, II-D; Frenzel 1976, 94–114; Aziza et al. 1978, 61f). I shall attempt to demonstrate the advantages of the structural approach, but a full comparison of the way the theme is treated in the two modes of thematics is beyond the scope of this paper. While the prominence of the theme in literature and in traditional thematics would by itself justify its selection for a structural reexamination, I have another, more special reason for my decision. The theme of the double is intimately linked with a semantic theory which, in my opinion, provides a most stimulating framework for the study of fictionality: the *semantics of possible worlds.* The theme of the double must have been invented by a Kripkean mind, expressing as it does the basic idea of the possible world model: when we think or speak about an individual, we do not think or speak about his or her actual existence only, but also about all the possible alternative life paths which he or she may follow or might have followed. Possible world semantics is a theory of reasoning and imagination which assigns an innumerable set of doubles to every individual.

The conceptual foundations and explanatory power of possible world semantics have been much discussed in contemporary philosophy, logic, linguistics and poetics; such discussions cannot be rehearsed here. I hope, however, that the pertinent notions of this semantics will be clarified as we analyze the theme of the double.

Literature is a semiotic system for constructing possible worlds which are commonly called *fictional* worlds. A fictional world may most simply be defined as a set of compossible fictional individuals (agents, characters). In this definition, 'compossibility' means capability for co-existence and interaction: Emma Bovary is compossible with Charles Bovary, but not compossible with Ivan Karamazov.[7] The feature of compossibility is crucial but not sufficient for the semantic representation of the theme of doubleness; it has to be complemented by the concept of personal identity. From manipulations of compossibility and personal identity, three kindred themes are generated:

a) One and the same individual, i.e. an individual marked by the feature of personal identity, exists in two or more alternative fictional worlds. This theme, which is popular in mythology under the name of reincarnation, will be called the *Orlando theme*.

b) The *Amphytrion theme* is generated by the coexistence in one and the same world of two individuals with distinct personal identities, but perfectly homomorphic in essential properties. In selective thematics, this theme is also known under the label 'doppelgänger' or 'identical twins.'[8]

c) The *theme of the double* arises when two alternate embodiments of one and the same individual coexist in one and the same fictional world. This is the theme in its strictest sense, the central, most conspicuous member of the thematic field of doubleness. The themes of the field are mapped out in Schema 2, but a more detailed description of their structures is called for.

The Orlando theme requires a multiple fictional world for its semantic representation. An individual (X) with a fixed personal identity exists in different alternate worlds in alternate embodiments (X', X'' . . .). The set of properties possessed by X undergoes changes as X moves from one world to another; any of these properties, including the most essential, can be altered. In her 1928 novel which gives this theme its name, Virginia Woolf has the protagonist exist as a man in one world, as a woman in others. Fictional semantics is a radically non-essentialist semantics.[9]

The construction of a multiple fictional universe in which the Orlando theme is located requires the erection of world boundaries. Various constructional devices may be used for this purpose. In Woolf's novel, the world boundaries are marked by substantial leaps in narrated time, taking the protagonist from Elizabethan England to the present day (1928). In O. Henry's story "Roads of Destiny" (1903), the world boundaries are established by the deaths of the protagonist David Mignot; the lives which David lives after each must be taken as lives in alternate worlds. It should be of some interest to note that it is precisely the lack of world boundaries in Kafka's "Metamorphosis" (1912) which leads us to recognize that it is *not* a manifestation of the Orlando theme.[10]

The second condition of the Orlando theme—the preservation of personal identity in moves across world boundaries—may be expressed in an explicit statement, as in Woolf's text: "Orlando had become a woman—there is no denying it. But in every other respect, Orlando remained precisely as he had been. The change of sex, though it altered their future, did nothing whatever to alter their identity." If an explicit statement is absent, the individual may be identified in each successive transmutation by identification "marks," one of the most powerful being the proper name, a *rigid designator* (Kripke 1972) which labels the individual in all possible worlds. Orlando and David Mignot both preserve their names in their different lives. Moreover, the three lives of Henry's hero share some common constituents. It is especially significant that all of them end with a shot from one and the same pistol belonging to the Marquis de Beaupertuy; once the pistol is fired by the Marquis, once by his companion and once by David himself.

In the Amphytrion theme we encounter in one and the same world two individuals (X and Y) with distinct personal identities, but sharing a set of properties in such a manner and to such a degree that they are indistinguishable: $X = Y$. The theme does not require an absolute identity of properties but, primarily, a perfect similarity of physical makeup and behavior, one which makes identification problematic. In Hoffmann's story "Der Doppeltgänger" (1822), the protagonists are not actually brothers, but they were born on the same day to families bound by close friendship; growing up "week by week and day by day the two children developed such a complete similarity, such a complete likeness, that it was quite impossible to distinguish them." When as young men they meet in the same place, they necessarily create a confusion of personal identity. Let us emphasize again that this confusion is purely epistemic, it exists in the minds of the fictional world's inhabitants; it creates the "mystery" of the Amphytrion plot. The revelation of the protagonists' different personal identities (made possible in Hoffmann's story by a hidden bodily mark) ends the confusion and reveals the authentic structure of the fictional world.

The theme of the double requires the most radical manipulation of the semantic features of compossibility and personal identity. As defined, the theme is generated when the alternative embodiments (X and X') of one and the same individual exist in one and the same fictional world. In other words, an individual characterized by personal identity appears in two alternative manifestations, usually as two fictional characters. Doubled individuals can coexist in one and the same space and time, as they do in Dostojevski's novel *The Double* (1846); or they may be mutually exclusive, as in Stevenson's story "The Strange Case of Dr. Jekyll and Mr. Hyde" (1886). Only in the first case may the incarnations of the double interact (verbally and physically): in the second case they cannot meet. Nevertheless, even in the second case the doubles live in one and the same world because they share the same set of compossible individuals and interact with the same set of co-agents.

In selective thematics, the theme of the double has usually been treated as a variant of the Amphytrion theme, under the common label 'doppelgänger.' Frenzel observes that the doppelgänger theme is based on "a physical similarity of *two persons*," but this does not prevent her from including in its scope "doppelgänger formations" which seem to correspond to "*two souls* or *two egos* of a single human being" (Frenzel 1976, 94f; italics mine). There is, admittedly, a semantic similarity between the two themes, and both of them raise the question of personal identity, but possible world semantics also makes us recognize their fundamental structural distinctness. In the case of the double we are forced to accept a fictional world in which one and the same individual can exist in two discrete embodiments. In the Amphytrion theme, the fictional world only appears to possess such an unusual structure; when the confusion of personal identities is cleared up, we recognize a standard world structure, where one personal identity corresponds to one and only one individual. Because of their semantic similarity, however, the themes are linked by a transitional zone of ambiguous and uncertain manifestations. In this zone individuals exist who seem to be doubles, or doppelgängers, or both.

In the Orlando theme, the epistemic confusion of personal identity does not arise, since the various embodiments of the protagonist exist in different worlds. Again, however, the theme is linked through a transitional zone to the theme of the double. This transitional zone contains individuals whose set of properties includes radical inconsistencies or who live a life of radically discontinuous stages. Such individuals then appear to be double or even multiple. Ultimately, the Orlando theme also creates a confusion of personal identity; this confusion is phenomenological, however, rather than epistemic.

4. Varieties of the double

Having identified a theme or thematic field, we must now take account of the fact that in different cultures and historical periods, as well as in individual textual manifestations, one and the same theme appears in many forms. The second basic problem of thematics, the correlation of invariants and variables, now has to be dealt with. Structural thematics does not perceive thematic variability as a result of random changes, but explains its systemic character by revealing the structural factors which mold the theme into different shapes. A theme is modified by being integrated into varying literary structures. The extant historical and cultural variants of a theme are actualized instances of its possible range.

Our comments will be confined to the theme of the double in the strict sense, and its variability within the narrative structure. Even such a specific task cannot be implemented systematically and exhaustively at this time. Every aspect and every regularity of the narrative structure can become a theme-modifying factor; the result is an extremely rich typology of the theme. Only a few of these types, hopefully the essential ones, will be delineated here.

a) Modes of construction

The most significant modifying factor is the manner of construction, i.e. the way in which the double is brought into fictional existence. Three modes of construction present themselves:

a_1) Two ORIGINALLY SEPARATE INDIVIDUALS ARE FUSED TO FORM THE DOUBLE. This is the procedure used in Poe's "William Wilson" (1840). Two schoolmates, who already hold some semantic features in common, grow more and more similar by imitation, until the stage of perfect similarity (doppelgänger structure) is reached. This stage is transcended, however, when the narrator's life path is mysteriously crossed at decisive moments by the second William. Finally, when the narrator kills his *alter ego,* he discovers an "absolute identity" and perceives that he has murdered himself. In contrast to this gradual merging of two personal identities, the double may enter the fictional world and join the individual suddenly, like an apparition; such a mode of fusion is exemplified in Dostojevski's novel. In Wilde's *The Picture of Dorian Gray* (1891) the link of doubleness between the young hero and his portrait is established with the same degree of suddenness; this time, the constructive device is the hero's wish which magically acquires a performative force.

a_2) THE DOUBLE IS GENERATED WHEN AN ORIGINALLY SIMPLE INDIVIDUAL IS SPLIT IN TWO. Gogol's story "The Nose" may be cited in this context. The nose of a clerk, separated from its owner, assumes the form of an official who strongly resembles its "master" (Pomorska 1980, 33). In Hans Christian Andersen's fairy tale, a shadow divorced from its human bearer becomes a man and ends up reversing the roles. It should be noted that the operation of splitting affects an "inalienable possession," a constituent or part of an individual which under normal circumstances could not lead an independent existence.

a_3) THE DOUBLE IS GENERATED BY A PROCESS OF METAMORPHOSIS. One well-known example of this variant is Stevenson's double. Metamorphosis is a rather general plot pattern, not specific to the generation of doubleness. It is common in mythological tales, dominates the Orlando theme and reappears in the modern myth of Kafka. Metamorphosis links the theme of the double to more general narratological patterns.

b) Paradigmatic variants

We have already noted that the theme of the double, unlike the Amphytrion theme, does not require that the embodiments be similar; in fact, the paradigmatic relationships between the doubles can range from perfect similarity to absolute contrast. In the paradigmatic typology, Dostojevski's double represents the variant based on absolute similarity and substitutability; Stevenson's doubles are manifestations of the contrary variant, being totally different in their physical appearance and moral attitudes. A still more radical contrast is achieved when one of the embodiments is a non-human fictional entity; such is the case with Wilde's portrait or with the willow tree in a popular Slavic fairy tale.

Similarity is only one possibility for a paradigmatic relationship between the doubles, one which generates variety within the theme; the interactional relationship, while equally important, seems to be rather static. As a rule, the doubles act as antagonists, as if to demonstrate that there is no place for two embodiments of one and the same individual in a single world. Projected into a plot, the antagonism generates a tragic story; this is why the story of the double so often ends in a murder—which is, at the same time, a suicide.

c) Syntagmatic variants

An opposing pair of syntagmatic relationships between the doubles—simultaneity and exclusivity—produce the two basic varieties of the theme. Simultaneous doubles share the same space and time and are therefore capable of interacting, whether physically or verbally. Dostojevski's double is a case in point. By contrast, exclusive doubles—such as Dr. Jekyll and Mr. Hyde—cannot coexist; the syntax of the theme is formed by shifts from one embodiment to another. In this latter case, we may observe a correlation between two modifying factors: the doubles generated by a process of metamorphosis are bound to be exclusive doubles. This, I feel, serves to indicate the peripheral nature of metamorphosis in the typology of the double. The true essence of the theme can only be carried by simultaneous doubles; only face-to-face confrontation between two embodiments of one and the same individual can exploit its full semantic, emotive and aesthetic potential.

d) Varieties of authenticity

One of the most flexible structural factors in the narrative genre is the procedure of authentication.[11] It operates here in full force, generating a variety of doubles, from the fully authenticated to the totally ambiguous. A clear case of a fully authentic double is manifested in Stevenson's text: the fictional existence of the metamorphosing identity is asserted by conventional devices of authentication, i.e. the protagonist's confession, confirmed by a statement from an independent witness. In the manuscript version of Gogol's "The Nose," the double is disauthenticated by a final narrative statement which relegates the story to the realm of dreams. In this form, the story is a typical instance of the fantastic genre, as defined by Todorov (1970). In the printed version, however, Gogol deleted the final statement, leaving the question of the double's fictional existence wide open. Thus Gogol pioneered the ambiguous variant of the theme, one which was fully developed in Dostojevski's *The Double*. Dostojevski's double constantly hovers on the borders of fictional existence, appearing both authentic and purely hallucinatory.[12] This ambiguity becomes even more radical in Fourré's *Tête-de-Nègre* (1960). While almost every character (including the author) appears in a double form, there is no way to assess the authenticity of the doubles; in fact, Fourré's entire fictional world lacks authenticity, as the very mechanism of authentication is undermined in his text. The fictional world is like a house of cards erected and destroyed at the whim of its playful constructor.

The various types of double which we have been able to isolate attest to the flexibility of the theme. It seems safe to say that this flexibility is a decisive factor in its longevity. A theme remains alive as long as it is capable of modifications. For the life of a literary structure depends, of course, on its ability to produce new aesthetic effects. Structural thematics, by studying the dialectics of invariants and variables, of stability and modification, of tradition and innovation, finds itself fully integrated into poetics and aesthetics. With this ultimate and decisive step, structural thematics seals its divorce from selective thematics which has always treated themes as aesthetically irrelevant.[13] Themes and their variability are central to the precarious balancing act which every artist has to perform in order to create a work of art.

Schema 1

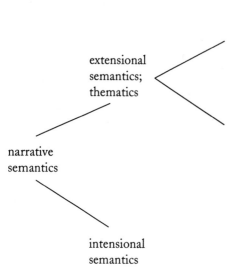

narrative
semantics

    extensional
    semantics;
    thematics

        interpretational thematics: function (Propp), actant (Greimas), rôle (Bremond), motifeme (Dundes)

        representational thematics: motif (Tomashevski, Mukařovský), proïrétisme (Barthes), domain (Pavel), frame of reference (Hrushovski), fictional world (Doležel)

intensional
semantics

Schema 2

1. The Orlando theme:

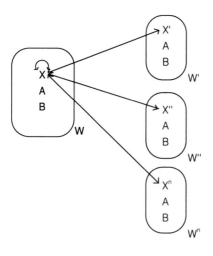

2. The Amphytrion theme:

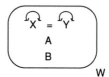

3. The theme of the double:

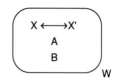

W, W'... fictional worlds
X, X', A, B... individuals
↔... relationship of personal identity

References

Aziza, Claude et al. 1978. *Dictionnaire des types et caractères littéraires.* Paris: Nathan.

Bremond, Claude. 1982. "A Critique of the Motif." In *French Literary Theory Today.* Ed. Tzvetan Todorov. Cambridge: Cambridge University Press—Paris: Editions de la Maison des Sciences de l'Homme. 125–46.

Chizhevsky, Dmitri. 1962. "The Theme of the Double in Dostoevsky." In René Wellek, ed. *Dostoevsky. A Collection of Critical Essays.* Englewood Cliffs: Prentice-Hall. 112–29.

Dimić, Milan V. 1975. "Motiv dvojnika u srednjevekovnom ruhu: Toma o Amiju i Amilu." *Filološki pregled* 1975: 33–53.

———. "The 'Double' in Renaissance Literature." In *Proceedings of the VIIIth Congress of the ICLA.* Budapest: Akadémia Kiadó. 133–40.

Doležel, Lubomír. 1976. "Narrative Semantics." *PTL: A Journal for Descriptive Poetics and Theory of Literature* 1: 129–51.

———. 1980. "Truth and Authenticity in Narrative." *Poetics Today* 1, 3: 7–25.

———. 1982. "The Conceptual System of Prague School Poetics: Mukařovský and Vodička." In *The Structure of the Literary Process: Studies Dedicated to the Memory of Felix Vodička.* Eds. P. Steiner, M. Červenka and R. Vroon. Amsterdam: Benjamin. 109–26.

———. 1984. "Kafka's Fictional World." *Canadian Review of Comparative Literature/ Revue Canadienne de littérature comparée* 10: 61–83.

Fischer, Otokar. 1929. "Dějiny dvojnika." In *Duše a slovo.* Prague: Melantrich. 161–208.

Frenzel, Elisabeth. 1963 (2nd ed.). *Stoffe der Weltliteratur.* Stuttgart: Kröner.

———. 1976. *Motive der Weltliteratur.* Stuttgart: Kröner.

Jauss, Hans Robert. "Poetik und Problematik von Identität und Rolle in der Geschichte des Amphytrion." In Odo Marquart and Karlheinz Stierle, eds. *Identität* (Poetik und Hermeneutik 8). Munich: Fink. 213–53.

Jost, François. 1974. "Grundbegriffe der Thematologie." In *Theorie und Kritik: Festschrift für Gerhard Loose.* Ed. Stefan Grunwald. Munich: Franke. 15–46.

Kripke, Saul A. 1972. "Naming and Necessity." In Donald Davidson and Gilbert Harman, eds. *Semantics of Natural Language.* Dordrecht: Reidel. 253–355.

Linsky, Leonard. 1977. *Names and Descriptions.* Chicago: The University of Chicago Press.

Mukařovský, Jan. 1928. *Máchův Máj: Estetická studie /*Mácha's May: An Aesthetic Study/. Prague: Facultas Philosophica Universitatis Carolinae Pragensis. Rpt.

in *Kapitoly z české poetiky* /Chapters from Czech Poetics/. Prague: Svoboda, 1948, 3, 9–202.

Perrot, Jean. 1976. *Mythe et littérature sous le signe des jumeaux*. Paris: PUF.

Plantinga, Alvin. 1977. "Transworld Identity or Worldbound Individuals?" In Stephen P. Schwartz, ed. *Naming, Necessity and Natural Kinds*. Ithaca: Cornell University Press. 245–66.

Pomorska, Krystyna. 1980. "On the Problem of Parallelism in Gogol's Prose: A Tale of Two Ivans." In Andrej Kodjak et al., eds. *The Structural Analysis of Narrative Texts*. Columbus: Slavica Publishers. 31–43.

Thompson, Stith. 1955–58. *Motif-Index of Folk Literature*. 6 vols. Bloomington: Indiana University Press.

Todorov, Tzvetan. 1970. *Introduction à la littérature fantastique*. Paris: Seuil.

Trousson, Raymond. 1980. "Les études de thèmes: questions de méthode." In Adam J. Bisanz and Raymond Trousson, eds. *Elemente der Literatur. Elizabeth Frenzel zum 65. Geburtstag*. Vol. 1. Stuttgart: Kröner, 1–10.

Vodička, Felix. 1942. "Literárni historie. Jeji problémy a ukely / Literary History. Its Problems and Tasks/. In *Čteni o jazyce a poesii*. Eds. Bohuslav Havránek and Jan Mukařovský. Prague: Družstevni práco. 309–400. Eng. trans. (part) in *Semiotics of Art: Prague School Contributions* Eds. Ladislav Matejka and Irwin R. Titunik. Cambridge MA: MIT Press, 1976.

———. 1948. *Počátky krásné prózy novočeské* / The Beginnings of Czech Artistic Prose/. Prague: Melantrich.

Weisstein, Ulrich. 1973. *Comparative Literature and Literary Theory*. Bloomington: Indiana University Press. German orig. Stuttgart: Kohlhammer, 1968.

Wellek, René, and Austin Warren. 1956 (2nd ed.). *Theory of Literature*. New York: Harcourt, Brace & World.

VARIATIONS ON THE THEME OF FAUST

Jean-Marie Schaeffer

In Valéry's *Mon Faust,* the well-known doctor and charlatan complains: "So much has been written about me that I no longer know who I am."[1] The same could be said for the Faustian corpus: everything and more has been written on these texts. The only excuse I can find for adding some words of my own, and it is a small one, is that what interests me is not so much the theme itself as some of its generic incarnations.

To begin with, I should like to propose a distinction between 'subject' and 'theme,' a purely *ad hoc* distinction, without any pretensions to originality or theoretical import. When I say 'subject,' I am referring to the set of events and facts (historical or fictional) related by a text or set of texts. If the proper name to which these facts and events are attached is identical, I shall accept this as a criterion for transtextual equivalence. Thus two texts need not necessarily share *all* of the articulated facts and events in order to be part of the same subject. They may even contain elements—like Faust's damnation and Faust's salvation—which would be mutually exclusive within a single text. When I say 'theme,' I am referring to any comprehensive actantial or hermeneutical construct which may be used to pick matching textual segments out of a given set of texts. In such cases I shall say that a text *exemplifies* a theme or themes.

These two terms need not overlap extensionally: thus Thomas Mann's *Doktor Faustus* exemplifies the Faust theme without being a instance of the Faust subject. Conversely, the various instances of the Faust subject do not necessarily exemplify the same theme. In fact, it would seem preferable to divide the corpus of Faustian literature into two themes, the first being the damnation of the arrogant man who loses his faith in the omnipotence of Divine Grace.[2] This is the theme which is originally exemplified by the Faust subject: we find it in the *Historia*—the founding text for the whole tradition—as well as in Marlowe, and in the puppet shows based on his version. It is connected with a specific genre, the anti-legend. The second theme is the salvation of a man in spite of his sins and aberrations: this of course is what Goethe's *Faust* is all about, but it is also to be found earlier, in Weidmann's "allegorical drama" *Johann Faust*. Thus the same subject has yielded two very different themes, grounded in radically incompatible views on life: what, in the anti-legend tradition, contributed to Faust's damnation—his thirst for the absolute—here ensures his salvation. The difference in theme lights on a specific textual segment, that of the dénouement; as this segment must be dramatically or narratively motivated, however, other textual segments (such as the pact) fit in with it. *A priori*, there is nothing to prevent the Faust subject from exemplifying a third, completely different theme in the future.

There are also texts with facts and events similar to those of the Faust series, but which neither provide an instance of the Faust subject nor the exemplification of one of its themes. This holds for Calderón's *comedia, El mágico prodigioso* (1637). It is not an instance of the Faust subject, as its facts and events are attached to a different proper name, that of Cyprian the wizard: what is dramatized, then, is a similar subject, but not the Faust subject itself. What is more, it exemplifies neither of the latter's themes, as an analysis of the pact soon makes clear. With Cyprian, it hinges on a double blindness: the magician, being pagan, does not yet know the Christian God, and is consequently unaware that the demon to whom he sells his soul is the Devil. As soon as he meets the Christian God, and realizes that the demon is in fact the Devil, he repudiates the pact and appeals to God for help;[3] thanks to which he is not only redeemed but made into a saint. When Faust makes the pact, on the other hand, he is perfectly aware of its possible consequences; it is either an act of defiance (Theme I) or a bet (Theme II).[4]

I would also suggest we distinguish between the instantiation of a subject and the exemplification of a theme. The two phenomena do not work at the same level: a subject is instantiated by a *text*, whereas a theme is exemplified in one or more *textual segments*. 'Subject' is a purely extensional category made up of facts and events, only constrained by the identity of the proper name or names to which these facts and events are attached. A theme, on the other hand, is an intensional category, a set of properties which pick out textual segments in which to be exemplified. By force of circumstances, it never marks out the set of all properties held by a given text or group of texts—an infinite set—but only selected properties. The theme, then, is never the matrix of a text, nor its genetic definition.

Secondly, a relationship of exemplification between theme and textual segments does not require segments to be identical from one text to another, but only that the exemplification be the same. A theme, then, can only be used to determine whether two exemplifications are equivalent, and not two texts: one text cannot be reduced to another on the same theme, even at the level of the elements which exemplify it. A theme is rarely exemplified in the same way twice.

Thirdly, the textual segments which exemplify the theme can exemplify other features at the same time—often generic ones, for the simple reason that themes are usually linked to generic orientations. On the one hand, a theme's transtextual trajectory quite often involves generic transformation: when this happens, the thematic features start to connect and indeed conflict with generic orientations independent of the theme. On the other hand, the generic orientations of a text are rarely monolithic. The segments which exemplify the theme may therefore come into conflict with other textual segments picked out by different generic features. Very often, these different generic features possess a conventional thematic horizon of their own, which may not coincide at all with the dominant hypertextual theme. In other words, it may be relatively easy to abstract a theme from a class of texts, but it is extremely difficult to work back from a theme to a given text taken as a whole. This stems from the fact that theme is an analytical concept: the mechanisms of textual synthesis which exemplify it, thanks to their own contextual and transtextual dynamics, cannot be transposed from one exemplification to another.

To illustrate these remarks, I would briefly like to discuss some genre-theme conflicts from the Faust tradition. I shall only be dealing with Theme I, which will allow me to pass over Goethe's *Faust;* in fact, I shall confine myself to three examples, the *Historia,* Marlowe's *Doctor Faustus* and Thomas Mann's *Doktor Faustus.* The first serves to show how the multiplicity of generic factors tends to undermine thematic unity; the second illustrates the fact that a theme always acts according to an additional hypertextual logic, which in turn affects the writing process; and the third helps us see that between the theme and the text itself, there is always the thickness of the text's hermeneutical projection.

In the case of Faust, we are fortunate in being able to locate the zero-degree of the textual series fairly easily: it is none other than the *Historia von D. Johann Fausten, dem weitbeschreyten Zauberer und Schwarzkünstler,*[5] dated 1587, printed and published by Johann Spies. From a narrative point of view, it comes across as a biographical chronicle (it records the life of Faust from birth to death), but functionally, as André Jolles has shown,[6] we are dealing with an anti-legend. In this respect it is comparable to the myth of Don Juan.

Right from the subtitle, which indicates that the *Historia* is to be "allen hochtragenden/fürwitzigen und Gottlosen Menschen zum schrecklichen

Beyspiel" ("a fearful example for all vain, curious and impious people"[7]), the tale defines itself by its function of negative exemplarity. This motif is reiterated in the dedicatory letter, interspersed at frequent intervals and summed up one last time in the *envoi*, this time in the form of a biblical reference: "Seyt nüchtern und wachet/dann euer Widersacher der Teuffel geht umbher wie ein brüllender Löwe/und suchet welchen er verschlinge/dem widerstehet fest im Glauben" ("Be calm but vigilant, because your enemy the devil is prowling round like a roaring lion, looking for someone to eat. Stand up to him, strong in faith . . ."[8]) The very identity of Theme I is linked to this generic functionality, the only thing capable of providing the subject with a religious meaning, by interpreting Faust's calamitous destiny as the result of an act of pride and despair.

In terms of its narrative structure, however, the *Historia* goes well beyond the functional framework of the anti-legend. Unlike Don Juan, Faust is no out-and-out miscreant: even after the pact, he manages to act with nobility from time to time. What is more, the narrator presents in great detail all of the secret knowledge Faust acquires after the pact. This can only mean one of two things: either the act of recording this knowledge purges it of its demonic character, or the narrator himself is the accomplice of Doctor Faustus. In as much as the knowledge in question is vital to humanity, since it bears on its ultimate purpose, Faust is liable at any moment to turn into some sort of Prometheus figure. In other words, the thirst for absolute knowledge is liable at any moment to escape the hermeneutical framework of the anti-legend, and to establish itself as an autonomous narrative end. Furthermore, Faust repents of his wrongs before being carried off to Hell, a difficult feature to reconcile with his role as a purely negative example. For all these reasons, the thematic univocality, suggesting an exclusively religious reading, is clearly compromised.

Far from being a simple anti-legend, the *Historia* is a complex amalgam in which diverse generic impulses collide to form a strange concoction: antipapal polemic, grotesque anecdote, theological *quaestio* (the questions Faust asks Mephistopheles about Hell), cosmological critique, sermon, religious lament ("Dr. Fausti Wehklag,"[9] which has a paradoxical model in the lamentations of Job), and doubtless more besides, which my unfamiliarity with the literature of that period prevents me from identifying. From the point of view of thematic unity, this series of characteristics is of course centrifugal. By foregrounding the autonomy of the various episodes, the paratactic structure of the tale only serves to accentuate the thematic dispersion. If the theme associated with the anti-legend still manages to make its presence felt, this is because the text is caught in a pincer movement by the anti-legend model which intervenes at strategic junctures, not only within the text itself—the pact, the grisly ending—but also, and especially, as a hermeneutical principle explicitly formulated in the paratext: the subtitle, dedicatory letter and final *envoi*.

Clearly this text could never be deemed an instantiation of the theme: it overflows the latter on all sides. Some of its features do exemplify it, but this exemplification is in turn closely bound up with that of a specific genre, the anti-legend. It is only because the anti-legend adopts the series of centrifugal generic elements in the text that the latter can be seen as exemplifying the original theme of Faust: the damnation of the proud man who defies God and loses his faith in the omnipotence of Grace.

Marlowe's *Doctor Faustus* (1594)[10] differs from the *Historia* both in mode and in genre. I shall not address the change in mode from narrative to dramatic—although, as it happens, this is full of issues relating to the highly paratactic structure of the *Historia:* no less than 68 episodes can in fact be counted (96 in the 1599 version), most of which are entirely freestanding. Marlowe is clearly forced to reduce the profusion of independent narrative units; it would be interesting to study the forms this compression takes from the point of view of the work's thematic status.

Alongside this modal transformation, at least two shifts in genre are discernible here, both due to the pressure exerted by the Elizabethan dramatic tradition. The first involves one of the textual features which exemplify the thematic structure. In the German text, Faust abandons the study of theology in order to turn to medicine, astronomy and magic, with the explicit aim of penetrating the secrets of nature: he would "die Elementa speculieren"[11]—in other words, what he wants to study are the fundamental forces of the universe. The main function of the pact with the Devil is to give him access to the Tree of Knowledge; one third of the *Historia* is devoted to Faust's various questions about ultimate truths. In Marlowe, this aspect takes a back seat: Faustus no longer differentiates between theology and other forms of knowledge. He turns to magic out of a disenchantment with knowledge *per se*. What attracts him this time isn't knowledge but power, a resonant and ubiquitous motif of Elizabethan drama. By means of the pact, Faustus hopes to win "a world . . . of power, of honor, of omnipotence,"[12] not to mention the status of a demi-god. Marlowe's decision to retain the tripartite structure of the events in Faust's life (quest for knowledge, sexual adventures, politico-grotesque episodes) makes this change in motivation all the more remarkable. Events which have something in common with those of the *Historia* are fitted into a new hermeneutical horizon: Faust's main sin—seeking to exceed theologically legimated power—is here no more than a minor aspect of Faustus' crime, which is more along the lines of a comprehensive challenge to divine omnipotence. Thanks to this change in the very nature of the crime, Marlowe's exemplification of the Faust theme cannot be superimposed onto that of the *Historia.*

The second shift is strictly dramaturgical. Marlowe reduplicates the plot structure: his Faust is imitated, in grotesque form, first by his *famulus* Wagner and then and above all by Robin and Dick, the clowns. The actantial universe—the universe of the *agents*—is thus divided into two levels, corresponding to two tiers of society, with the serious plot on the upper level and the burlesque action at the lower level. This dichotomy is of course recognizable as a quasi-ubiquitous aspect of Elizabethan theater. The *Historia* knew no such dichotomy: there, the *famulus* Wagner is no more grotesque than Faust, and the Robin and Dick characters do not exist. There is, however, one feature of the *Historia* which Marlowe retains and even reinforces, and that is the combination of serious and grotesque passages on a single actantial plane, making Faust ridiculous and tragic at once. This goes for the scene at the papal court. Not only does Marlowe insert it into a general situation—the anti-pope episode—which is not in the *Historia;* he also increases the number of indignities suffered by the Pope at the hands of Faustus.[13] The result is constant dramaturgical interference: the semantic tension emanating from the actantial dichotomy of Elizabethan drama is impeded by the doubling which already exists within the upper level, the serious plot, and which comes straight out of the *Historia.* As this phenomenon clearly shows, Marlowe borrows more than just the theme of Faust: he also takes a specific textual exemplification of it, performing a purely hypertextual operation, rather than an analysis of thematic abstraction from which to generate his own independent exemplification.[14] In this respect, his approach differs radically from that of Thomas Mann.

Marlowe's *Doctor Faustus* has often been compared with the morality play.[15] Certain dramatic features, like the good and bad angels and the chorus, undeniably derive from this tradition. On many counts, however, Marlowe's play departs from the morality model. First of all, as far as I know, morality plays (like *Everyman*) usually have an edifying purpose. Admittedly, like the legend or anti-legend, their function is an exemplary one; but instead of presenting a model to imitate or an example to avoid, they simply submit a case for contemplation. And admittedly, Marlowe's play is no clear-cut anti-legend: witness the last great monologue, which raises Faustus to truly tragic stature, and which is quite difficult to reconcile with its function of negative exemplarity. Here, the hero comes across as the victim of a divine force more terrifying than just; Faustus' monologue comes perilously close to the despairing cry of the creature sacrificed by its creator. The difference between this and Don Juan's demise could not be greater: the latter goes to Hell blaspheming, while Faustus repents of his wrongs. At the same time, the fact that he is damned anyway is liable to cast divine justice in an equivocal light. This feature, as we have seen, was already present in the "Dr. Fausti Wehklag" section of the *Historia;* in Marlowe, it is expanded.

Still, Marlowe's Faustus inherits certain grotesque features from the Faust of the *Historia*—a fact which fits in poorly with the tragic aspects here, highlighting those of the anti-legend instead. The use of the chorus, a dramatic technique typical of the morality play, goes some way in the same direction. This chorus is not just there to summarize the action: in the prologue and epilogue, it also serves to insert the function of negative exemplarity (belonging to the anti-legend) into a dramatic structure (Elizabethan drama) from which this function is absent. In the prologue and epilogue, the chorus comments upon and judges Faustus' progress from the point of view of Christian theology. It thus fulfills a similar function to that of the subtitle, *envoi* and narrator's sermons in the *Historia.*

I would just like to add one last point. Marlowe, as has often been remarked, retains the paratactic structure of the *Historia,* albeit in somewhat pared down form. The chief reason for this undoubtedly lies in his desire to preserve the biographical chronicle framework and to account for the twenty-four intervening years from the signing of the pact to Faust's damnation. Given its function in the anti-legend framework, the conclusion of the pact makes any real dramatic evolution impossible. The play moves into the wholly static world of negative exemplarity. The biographical chronicle suits this state of affairs well, as it can give the same value to every event, seen as just another illustration of a single *vita.* Whence the second function of the chorus: it effects the transition from one exemplary situation to another, even as it compresses narrative time.

If this abolition of dramatic temporality is to be avoided, either the dramatic tension must be displaced onto another character (like Gretchen in Goethe's *Urfaust*—assuming, that is, that the *Urfaust* still falls within the anti-legend framework) or the pact must be confined to the end of the narration, immediately before the descent into Hell (as in Berlioz's *Damnation de Faust*), or replaced by a motif which allows for dramatic progression. Thomas Mann, as we know, opted for the last solution: by replacing the pact with the contraction of syphilis, a slow disease, he re-introduces narrative progression into the novel, while at the same time allowing it to acquire a hypotactic structure.

—⊪—

Thomas Mann's *Doktor Faustus* (1947) occupies a place of its own in the Faustian hypertextual series. Mann, unlike just about everybody else who engages with the Faustian thematics, does not use its subject: he tells instead the apparently unrelated story of a twentieth-century musician, Adrian Leverkühn. Neither by name, conduct nor individual destiny could this man be confused with the Faust of the tradition. And yet, if he cannot be Faustus himself, Leverkühn still is *a* Faustus, just as he is a musician. This apparent paradox is tied in with the hypertextual status of *Doktor Faustus,* the fact that it is—to use Gérard Genette's terminology[16]—a transposition, transforming the proper name, time, events and so on; in fact, every element of narrative substance which lends the Faust subject a degree of unity. Here, then, we have a text which constitutes an exemplification of the Faust theme without using its subject. In this respect it sets itself apart from all other exemplifications of the Faust theme: even if they expand the old episodes and invent new ones, or couple Faust with characters from other thematic traditions, they always tend to preserve the identity of the hero. And when the hero's identity stays the same, so must the epoch and the universe in which he moves, since his (narrative) identity is inextricably bound up with them. Apart from Mann, the only writer to break this rule is Valéry; but in the latter, Faust is no longer a fictional character: he is a literary *effect* in the true sense of the word. As the passage I began with reveals, Valéry's Faust consciously thinks of himself as a hypertextual character: he is a creature of paper whose continued existence is a direct result of the hypertextual tradition, as are his changes in historical universe. In other words, Valéry's Faust—and again I am using distinctions introduced by Genette[17]—is an *extension* in which personal identity is preserved.

Nothing of the sort in Thomas Mann: Adrian Leverkühn is Adrian Leverkühn. The whole of his career makes perfect sense, and the text can thus be read without reference to theme of Faust. All of the scattered hypertextual indices, like the visit from the Devil and Adrian's use of archaic German during his fits of madness, can also be explained from within the narrative universe of Adrian's life: by his illness, and by the fact that he is composing a piece based on the *Historia.*

This transposition theory has had its fair share of critics, the most prominent being Käte Hamburger. Hamburger points out that the two heroes in question are "only" connected by the title, which the tale could very well do without and which it even partially undermines, or, at the least, obstructs. According to her, the reader's experience of Leverkühn is in no way that of a modern Faust, since he is missing the character trait in which Faust is grounded *(gegründet),* as she puts it: the obsession with absolute knowledge, pleasure and action.[18] But could the novel not lead us to do the opposite—to see Faust as a proto-Leverkühn, to read the first from the perspective of the second? Why shouldn't the thematic dynamics, which is in any case interpretive, work in both directions?

Hamburger would undoubtedly reject this solution. Clearly what bothers her is the fact that the Faustian thematics in *Doktor Faustus* resides exclusively in a paratextual element, namely the title and subtitle *(Doctor Faustus: the life of the German composer, Adrian Leverkühn, as told by a friend)*. As "Doktor Faustus" is not the title of a work by Leverkühn (*his* Faustian oeuvre is entitled "Dr. Fausti Wehklag"), obviously the term can only be applied to Adrian himself. What generates the Faustian thematics, then, is the identification of the emblematic name in the title with the proper name in the subtitle. Here, "Faustus" is not a proper noun; it designates the *class* of beings to which Adrian belongs. This is why, if he cannot be *the* Faustus, Leverkühn still is *a* Faustus. "Faustus" is not—and especially not in Germany—the same as "Faust"; by choosing the former over the latter, Mann clearly steers the reader toward Theme I, and, in consequence, toward the generic structure of the anti-legend.[19]

In her own terms, of course, Hamburger is perfectly right. The events in Mann's novel which exemplify the Faust theme, attached as they are to a different proper name, remain outside the framework of the Faustian subject; they don't look much like those of the subject either. What drives Adrian is neither the thirst for knowledge nor the will to power; the book's underlying problematics contains no kind of theological perspective. Furthermore, the intratextual indices which establish associative analogies between certain segments of the novel and certain segments of the Faust subject only become relevant if we *already* see Adrian in the context of the *Historia*. This goes for Adrian's theological studies, for his musical treatment of a subject from the *Historia,* for the visions of the Devil and the old German idiom; it also goes for more scattered indications such as his father's predilection for the occult, the name Capercailzie (English for *Auerhahn*,[20] the diabolical spirit serving Faustus' footman Wagner in the *Historia*) and the disturbing presence of the dog on the farm he retires to. All of these indices merely serve to reinforce the hermeneutical projection which the title and subtitle have drawn up as a contract for reading: they would doubtless have little effect on their own.

Once this hermeneutical projection is established, however, the novel fits in perfectly with the Faustian thematics. At this point, a distinction should be drawn between those textual segments which function as indices and those which exemplify the thematics. The textual segments mentioned earlier, the ones which evoke certain segments of the *Historia* by analogy, are merely indices. The real work of exemplification is performed by other elements which are not analogically linked to the *Historia* but which, in functional terms, take the place of some of its features. The cult of dionysiac creation replaces the thirst for knowledge or power; the contraction of syphilis replaces the pact; insanity replaces damnation. These last elements exemplify the overarching hermeneutical projection generated by the title and the indices.

This overarching projection places the text within the generic tradition of the anti-legend. It applies, of course, not only to the tale itself but also and above all to the narrative framework, which details the historical consequences of a collective pact far more horrible than that of Leverkühn: Germany's pact with Nazism. This being said, certain qualifications should be made. The fact that the novel is placed within the anti-legend genre does not imply that this functions as a hard and fast hermeneutical model. Thus, in terms of Leverkühn's individual destiny, the pact is not only a deadly threat to rationality but also the precondition for artistic creativity, or at least for dionysiac artistic creativity; the novel maintains a fundamental ambiguity in regard to the meaning of this contradiction. No such ambiguity as far as the Faustian pact of Nazi Germany is concerned, even if the acceptance of Germany's damnation is accompanied by a feeling of compassion: the book is also a plaint, a *Wehklag* for the fate of Germany. So the hermeneutical horizon of the anti-legend, rather than authoritatively interpreting the novel, hovers above it in the shape of a question.

The case of *Doktor Faustus* clearly shows the scope of thematic exemplification. Here this relationship is essentially established by a reading contract formulated in the paratext; without this, it would simply not exist. The disposition of this particular novel is obviously not the rule for thematic exemplification, but it is *one* possibility. Add to that the importance for thematic recognition of generic identification (here, the anti-legend), as well as the instability of this recognition, given the multiplicity of generic exemplifications to be found in most texts, and I think it must be agreed that the movement from the analysis of a text's theme to the study of a theme's text seems less like a guided tour than a voyage of discovery.

RACINIAN SPACES

Thomas Pavel

Claude Bremond and I have called for a conception of thematics which gives *attention* and *aboutness* their due.[1] Recognizing at the same time the incurable mobility of both, we concluded that the theme can never be confined, once and for all, to a given level of the literary text. In an attempt to give the concept of *thematic universe* a new lease on life, we claimed that its most general categories—such as space, time, causality and action—constitute a kind of thematic framework, forming the very conditions of possibility for more concrete thematic choices.

To illustrate this idea, I shall draw upon the thematic space of Racinian tragedy. As the mobility of attention and aboutness automatically precludes the discovery of a single Racinian space, I shall show that there are at least *two* contiguous and antagonistic spaces here, which I shall designate respectively as the open peristyle and the closed doors *[huis clos]*. My analysis of these spaces will lead into discussions of the more specific themes which inhabit them, the organization of Racinian texts, and the evolution of tragedy and neo-classicism in general. Thematic worlds, I shall conclude, can only be understood in strict relation to the history of aesthetic activity.

I. The Sleep-Walkers

There can, by all accounts, be no better guide to Racinian topography than Roland Barthes himself.[2] Barthes identifies two spaces in Racine: the Chamber, a secret space of power, and the Antechamber, in which victims patiently await the hidden tyrant's decree. This structure accounts for Néron's impenetrable lair, at whose door Agrippine waits to be received (*Britannicus* I:1), and also—to some extent—for Titus's unpredictable appearances in

Bérénice, a play in which the hero prefers to run away ("Let us go. I can say nought to her"[3]) rather than break the bad news to the heroine. Yet what one senses behind the stage is not so much that "vestige of the mythic cave," the terrifying Chamber of the Minotaur, as the sumptuous suite where the disconsolate emperor hides to cry in peace and quiet.

The protagonists in *Bajazet* know that they are near the center of a labyrinth ("I'm led here by a slave, through hidden paths"[4]) if not actually *there,* in the Chamber itself. Roxane's supremacy derives less from her withdrawal into some mysterious space behind the scenes—after all, everything we see on stage is *already* behind the scenes—than from her ability at any moment to expel the intruders from her realm. When the tender object of her desires fails to promise to marry her, her order is peremptory:

> Go: henceforth the harem shall be closed,
> And all return to its accustomed state.[5]

Still, these images—Titus running off to sob on his imperial bed, Roxane threatening expulsion from the inner sanctum—are not necessarily *similar;* they may also be *complementary.* In fact, the stage displays an almost protean flexibility. In *Athalie,* for example, it becomes a trap, catching the renegade queen off her guard: first a curtain is raised, revealing Joas, and then—just as she is threatening the High Priest—the back of the stage opens up, and an army of Levites invade the space.

Whether it be an Antechamber, a transitional zone between two antithetical spaces, some dark corner of a labyrinth or a temple that turns into a trap, Racine's stage is always crossed by hesitant characters, unsure of their whereabouts and ready to flee at any moment:

> What have I done? What shall I do? Where am I?
> What pain devours me? What comes over me?
> I wander in the palace aimlessly.
>
> Ah, Princess, whither now? What blinding frenzy
> Provoked these sad attempts upon your life?
>
> Flying with but one thought to aid his son,
> I tore myself from pale Oenone's arms . . .[6]

Racine's heroes seldom walk; usually they dash from one place to another, and if they cross the stage it is apparently quite by chance, on their breathless journey to some indeterminate end. Meetings are always something of a surprise, as if the presence of another character awakened them from their sleepwalking ("But who is this?/God! it's Achilles.")[7] Most often, however, they simply avoid one another, leaving as soon as the other arrives:

> She flees. Am I awake, or do I dream?
>
> The King is coming. Flee, make haste.
>
> What! you were leaving, prince? Wherefore this haste,
> This unforeseen departure, nay, this flight?[8]

Often they must be begged, cajoled or pressed to cross the stage: "Come, daughter, we were waiting but for you."[9] And sometimes it is only because another character is blocking their path, or because their strength has given out, that they stop in front of us.

> No further. Here, Oenone, let us stay.
> I faint, I fall; my strength abandons me.[10]

Their relationship with the stage is fluid, ever-changing. They step in hesitantly and stop with reluctance, as if haunted by a seductive *elsewhere,* as if their short stay in front of us epitomized caesura, the brief interval between two beats, the space between stabler platforms, firmer grounds.

And yet, as has often been noted, when they *should* flee, they don't. The ships awaiting Acomat, Oreste and Hippolyte ("on a vessel ready in the port . . . / I pondered an escape to foreign lands"; "Our ships are ready and the winds blow strong"; "If you will leave, the sails are all unfurled")[11] never will set sail. Like a repetitious operatic chorus—or like Beckett's Vladimir and Estragon—the *Bérénice* trio are endlessly declaring their intention to leave, but never do so, making one wonder what keeps them in place. Or—to look at it another way—why, once caught in the tragic space, do they constantly, aimlessly wander about?

Racine's spectators noticed this aimless movement very quickly, and reacted in dismay. "I haven't seen anyone fail to laugh," writes Subligny in *La folle querelle,* "when Pyrrhus comes up to Oreste saying '*I looked for you everywhere, Your Majesty.*'" Pyrrhus, of course, is a king, and "a Royal Majesty should not run around like this from one room to the next."[12]

The Romantics (in particular, Victor Hugo and Alfred de Musset) were acutely aware of this tension between aimless wandering and impossible flight. Musset, writing in 1838, proposes a somewhat anecdotal explanation: Racinian tragedy, he claims, cannot be understood outside of its conditions of performance.

What! all these beautiful theories of Racine, these pompous thoughts in so elegant a dress, these concise prefaces, so noble, this gentle method of proceeding, so tender and so passionate, may trace their true origin to the fact that there was only a space of ten feet in which to act, and also to the benches in front of the stage. May it not be possible that the numerous confidants only make these fine speeches, so well delivered by enamored princes, to fill up the scene without doing much, for fear of striking the legs of the marquis in passing?[13]

If Racine's characters cannot "do much," this is because of the limited size of the stage, crowded as it is with elegant spectators. Dramatic *distance* being lost, the imaginary world lies literally at arm's length—which rather tends to prohibit sweeping movements and violent endeavors, favoring instead this incessant quivering and dithering about. As long as the stage lacks breadth and scope, Musset seems to be saying, the heroes have to wriggle around like tropical fish in a crowded aquarium. As soon as the benches are removed from the stage in 1759, French classical tragedy becomes practically static:

this is the reason that Andromache, Monime, and Emilie now have peristyles to themselves, with nothing to interfere with them; there they can have a space of sixty square feet to walk in, and no marquis is there interfering with the actors, to say something pleasant after every tirade, to pick up Hermione's fan, or to criticize the legs of Theseus. Orestes, sword in hand, needs no longer scatter the crowd of dudes, saying: "Gentlemen, allow me to pass. I am on my way to kill Pyrrhus."

On the new stage "we find that the action lags, and are astonished that, all the doors being open and the palace deserted, no one enters, acts, or makes the play progress."[14]

Interestingly, while for Barthes (who may, without saying as much, have Sartre's *Huis clos* in the back of his mind) the Racinian space closes tightly round its characters—literally to the point of suffocation in *Bajazet*—Musset is disturbed by the vast, drafty emptiness of the stage, its deserted openness, its depopulation. One may, of course, dismiss this contradiction as irrelevant: from Madame de Sévigné and Saint-Evremond to Thierry Maulnier and Leo Spitzer, almost every aspect of Racine has been described in contradictory terms. Is it a ballet of empty elegance, or a burst of savage violence? Are its characters just courtiers of Louis XIV, thinly disguised in classical costumes, or are they tortured Jansenist souls, torn by heroic demands and by the absence of Grace? Are the speeches conditioned by humanist rhetoric, or do they express a more personal desire for moderation?

I shall not attempt to resolve these paradoxes here; there may, in any case, be no solution to such conflicting claims, pertaining as they do to the infinite work of interpretation. Saint-Evremond's criticisms and the eulogies of Thierry Maulnier are, after all, both subject to historical analysis. For a reader of Racine at the end of the twentieth century, these contradictory images pose no problem; they merely indicate the existence of several possible worlds, each containing possibly similar but ultimately incompatible structures and themes. Or we may view them as twin sets of lights, one on either side of the stage, and—like a good director—use them in turns, each time bringing out a new *aboutness*.[15]

II. Tragic Circles and Blowing Winds

> Neo-classical characters are less interested in living life than in *speaking* it.
>
> —Thierry Maulnier, *Racine*

First let us view the Racinian stage as if it really were the vast, empty peristyle Musset describes, its doors wide open to let the spellbound heroes shuffle through. It is a vague terrain, crisscrossed by multiple paths and surrounded by seas—far beyond which lie other lands, sometimes lending the tragedy a deceptive horizon of hope, sometimes suggesting the depths of despair.

Andromaque is set in Epirus, where Pyrrhus is king. Outside his palace—possibly adjoining it, in fact—are a temple (where he will meet his death on his way to marry Andromaque) and a prison (for Astyanax, her son with Hector). Away in the distance stretches the sea, separating all this from the rest of Greece.

The peristyle in *Bérénice* links Titus's quarters with those of the Queen. A glimpse of imperial Rome—and perhaps, as Lucien Goldmann was so keen to suggest, of the Romans as well—is visible through the open doorway. We can certainly see the Senate, and then once again the sea; beyond that lies the Orient, a space of solitude, dreaded with equal intensity by Antiochus and by Bérénice: "How will we pine a month, a year, from now/When we're divided by a waste of seas . . . ?"[16]

In *Bajazet* we descry, through the loopholes of the labyrinth, a narrow sound bounded by a massive continent; at its end lies Babylon, besieged by the forces of Sultan Amurat. A path leads past the gates of Phèdre's palace, out to the forest where Hippolyte goes hunting and the beach where the monster will eventually destroy him; on the opposite shore lies Athens.

Just as space is arranged in concentric layers, so the temporal structure carefully stratifies events preceding the start of the play. *Andromaque*, like

Athalie, opens with a *yes:* "Yes, since I find again so true a friend . . . "[17] Critics like Jacques Scherer and M. C. Bowra have pointed out how *late* neo-classical tragedies, especially those of Racine, tend to begin; this play is clearly a case in point, the "yes" connecting the meeting on stage to a long series of prior events, each of which corresponds to a different spatial layer. Thus, before deciding to head for Pyrrhus's palace, Oreste has spent an indeterminate length of time in the grip of his unrequited love for Hermione. This eventless period of torment and indecision, dominated by a sterile passion, I would label *pre-tragic.* It surrounds the tragic time just as the seas encircle the palace.

Oreste explicitly associates his pre-tragic suffering with the sea:

> You witnessed my despair, and ever since
> I've dragged my sorrows over endless seas.[18]

Other characters—like Andromaque ("A captive, always hateful to herself"), Pyrrhus ("Vanquished, in thrall, devoured by keen regrets,/Burned with more blazing fires than e'er I lit"), and of course Phèdre ("All things contrive to grieve and thwart me, all")—may not make this connection, but they still undergo the same indeterminate tortures.[19]

The Waste Sea these heroes are forced to wander does not, however, extend to the very margins of the world, beyond the beginnings of memory. Before the period of pre-tragic tribulations, they once inhabited *terra firma,* those territories that glitter on the other side of the water: Oreste's Greece, Andromaque's Troy, Bérénice's Palestine, Phèdre's Athens. There in the distance we can just make out the shimmer of weapons, the glow of fires, the movements of troops:

> My soldiers for the nonce were barely clothed,
> The darkness magnified our fears. The lines
> Were weakened everywhere and poorly held;
> Complete disorder caused bewilderment.
> Sometimes we turned our arms against ourselves,
> The frightful cries re-echoed from the rocks—
> In short, we knew the horrors of a clash
> In darkness . . . [20]

This faraway landscape I would call the *epic horizon.* It is the time and space of Troy, the Roman Wars and the conquest of Palestine; it favors sincerity and closeness to oneself; love and speech enjoy an unproblematic relationship: "I did not don the cloak of silence, but . . . / Followed the promptings of my heart alone."[21] Glorious victories and noble defeats notwithstanding, the heroes cannot stay on epic ground forever. At some point they detach themselves from their military surroundings, falling victim—in spite of themselves—to what I would call the *initial catastrophe*.

The Jansenists' Original Sin may, of course, be read between the lines here, *à la* Lucien Goldmann and F. J. Tanquerey: following a state of pretemporal innocence, the Fall gives rise to conflict, Eros and Time. In Racine, however, the horizon against which the initial catastrophe occurs already contains both history and conflict; as for erotic fulfillment, the outcome of this catastrophe—which consists, more often than not, in the birth of an impossible love—tends to cancel its possibility. Whether it transgresses every human rule or is merely impeded from without, tragic passion clouds the stream of speech, silencing the sincere protagonists, deadening their energies, dividing them against themselves and making them lose their bearings:

> My peace of mind, my happiness seemed sure.
> Athens revealed to me my haughty foe.
> As I beheld, I reddened, I turned pale.
> A tempest raged in my distracted mind.[22]

Unrequited love is not, however, the only cause of the initial catastrophe. In *Athalie* it instantiates the work of the unconscious, the sudden rush of guilt bursting frail films of repression. Athalie's prophetic vision—"A dream (should I be worried by a dream?)"[23]—is the equivalent of Phèdre's tortured love.

Stunned as they are by the sudden fall that lands them in the Waste Sea of suffering, characters still try to free themselves from their predicament. Phèdre attempts to extricate herself from the clutches of Hippolyte, like Oreste from those of Hermione, by her own unaided efforts:

> Against myself at last I dared revolt.
> I spurred my feelings on to harass him.
>
> Anger seized my heart.
> I strove for vengeance by forgetting her.[24]

The calm obtained is short-lived, however. All it takes is for Phèdre to be back near Hippolyte, or for Oreste to learn that Pyrrhus has rejected Hermione, and the old pain returns, more poignant than ever:

> I saw my passion's embers blaze again;
> I felt my hatred was about to end;
> Or rather felt that I adored her still.
>
> Ah vain precautions! Cruel destiny!
> Brought by my lord himself to Troezen's shores,

> I saw once more the foe I had expelled.
> My open wound at once poured blood again.[25]

At this point—which we might designate the *re-lapse*—the intensity of suffering ("Venus in all her might is on her prey"[26]) becomes such that they must needs renew the pursuit after the object of their scandalous desire; or die. Oreste leans toward the first alternative, Phèdre toward the second:

> Since stubborn, long resistance is in vain,
> I follow blindly my impelling fate.
> I love, and come to win Hermione,
> Carry her off or die before her eyes.
>
> Dying, I could have kept my name unstained,
> And my dark passion from the light of day . . . [27]

Before dying, however, she simply cannot keep herself from speaking; and neither can Oreste. It is in fact precisely at the juncture when the excess of silent—pre-tragic—suffering crystallizes into language that the tragedy proper begins. Oreste's acceptance of speech ("*Yes,* since I find again so true a friend . . . "), like Phèdre's confession ("I to Hippolytus have bared my shame,/ And hope, despite me, has seduced my heart . . . "[28]), sanctions the encounter of passion and language, setting up a fragile space where discourse and destiny may question one another.

The imaginary universe, a framework for thematic reflection, thus leads us to construct a Proppian chain of narrative (or dramatic) functions: epic horizon—initial catastrophe—pre-tragic torment—attempt to escape—relapse—entry into language. As a side-effect, such an analysis serves to indicate the hermeneutic nature of structural description. More importantly, it may also throw some light upon the *history of structures*.

If neo-classical tragedy tends to start "late," this is not just for the sake of the unity of action—best obtained, according to such contemporary theoreticians as Mairet, d'Aubignac and Corneille, by means of a "sudden and violent psychological crisis"[29]—but also due to the gradual specialization of genres, thanks to which tragedy begins to eliminate its epic openings. A principle of textual differentiation is at work here, emphasizing what is particularly theatrical about the theater: the characters' ability to *speak for themselves*. In other words, between the "irregular" works of the generation before Mairet—most notably those of Alexandre Hardy, but also some early Corneille—and the time of *Sophonisbe* (Mairet, 1634), *Pompée* (Corneille, 1642) and *Andromaque* (Racine, 1667), there is a noticeable effort to remove everything epic, everything that can be narrated as well as enacted, from the stage.

When we compare the dramatic construction of French classical tragedy with that of its counterparts in Elizabethan and Jacobean England, this process soon becomes apparent. Of the several sub-genres of English Renaissance drama, only one typically opens "late," and that is the *revenge tragedy,* in which the murder to be avenged is required by convention to take place before the curtain rises. Most often, as in *Hamlet,* this rule is carefully respected; in some cases, however, the original murder is only a pretext for the action, one which will contain *more* murders and *more* acts of vengeance. The real revenge in *The Spanish Tragedy* is for Horatio's death (in Act II scene 4) and not Andrea's (before the play started). And in spite of their "late" start, *Hamlet* and *The Revenger's Tragedy* are so full of adventure, reversal and recognition that the *in medias res* technique is very soon forgotten. In the other sub-genres of Elizabethan tragedy, the plot begins as soon as the curtain rises.

Imagine a *King Lear* written by Racine: would it begin much earlier than Edmund's capture of Lear and Cordelia? Would it contain anything more than the hangman's hesitation before an execution? Edmund would love Cordelia with a dark passion, while Cordelia would feel a sisterly fondness for Edgar. Lear's life would be in her hands: if she agreed to marry Edmund, the old king would be freed; if not, he would die.

This hypothetical plot is actually less idle than it seems. Given that *Lear* begins so early, from the very sowing of the seeds of strife, and that it includes so many episodes—Edmund's machinations around Lear's elder daughters, the series of blows and counterblows exchanged by Lear and the latter, the tribulations of the King and Gloucester—its structure is clearly still an *epic* one. English tragedy has not yet managed to free itself from the strangle-hold of the narrative genres: just as Renaissance comedy is still under the influence of medieval romances and pastoral prose, so the tragedies still bear the unmistakable stamp of the historical narrative, the folktale and the novella. Shakespeare's *Antony and Cleopatra* reproduces Plutarch's *Life of Antony* with all the fidelity of a best-selling novel made into a film.

By contrast, French classical tragedy swiftly and expressly defines its program as that of *emptying out* the play, eliminating the plethora of events it once contained. As Mairet writes in 1631,

> It must be understood that the same Euripides, Sophocles and Seneca plays we now find so simple and devoid of plot *[sujet]* were considered quite full in their own day . . . [30]

Richness and variety of event are felt to be improper for the theater; what Musset loses sight of entirely, in his belated amusement at benches filled with noisy nobles, is the deliberate effort of classicist writers to purge the stage of every epic trace, to clarify the design of tragedy, to let some air into the vast imaginary spaces. The elimination of event in favor of speech is so clearly the intention of most Cornelian tragedies (*Le Cid* excepted) that some of their most striking singularities simply cannot be understood otherwise. How else is one to account for the interminable opening scenes of *Rodogune, Héraclius, Pertharite* and *Suréna,* in which a pair of characters tell each other endlessly intricate stories—supposedly indispensable to an understanding of the plot—if not as a sign of the pleasure they must have taken in those days, playwright and audience alike, every time *diction* took over from *action?* How else are we to comprehend the effect of *Horace*—a play in which the characters are constantly narrating, on stage, events which happened off-stage a few moments earlier—except as a victory of articulation over representation? Rhetorical techniques provided, admittedly, a ready-made tool for the task; but if the shape of the genre had not undergone such a structural alteration, they might never have been used at all. The whole of the immense, wide-open set with its windows overlooking temples, harbors, seas and continents was nothing but the *resonance space* of articulate speech.

By the time Racine was active, the stage had long been cleared of enacted events, and the supremacy of rhetoric was firmly established.[31] The disturbing rigidity, inexorable maxims and relentless syllogisms of *Cinna, Horace* and the later *Sertorius* arguably represented little more than a youthful infatuation on Corneille's part with the pithiness of language, the pride of a recent victor over the baroque proliferation of events. The women in *Horace,* Sabine, Julie and Camille, stand almost motionless throughout the play, listening to the conflicting reports of the battle and nobly reasoning with one another:

> When one of them must die at the other's hands,
> I find your arguments most unconvincing.[32]

"Arguments!" Charles Péguy writes (in his *Note conjointe*) of those young Cornelian heroes who love honor with a love that is true, and honor love with an honor that is true; they also speak candidly of love, one might add—and candidly love to speak.

Faced with a vacant stage from which events had quite effectively been outlawed, Racine's innovation is to narrate the birth of language, now that it reigns supreme. From its epic beginnings, through the various stages detailed above (initial fall into pre-tragic limbo, attempt to fight back, subsequent relapse), desire advances toward its encounter with language; and everything takes place as if tragedy itself were nothing more than the brief interval between the entry into language and the tragic end—death or madness—which reinstates the reign of silence. This entry into language is no culmination of a rational effort toward expression, but is provoked by an explosion of suffering, one which sends the relapsed heroes scurrying toward the shelter of articulate language—the tragic space, in other words. The energy such explosions liberate—what I would call the *tragic whirlwind*—causes the characters' incessant motion, their breathless haste, their fears and their hesitations. It provides an answer to the perennial question, "Ah, Princess, whither now?"

And it also explains why the spurious ships can never leave the harbor: for the whirlwind blows toward the stage, instead of out to sea. The open peristyle may have seemed empty to the Romantic eye, but the attentive ear can hear the winds blowing through its columns, carrying the heroes onward to their meeting with the word.

III. The Privilege of the Stage

A whole new set of features will emerge if we follow Barthes' perspective on Racine. As we have seen, certain plays neatly instantiate his "closed doors" structure: *Britannicus,* for one, exemplifies the opposition between the secret Chamber, where the power figure makes its fateful decisions, and the accessible Antechamber. We have also seen how this distinction fails to operate in all of Racine's plays. Titus's Chamber is a space of weakness and remorse, a refuge for the over-sensitive emperor; and while Pyrrhus may, in the depths of his palace, have some means of restraining Andromaque, his power hardly extends to Hermione or to Oreste. In *Iphigénie,* the stage borders on a place of sacrifice, a sacred area where divinities speak and miracles come to pass. In *Bajazet,* the scene is the Chamber itself; and in *Phèdre* the distinction between Chamber and Antechamber simply does not seem to apply.

Barthes' description may not fit every play in detail, but one cannot help feeling that there *is* a second principle at work here, opposed to the tragic whirlwind and offsetting somewhat the openness of the vast peristyles; a factor I shall dub the *privilege of the stage.* With habitual perspicacity, Barthes also notes that for the Racinian hero, leaving the stage amounts to death. He points to Bajazet, whose continued existence depends upon his being allowed to stay with Roxane. Pyrrhus hurries off to the temple, in spite of his confidant's warnings (*Andromaque* IV:6), and duly meets his end there; Britannicus dashes to Néron's apartments, relentlessly deaf to Junie's misgivings ("I must go. I'm waited for"[33]); and Hippolyte, even more unfortunate than the rest, is driven by his fiancée to hasten to his death (*Phèdre* V:1).

The exception, of course, proves the rule once again, most notably in the case of *Iphigénie:* after lengthy deliberations, and in spite of Clytemnestre's staunch opposition, Iphigénie leaves the stage—only to be saved by the hands of the gods, and not sacrificed at all. Mithridate goes off to war; and Bérénice's freely-chosen exile, even if this deserted Orient bears some resemblance to death, has nothing in common with the unexpected ends of Hippolyte, Pyrrhus and Britannicus.

Most of the time, however, the visible stage is a kind of stronghold in which nothing and nobody may harm the hero—a feature which Corneille adopts as well. When Suréna is banished from the palace, his sister Palmis begs him not to leave; the ageing general refuses to listen, and

> Hardly had he gone out into the street
> When from an unknown hand an arrow sped . . . [34]

This late tragedy (1674) may well owe something to *Andromaque* and *Bérénice;* but similar situations can also be found much earlier. Thus, in 1662, Sertorius— not unlike Britannicus seven years later—is poisoned at a feast behind the scenes. *La mort de Pompée* (1642) provides an interesting variation, as the character who gives the play its name never even manages to show his face: Ptolomée's soldiers run him through before he can reach the safety of the stage. And although Polyeucte's early visit to the pagan temple *ultimately* brings his doom, Corneille's contemporaries were disappointed—aware as they were of the privilege of the stage—to see him returning at all. Having left, they felt, he should have died without delay, leaving his wife in the arms of Sévère.

To clarify the privilege of the stage, we may connect it to three types of formal development, each with its own thematic inflection and structural consequences. The first is intrinsic to Racinian space. The stage owes its conspicuousness to the explosion of pre-tragic energy—from which, as we have seen, the shelter of language is born. Chaotic winds still traverse the newly-formed enclosure, but the excess of pain has been channeled, allow-ing language to encounter passion right before our eyes. The privilege of the stage thus hinges on a previous accumulation of suffering; it does at least grant the heroes' despair a chance to find expression, even if the irrational forces which roam the pre-tragic wilderness are never completely defeated. And even though the entry into language offers them no more than a *symbolic* prospect of victory or survival, the privileged stage provides these haunted heroes with the only—imperfect—protection they may hope for: the gaze of the spectator.

Secondly, we may well be mining an ancient seam. Long before the time of Racine and Corneille, their Greek predecessors made the stage a protected area reserved for parley, meditation, lamentation and song, an area from which more violent events were usually excluded: perhaps, then, we should see this as a relic of tragedy's religious origins. Born from the cult of Dionysus, it may have preserved within the visible performance space an echo of the ceremonial sanctuary. The dance around the *thymelé,* the small round altar, had traced on the ground the magical, musical circle of the *orchestra,* protected by its proximity to the altar and exposed to the view of the *theatron*: the place from which one sees. A descendant of archaic religion, the recitation on stage did not represent the Dionysiac mysteries in all their secret horror, but extracted from the savage initiation process only that which could safely be pronounced in front of a crowd of uninitiates, confining itself to commemorating the adventures of the gods. Thus, in a strange turn of events, it is only by being protected themselves—from the dangerous vitality of the sacred mysteries—that the audience, in turn, may protect the tragic heroes with their gaze. The fact that these protective measures were later interpreted as rules of propriety should come as no surprise: it is the way of all taboos gradually to fade into decorum.

Thirdly, and perhaps unrelatedly, the privileged stage has thematic ties to the heterogeneity of fictional space, one of the latter's most striking features. In most fictional worlds there are neutral spaces where nothing ever happens, and then there are highly-charged areas by which characters are clandestinely attracted or repelled. Elizabethan and Jacobean drama is simply saturated with asymmetries of this type. In *King Lear,* for instance, people often turn up where they have no special reason to be. Why do Cornwall and Regan live in Gloucester's castle? Why should Gloucester decide to commit suicide at Dover, rather than somewhere else? The magnetism of the space is the only plausible explanation: the characters are drawn towards Gloucester's castle by the thrill of the oncoming conflict; an intuitive sense of the dénouement then attracts them to Dover. If this is so, then both the visible stage and its dark side may be governed by tacit rhythms of attraction and repulsion, more powerful in their overwhelming silence than all the passions and plaints of the protagonists. When a tragedy begins, the magnetic stage contracts, relentlessly drawing its heroes onto the platform of language; later, as inexorably as the turning tide or the outward flow of breath, it expands again, expelling them into darkness and into death.

IV. Coda

Once a thematic framework—that is, the curvature of the thematic universe, revealed by the inflexions of its space—has been posited, every local theme then finds its place within it. This goes for the two types of freedom thematized by Racine, following Arnauld and his Jansenist theology—freedom of choice *(libertas a coactione)* and freedom of refusal *(libertas a necessitate)*[35]—granted, respectively, to the possessors of power and to the objects of their unrequited love. Indeed, the conflict between these two types of freedom, so accurately rendered in *Britannicus, Bajazet, Mithridate* and *Phèdre,* replicates the tension between the privileged space of consciousness and the open, stormy stage. Perhaps Racinian love, whose complicity with power relations has been registered by Barthes, means little more than the actors' appropriation of the space in which they move. Moving onto the level of textual stylistics, this fundamental topographical uncertainty might also be responsible for what Jean Starobinski has called the *poetics of the gaze,* as well as the Racinian thematics of bright surfaces—appropriate as it is to this privileged stage, offered for our inspection.

Further, these topographical themes which emerge from the meeting of *attention* with *aboutness* do not exist independently of formal and aesthetic evolution. Whether in search of specific seams of *aboutness* or of its more general forms of organization, thematics simply cannot do without a historical horizon. The presence of history makes itself felt in the movement of structures themselves, whether they be formal or thematic.

One of the most enduring characteristics of Barthes' *Sur Racine* is its unremitting endeavor to demonstrate how, on an intentional level, structural regularities reveal the shape of human destiny. Over a period of time, structuralism and post-structuralism subsequently abandoned the attempt to link the structure of a work to its intentional properties in a thematic manner; these links cannot stay neglected forever. Form, as the younger Barthes knew so well, is saturated with thematic implications; and unless we link it to the thematic universes—fictional or actual—from which it derives its vitality, we can never hope to grasp its full extent.

Part III

OTHER ARTS

PAINTERS AND THEIR MOTIFS

Georges Roque

I. Theme and Assemblage

It would be hard, if not impossible, to give even a rough idea of the concept of theme in the visual arts as a whole. Each of the disciplines concerned has its own problems to face, requiring a specific method—or rather several specific methods—for their elucidation. The thematic study of cave paintings, which has expanded our knowledge of prehistoric religions considerably, has little in common with the thematic analysis of Greek vases: these raise different questions for archaeologists (questions which also vary according to the ideology of the given archaeologist).[1]

In addition to the problems besetting the various disciplines and periods involved, the classification of pictorial themes poses other, more general difficulties; and although a distinct degree of progress has recently been made—at least in the classical period, doubtless the easiest to classify in this way—these difficulties are far from being settled.[2]

So I shall not address pictorial themes and motifs so much as some of the ways in which they can be analyzed; I shall also confine myself to the contemporary period, which has brought to light a certain number of questions. Before proceeding to analyze a single motif in the work of a single artist, I shall limit myself, in the first part of this paper, to a series of remarks which will attempt to bridge the gap between pictorial problematics and theoretical approaches to literary themes.

I shall take Panofsky's iconological method as my point of departure, as it explicitly theorizes the theme-motif relationship. In his analysis of the image, Panofsky sets up three distinct levels of meaning:

(1) Primary or natural meaning

We perceive this level by recognizing pure forms (configurations of lines and colors) as the representation of natural *objects* (animals, people, plants) and by identifying their mutual relationships as events.

> The world of pure forms thus recognized as carriers of *primary* or *natural meanings* may be called the world of artistic *motifs*.[3]

The enumeration of these motifs constitutes a *pre-iconographic* description of works of art.

(2) Secondary or conventional meaning

We perceive this level of meaning by realizing, for example, that a male figure armed with a knife represents St. Bartholomew. Artistic *motifs* and combinations of artistic motifs *(compositions)* are thus placed in relation to *themes* or *concepts*. This level of description constitutes the domain of iconography.

(3) Intrinsic meaning, or content

We perceive content by discovering the underlying principles which express the fundamental mentality of a nation or period, refracted by the personality of a given artist and condensed into a given work of art. These elements must be interpreted as symbolic values in Cassirer's sense. This third level constitutes iconology proper.

This method calls for some remarks. First of all, a work's actual content—its "intrinsic meaning"—is not the theme, even if the latter can help us to reach it. While the theme must be "extracted," the content has to be *inserted* into the general cultural context of the work; as a result, the latter's meaning is considered to be immanent, and not—a view with many attendant difficulties—transcendent. Here, Panofsky is referring to the idea of a *synthetic intuition* which allows one to grasp the actual content of a work and which must be guided by an investigation into "the way in which, under different historical conditions, the *general and essential tendencies of the human mind* were expressed in specific *themes* and *concepts*."

Panofsky uses *theme* and *concept* interchangeably. From his point of view, the two notions are equivalent in their common opposition to the *motif*. For the strong contrast lies between *theme* and *motif*: this is a difference in nature, in level of analysis. Such a difference is indeed required for the two terms to form a *structure*, as is the case in what Panofsky, in his discussion of the Middle Ages, calls the "principle of disjunction":

it is significant that, just at the height of the mediaeval period (thirteenth and fourteenth centuries), classical *motifs* were not used for the representation of classical *themes* while, conversely, classical *themes* were not expressed by classical *motifs*.[4]

Thus the Orpheus figure served to represent David; the Hercules type, snatching Cerberus from Hades, was used for Christ wresting Adam from Limbo. Conversely, Medea and Jupiter were drawn in the respective guises of medieval princess and judge.

Still, this principle of disjunction, which Panofsky claims would also hold for literature,[5] limits the method with its presuppositions. For the medieval disjunction, defined as the "failure to realize the intrinsic 'oneness' of classical *themes* and classical *motifs*,"[6] is only meaningful in opposition to a *con*junction, the Renaissance appearing as a period of reunification, as "the reintegration of classical *themes* with classical *motifs*."[7] In fact, this thematic reading called iconology, a cross section through the history of European art and culture, can only take the form of a narrative, one whose (implicit or explicit) aim is to valorize a specific historical period—the Renaissance, in this instance. Irrespective of its particular premises, this iconological reading will be seen to favor diachronic and "macroscopic" analyses, i.e. ones dealing with very long periods of time. (Thus, Panofsky's analysis of the Pandora theme stretches all the way from Hesiod to Paul Klee and Max Beckmann.)[8]

This is to say that there is a great danger of slipping into a mere index, a catalog of names. Panofsky needed all the resources of his erudition and all the wiles of his intelligence to keep himself from this pitfall, by structuring most of his iconological studies like criminal investigations. In other words, if we don't want our iconological reading to become a catalog—which can never be exhaustive anyway—we must give it a narrative form. Panofsky's most brilliant cases are organized around an inversion of meaning (due, for example, to a misunderstanding of a philological order, in the transmission of a theme from one era to another). To put it another way, ruptures and discontinuities are overlooked, in as much as the thematic elements which are retained—removed from the flux of the history of art—tend to form a continuous chain, the diachronic length of the analysis. As a result, those periods and cultures for which literary sources are sparse are left aside.[9]

To return to our theme-motif nexus, we should bear in mind the extent to which the latter is subordinate to the former: the motif is almost always defined in negative terms, and its description belongs to the *pre-iconographic* level. It is iconographic interpretation which confers a title of nobility upon it, raising it, as it were, to the level of "conventional meaning"—a level which requires a knowledge of *literary sources*. In short, the image is subservient to the text. This is a function of iconology's logocentrism, which, having already received due attention,[10] requires no further emphasis; except to note that it is no accident if this chiefly literary colloquium devotes only one session to the visual arts, placing them after music. Its very organization appears to reproduce the time-honored relationship between art and literature: one of subservience, especially where thematics is concerned. We see this, for example, in the classical theory of art, which twists the meaning of the *ut pictura poesis* formula in order to "raise" painting to the level of dignity acquired by poetry, transforming the ancient parallel into a rigid principle; the net result being that the aesthetic qualities of a work of art are judged, from this point onward, purely in terms of its fidelity to a theme it must force itself to "describe," without digression.

Literature and the Visual Arts

I would, however, be a poor defender of the visual arts if I merely confirmed a subordination which contemporary developments have, to say the least, put in doubt! Things have changed a lot since Lessing's *Laocoon*, as far as the relationship between literature and the visual arts is concerned. Nowadays, as Robert Klein notes in his "Thoughts on Iconography,"[11] the motif is not automatically identified as the subject of a work. In this respect, the problem resembles that posed by the identification of motifs in the analysis of *literary* texts, and it merges with the set of questions relating to literary aboutness.

Contemporary artists have pondered this issue, a number of them challenging the general notion of theme by asserting a position of self-referentiality whose formulation is often tautological. Ad Reinhardt's comment bears repetition:

> The one thing to say about art is that it is one thing.
> Art is art-as-art and everything else is everything else.
> Art-as-art is nothing but art. Art is not what is not art.[12]

—a statement which conceptual art, and Kosuth in particular, will later attempt to formalize.

Still, this movement toward pictorial autonomy has deeper roots. One finds it clearly expressed by the Russian Futurists. In his introduction to Shklovsky's *Resurrection of the Word*, Andrei Nakov shows very cogently how Russian Formalist theories developed out of Futurist experiments—the poetic ones, of course, but also and primarily the visual ones. "In the art of our time," writes Olga Rozanova in a manifesto for the Union of Youth (1913), "painting plays the starring role."

It is a fact that painters, directly subjected to the tyranny of theme over motif, of idea over process—or, in short, of literature over art—were very quickly driven to shake off this yoke, foregrounding physical material in its autonomy from meaning:

> The subject, having detached itself from the *theme* (literary or otherwise), can no longer be transported at will from one material to another. The material becomes the main determining factor behind the new conception of the work. Hence the statement: "Word transcends meaning."[13]

And hence also Kruchenykh's proposition: "Form determines content." As regards the general framework of relationships between Futurist painters and Futurist poets and theoreticians, Nakov reminds us that

> most of the Futurist poets and theoreticians knew more about art than they learned from their visits to the painters' studios: very often, they had received a highly serious artistic training of their own. The Moscow School of Visual Arts was the seed-bed of this generation. David Bourliouk studied here with Mayakovsky, Kruchenykh received an art teacher's diploma . . . and Shklovsky states in his memoirs that he did some sculpture at the time.[14]

That is what allows us to reread certain works from a new perspective. In the very first paragraph of his important text on thematics, Tomashevsky writes:

> Every work written in a meaningful language has a theme. Only the transrational work has no theme, and for this reason it is but an experimental exercise, a laboratory experiment for certain schools of poetry.[15]

It is, perhaps, permissible to invert the axiom, by asking oneself whether what is somewhat disdainfully referred to as a "laboratory experiment" is not really the athematic "experimental exercise" which created the conditions for an *a contrario* approach to thematics in the first place. Not before it was foregrounded and questioned by poets and artists did we start to wonder how to analyze the theme.

What goes for the visual arts also goes for the cinema: Shklovsky, Brik and Tynianov worked as scriptwriters; Zholkovski, as Claude Bremond reminds us, was influenced by Eisenstein. Emboldened by these examples, I would now like to consider whether there are other indications of this change of course, one which caused the theorization of the theme in literature to rely upon an artistic movement or upon a methodology proper to the history of art.

There is indeed such a case, an utterly explicit one at that: Curtius, who dedicated his monumental *European Literature and the Latin Middle Ages* to Aby Warburg (as well as Gustav Gröber). Let us go a little further down this avenue which Carlo Ginzburg first explored.[16] Warburg's multidisciplinary researches certainly hold a great deal of interest; Curtius singles out one of their central concepts, *Pathosformeln* or "pathos formulae," for retention, taking it up in an article whose title quite unambiguously betrays his debt to Warburg: "Antike Pathosformeln in der Literatur des Mittelalters."[17]

Warburg's method of analyzing artworks consists in paying attention to dramatic forms which intensify physical and mental expressivity. What interests him in themes and motifs is, in fact, the dumb show, the set of typical expressive gestures, "die typische pathetische Gebärdensprache"; in other words, the permanence of a universally comprehensible sign language, betraying preoccupations of a theatrical nature in existence since antiquity and found in the Renaissance and Middle Ages. (These ideas were chiefly inspired by his reading of Darwin's 1872 essay "The Expression of the Emotion in Men and Animals."[18])

A cross-sectional investigation like this, aiming as it does to discover universally expressive gestures and postures, is independent of historical context; that is why it has been possible to relate Warburg's *Pathosformeln* to the *figurative topic* concept.[19] This is also the feature which Curtius uses to justify his parallel between the *Pathosformeln* and the *topoi* of medieval literature whose articulation they serve to reinforce.[20] This research by Warburg not only departs from what might otherwise become a mere inventory of themes and motifs: far from restricting itself to the semantic register, it recognizes polyvalency, i.e. the fact that a single pathos formula can quite easily see its meaning turned on its head from one context to the next; this is what Warburg calls *Bedeutungsinversionen.*

In his epilogue to *European Literature and the Latin Middle Ages* (as well as in the article mentioned above), Curtius explicitly acknowledges Warburg's contribution in terms of methodology:

> When we have isolated and named a literary phenomenon, we have established one fact. At that one point we have penetrated the concrete structure of the matter of literature. We have performed an analysis. If we get at a few dozen or a few hundred such facts, a system of points is established. These can be connected by lines; and this produces figures. If we study and associate these, we arrive at a comprehensive picture. That is what Aby Warburg meant by the sentence quoted earlier: "God is in detail."[21]

This definition is all the more interesting when one considers the metaphor it uses: a system of isolated points, forming a figure when connected. W. S. Heckscher, an excellent Warburg critic, readily relates this remark (which, incidentally, he considers the best description ever given of "the secret of Warburg's method") to the simultaneous appearance in 1912—when the latter's iconology produced its first results—of *papiers collés* and the Cubist collage.[22]

What makes this insight especially potent is that Cubism played an important role in Russia at the exact same time, in the brief, so-called "Cubofuturist" period. In other words, the collage and the *assemblage* may have provided the epistemological framework for a new approach to thematics. Clearly, the appearance of theoretical discourse on themes and motifs and their simultaneous shattering or scattering in the *assemblage* or *papier collé* presents a paradox. But this paradox fades when one considers that such works as Cubist *papiers collés,* Dadaist assemblages and photomontages, Malevitch's collages of 1914 and transrational poetry, by challenging the artificiality of a central and centralizing subject and of a dominant and dominating theme, emphasize the discontinuity of the work and hence more accurately reproduce the flow of thought.

In their works, which often eschew the security traditionally offered by titles that function as thematic indices ("I have seen pictures entitled Solitude containing many human figures," writes Apollinaire in his essay "The Cubist Painters," a chronicle of the demise of the "subject"[23]), the artists situate themselves in the same pragmatic conditions of deciphering, vis-à-vis the discontinuity of the ambient world, as the ones in which we find ourselves when we analyze them, or when we interpret any text.

So it is not surprising to find that the *assemblage* has been held up as a model for the way in which *thematization* operates. Shlomith Rimmon-Kenan's definition—"theme is a construct (a conceptual construct, to be precise), put together from discontinuous elements in the text"[24]—could, if adapted, be applied to many collages. Especially since the first of the three tightly linked operations which she sees as characterizing the thematization process is in fact assemblage (the two others being generalization and labelling). Whereas generalization is clearly alien to assemblage, whose disruptive effects it tends to deny, labelling calls to mind the titles of works, with which the artist may or may not play.

This is merely the suggestion of a line of inquiry concerning the possible influence of the visual arts on literature and literary theory. Along the same lines, the method used by Gide in the construction of his *Faux-monnayeurs* has been likened to Cubism;[25] and thinking of Gide, let us not forget that the first three examples of his infamous *mise en abyme* technique, readily held up as one of the paradigms of self-referentiality, are found in Memling, in Metsys, and in Velasquez's *Las Meniñas.*[26]

Themes in Crisis

It is time we considered whether the artistic theme possesses properties which literature and music do not share. At first sight, the answer would seem to be no. Quite clearly, a painting can force itself to "illustrate" a given

theme, whether religious, mythological or other, as is often the case in classical art; this does not prevent the artist from interpreting the theme, up to a
point. In this perspective, the art of reference, citation and parody which is
flourishing today proceeds in exactly the same way: artists choose a theme
(Actaeon and Diana, say, or the myth of Orion) and knowingly alter it.[27]

But the theme is not necessarily given in advance. Indeed, artists often
refuse to provide a theme; this ties in with their unwillingness to let a precon-
ceived idea dominate their work and reduce them to mere illustrators, as if
there were no effort involved in producing a painting, as if each material did
not exert its own resistance. The "subject" often emerges in the course of
execution, and sometimes involves a radical transformation of the project
(whether vague or specific) which the artist had in mind at the outset. As
Dubuffet puts it, in a formulation similar to that of the Russian Futurists:

> Art must be born from the material and the tool, and must retain the trace
> of the tool and of the tool's struggle with the material.[28]

If the theme as "subject" can appear so late, this is because numerous
artists refuse to "dominate" the theme, preferring to remain attentive to anything which may materialize under their hands as the brain interacts with the
material. To return to the concept of assemblage, canvases do not need to be
conceived as a series (whether variations on a given theme, e.g. painter and
model, or a combinatory work) in order to be perceived as one: an artist's
works—especially those designed such that each forms an independent whole—
often seem to reinforce one another anyway, simply by virtue of being put
together for an exhibition. (A phenomenon, it must be said, which is not
peculiar to the visual arts: thematically-organized journal issues usually sell
better than the rest, a fact which has led many scholarly journals to drop non-
thematic issues altogether). Perhaps one could go further and suggest a connection with thematic interpretation. If it is true that the process of
thematization is a construction produced by analysis, not a fact already present
for an interpreter to bring to light, doesn't the same often go for the production of a work? A theme is always the sum of its variants: no single work can
ever cover or exhaust it. Moreover, theme often emerges after the event,
thanks to the attention paid by an artist to what is allowed to appear in the
course of the work. Both producer and spectator, even if each sees something
different, would thus view the theme as a pattern, a schema, a post hoc
rationalization, functioning just like a *title:* that is, allowing one to orient
one's reading in the jungle which every image—and perhaps every text—
always is, or always would be.

The fact that an assemblage of works can generate thematic effects also
explains the abundance of theme-based exhibitions, in spite of their often

doubtful degree of interest. Just looking under "themes" in the index of an
exhibition catalogue gives a fair idea of their range. Here, for example, is a list
of thematic categories from the catalogue of a contemporary art library in
Paris, somewhat reminiscent of Borges' Chinese encyclopaedia:

> animal, body, box, color, cosmos, face (man's), horse, invisible (the), jazz,
> knots and ties, landscape, London as seen by painters, machine, music,
> paper, portrait, racism, science (general), sea, still life, tobacco, tondo, town,
> toy, tree, wall, water.

Such a list, though highly deficient, does at least have the advantage of
showing, as if this were necessary, to what extent anything or nearly anything
(why, even the invisible!) can inspire a thematic exhibition: objects, elements,
concepts, materials, "pictorial genres" . . . Taken on its own, each work may
not necessarily typify the artist's production; what takes shape and gains
coherence, through effects of repetition and variation, is the whole, the cross-
section, whether synchronic or diachronic, as long as the choice of theme or
motif, not unduly artificial, guarantees the minimum degree of consistency
necessary in order to function as such.

We come then to a definition of the theme based only on the formal
devices of recurrence and recursivity, a definition whose main interest lies in
its enhancing the presence of a "subject" or visible representation: the emphasis on and repetition of certain formal devices through a series of collected
works can also produce a "theme effect." At the first French retrospective of
Mark Rothko, Dora Vallier wrote an article with the emblematic title "Mark
Rothko, or the absence of theme as theme," stressing what her study owed to
the juxtaposition of a wide group of works:

> There, that dumb perplexity which the single painting had provoked simply
> dissolves under the pressure of numbers.[29]

This suggests a connection with music. To describe the musical theme,
musicologists first turned to figurative imagery, evoking its "face," its "figure"
or its "character," and later pictured thematic organizations with an underlying, hidden matrix—in short, one which was no longer "visible." The most
important thing, it seems to me, is not so much the fact that musicians and
painters both use the same word—"motif"—but that it comprises the same
double reality for each: a recognizable face and an iterative structure.

Such indeed is the double sense of the term, as far as the visual arts are
concerned: (1) the subject of a painting; (2) a single or repeated ornament
serving as a decorative theme. At this point, the whole problem is to keep this
double determination of the artistic *motif* in mind; otherwise, a large quantity

of figurative expressions are very likely to be misunderstood. And one should not distort this opposition between the motif as a subject which stands out from the background and the motif as a decorative element. Matisse, who worked extensively on these two levels at once, has this to say on the subject:

> For me, the subject of a picture and its background have the same value, or, to put it more clearly, there is no principal feature, only the pattern is important.[30]

Not the least interesting aspect of the term *motif,* still in the context of the visual arts, is the fact that it serves as a hinge or interface between figurative subject and abstract ornamentation, between figure and ground, between the static and paradigmatic nature of the motif as subject and the dynamic, syntagmatic, periodical, rhythmical nature of the decorative motif.

The Study of Motifs

The decline of the great traditional religious or mythological theme goes along with an interest in new motifs appearing on the artistic horizon. Some (like the bicycle[31]) are linked to technical innovation and sometimes form themes (like the machine[32]) by dint of their sheer scope. Others (like the goldfish bowl in Matisse) are tied in with the symbolic economy of the painting. In some ways, contemporary critical thought could be said to follow this trend, by taking more and more of an interest in motifs. But how is one supposed to study a motif, to weave a whole discourse around it?

It should be noted, first of all, that the theme-motif relationship parallels the opposition between the iconic and plastic aspects of painting, although without reproducing it down to the last detail. In a way, this opposition has been the implicit basis of my argument, in as much as the iconological study of a theme primarily involves content (the iconic aspect), whereas the study of motifs often lends itself more readily to a formal analysis of the plastic dimension.[33] Still, as I have mentioned, even the theme can be defined in terms of formal criteria (such as repetition or recursivity). Conversely, to extend the analysis of the motif beyond the strictly "formal" is not only possible but desirable.

When we are dealing with a representational motif like a landscape, we can obviously discuss how faithfully the canvas reproduces the motifs on the other side of the easel. Cézanne—who, incidentally, contributed greatly (along with the Impressionists) to the diffusion of the phrase "go for the motif"—is a case in point.[34] It seems to me that the interest of such a study,[35] though undeniable, is essentially documentary in character.

To stay with Cézanne, how are we to discuss his most common still-life motifs—like apples, for example? Why have so many apples been painted in the modern period? "Because the simplified motif gave the painter an opportunity for concentrating on the problems of form," replies Lionello Venturi.[36] A rather curt answer, it must be said, which makes the choice of motif a scantily-motivated gesture, positing a purely formal impulse and thus closing the subject.

This is precisely what Meyer Schapiro's article on "Cézanne's Apples" inveighs against. Here, in a reading prompted by psychoanalysis, the author reconstitutes the entire network of libidinal associations surrounding the apple, in order to explain the impulses driving Cézanne to choose that motif. This points up another temptation: that of attributing the choice of motif to the artist's unconscious. Schapiro does not stop here, however. After expanding his inquiry—for "in a type of theme may be found many qualities and connotations; to say which of these has attracted the painter is no easy task"—he ends up questioning the meaning of "theme" in general:

> Besides, in explaining the prevalence of a field like still-life—as of landscape or of subjects from religion, myth and history—we look for the common interests that give that field importance for artists of the most varied temperament and make it a characteristic choice during a period of history.[37]

In an unexpected slippage, then, the study of an apparently innocuous (albeit tenacious) motif begins by illuminating the artist's personality and ends up as an in-depth meditation on the still life as "subject." (Indeed, the article is subtitled "An Essay on the Meaning of Still-life.") In so doing, this analysis switches from the pre-iconographic to the iconological level, studying Panofsky's "direct transition from *motifs* to *content* . . . as is the case with European landscape painting, still-life and genre."[38] (In a later version of his text, Panofsky adds " . . . not to mention non-figurative art.") Doubtless these remarks would also apply, *mutatis mutandis,* to Hubert Damisch's study of the cloud motif, one which involves nothing less than the entire history of painting.[39]

Analysis has another course open to it, however, in the form of the *privileged motif*—the window, say, or the mirror—with its close, albeit metaphorical ties to painting. Most of the time, such interpretation highlights self-referential aspects. One would be hard put to open a study of the window motif without bringing up Alberti's famous description in which the rectangle traced upon the painting surface is viewed "as an open window" through which to observe the scene.[40] Similarly, any study of the mirror motif must mention da Vinci's formula: "The mirror is the master of the painter."[41] Self-reflexivity obviously culminates in the motif of the painting within the painting, whose frequency these days is attributed to the "radical subjectivization of art."[42]

This "subjectivization" also affects the personality of the painter, the disaffection with all forms of external justification for art producing a corresponding valorization of the artist as a human being. As a result, a certain number of themes and motifs which may have nothing to do with the material reality of painting still enable an artist to be identified with a manner, in a self-reflexive movement which analysis brings to light. As Jean Starobinski points out,

> the choice of the clown as an image is not just the selection of a pictorial or poetic *motif,* but an oblique and parodic way of raising the question of art;[43]

and the same could be said for a great many motifs. When I was studying contemporary artistic representations of hunting, it occurred to me that its social function no longer suffices to explain the presence of such images, and that these cynegetic scenes very often function as a symbolic or metaphorical representation of the artist's hunt for a motif. Shouldn't we, for example, take André Masson's *Chasse à l'élan,* a crisscrossing of lines with fragments of bodies, muzzles and paws emerging here and there, literally as a search for and chase after the spontaneity of the gesture, one that fuses the two meanings of the word "motif"?[44]

I see an obvious connection here with Jean-Yves Bosseur's comments on musical theater: in a way, the valorization of performers (and of their instruments) turns them into themes in their own right. This also ties in with Gerald Prince's remarks on "autothematism": the work of art being an end unto itself, he asks, what could be more normal than for it to foreground its own nature and to take itself as a privileged subject?

We should not, however, be misled by this convergence of different disciplines (painting, music and literature) and their associated theoretical approaches. For we risk losing sight of the motif itself, such is its danger of being smothered—along with all the questions it raises—by a circular, self-conscious and self-satisfied mode of criticism.[45]

II. The Bird in Magritte: To Catch a Motif

> What things do we write and paint, we mandarins with Chinese brushes, we immortalizers of things which *let* themselves be written, what alone are we capable of painting? . . . Alas, only birds strayed and grown weary in flight who now let themselves be caught in the

hand—in *our* hand! We immortalize that which cannot live and fly much longer, weary and mellow things alone!

—Friedrich Nietzsche[46]

The fingers of the hand gave birth to numbers; for the resources of desire are innumerable, and this is how the hand begins to grasp what it cannot yet reach: this bird's flight, those stars.

—Paul Nougé

After this lengthy preamble, an attempt to address various aspects of theme and motif in art, I come now to the study of one particular motif. When I mentioned the two meanings of the term "motif" in the visual arts, I provisionally left aside its primary and strongest meaning—that of *motive*—and I should now like to take this into account, restoring the full force of its etymology: the motif is *that which sets in motion*. In focusing on the motif as a fixed, immobile "subject," one loses sight of the *motive* in its double valency (the same, incidentally, as that of the "motif"); this motive force is what causes movement, what leads one to "*go for the motif*," as Cézanne would say. My aim, in short, will be to combine two meanings of the word *motif* (this time ignoring the decorative variety): (1) a motive; (2) the subject of a painting.

If there is such a thing as a motif specific to painting, perhaps this intersection of subject and motive is where it is to be found. No self-respecting painter can fail to question the motive behind the motif, the choice of such and such a "subject" for the painting. Whenever an artist investigates the choice of some or other visible motif, what is explored is the nature of painting, the very essence of art. In other words, it is one thing to show that artists take their own activity as a "theme"; it is quite another to uncover their investigation, via artistic motifs, into the motives for art.

To restore the motif's *motive* function is also to propose a dynamic form of reading, one which attempts to follow the evolution (or involution) of a motif through the chronological series of canvases in which it appears, catching the artist's attention as she wrestles with the work. (I use the "dynamic motif" concept in a broader sense than Tomashevsky: it affects—or transforms—not only a single work, as I see it, but the painter's entire artistic enterprise.)

The analysis I wish to perform here, using one of Magritte's motifs as my point of departure, is just this kind of reading. First, however, I have a word or two to say about the choice of this artist, dictated as it is by a variety of reasons.

For one thing, Magritte uses a considerable number of repeated motifs (apple, pipe, hat, stereotypical gentleman and so forth), all perfectly identifiable by virtue of their precise and polished contour but still offering a certain resistance to interpretation. This resistance is deliberate, planned and desired by the artist who has always refused to grant the status of "themes" to these enigmatic everyday objects, though they recur with a persistence bordering on the obsessive and though the temptation to decipher them is certainly great:

> Strictly speaking, there is no subject in my art. Every object deserves better than to be considered as a "subject" for painting: for the painter, who is only concerned with interpreting a subject in a more or less original way, the object has an indisputable reality. What appears in my art is not a collection of "themes" either. The world is not made up of "themes." My conception of the art of painting is all about the world and its mystery.[47]

Magritte, in other words, puts us on our guard against two things: a hermeneutics in which the "theme" becomes the key to a tautological interpretation of the motif, and the attribution of an extrinsic meaning to the latter. The motif is not "about" something; it *is,* period.[48] In this respect, a canvas like *La belle captive (The Beautiful Prisoner),* of which there are many versions, is indicative of his method as a whole. An easel is set up before a prosaic landscape; exactly that section of the landscape which it hides from view is represented on the canvas. Ironically, then, the painting takes its own emancipation from the motif as its subject, effacing it as it affirms itself, making all questions of referentiality academic. The choice of title serves the same strategic purpose of withholding thematic indices of any kind.

In his *Esquisse autobiographique,* Magritte has this to say for himself:

> It was in 1924 that René Magritte discovered his first painting. It represents a window seen from within. In front of the window is a hand, which seems to want to catch a flying bird.[49]

The information he provides is invaluable: *La fenêtre* may not be the first picture he ever painted, but it is the first he recognizes as such, just as he will view *Le jockey perdu (The Lost Jockey,* 1926) as his first Surrealist painting. A good reason, then, to take this picture as a starting point: it is the first in which the painter values the *motif* as it emerges from the years of trial and error. He emphasizes the contrast between this and the formal experiments which had absorbed him up to then, traces of which may still be seen in the work:

> Traces of past investigations still appear in this picture, in certain "plastically treated" parts, to use the already outdated jargon.

Though he elsewhere makes the point more strongly still, this clearly indicates Magritte's desire to free himself from the formal preoccupations peculiar to the small circle into which he had gravitated (Flouquet, Servranckx and company), in order to concentrate on a search for the motif or the subject. He says of this shift, which marked the beginning of his Surrealist phase, that he simply abandoned *how* to paint in favor of *what* to paint, something he thinks de Chirico was the first to worry about.[50]

According to Félix Labisse, the hand-trying-to-catch-the-bird motif was inspired by the mural Max Ernst created for Éluard's Eaubonne residence in 1922.[51] In fact, this motif is part of the Surrealist repertoire: Miró paints his own *Main attrapant un oiseau (Hand Catching a Bird)* in 1926, and Labisse himself takes up the same motif in *L'enchanteur (The Magician)* of 1938.

Whatever its derivation, the first suggestion of this motif may be found in *L'homme à la fenêtre (The Man at the Window*, 1920): there is indeed a man at a window, with a bird that appears to be inside and outside the room at the same time—which shows how far back this obsession goes, though the motif is not yet isolated and although questions of form clearly take precedence here. Unlike this canvas, however, the "first" picture has a figure (metonymically reduced to a hand) which is not inside the room—trying, for example, to catch a bird outside it—but, as Magritte clearly states in his description, "in front of the window"; it *"seems* to want to catch a flying bird" (my emphasis). Is this what makes him think he has "discovered his first painting?"

It is of course tempting to see in the subject of this (first) painting the subject of painting in general. What was Magritte looking for, if not an answer to the question "how to paint?" He was after a motif: that is, he was seeking to seize a fragment of reality—ever elusive, ever evasive—and to fix it on canvas. And this is precisely what he depicted: a hand which seems to want to catch a bird in flight! It is not by chance, then, that the bird and the hand occupy a liminal position in the representational space, between inside and outside, reality and desire. An intermediary, transitional position, or a space of de-realization, the space peculiar to the work of art?[52] On the borders of representation, the bird could stand for the elusive motif which the artist attempts to catch and which forces him to paint, the motif he seeks and whose quest he represents in this "first" picture.

The bird and the hand are found again in *La traversée difficile (The Difficult Crossing*, 1926), although in somewhat different form. The background, like theater scenery, shows a ship in a violent storm; on a table in the foreground, by a large peacock-feather pen, sits a severed hand grasping a bird. It is of course easy to put this "typically" Surrealist motif—so Surrealist that "the mere presence of a severed hand in a painting or a novel will immediately make people say 'how Surrealist!' "[53]—down to castration anxiety, the expression of an inability to seize the living, moving, flying motif which can, at best, be immobilized—killed—at the price of one's own hand. (In *La femme introuvable* [*The Elusive Woman*, 1927–8], four fumbling disembodied hands try in vain to touch a naked woman; they, too, are frozen, sealed forever in the cement of a stone wall which they animate . . . just like a motif does, perhaps?)

The key to the image of the bird in the disembodied hand—if there *is* a key, that is—must be the small ink drawing of the very same motif which also bears the legend "maintenant" (now).[54] A whole complex of feelings is condensed within this play on words and images. *Main-tenir*, "to maintain," "to hold in the hand": to seize the bird, to hold the motif, to maintain desire and reality, here and now—*maintenant*. It is also to check the flow of time: now is the present which I wish to seize, the motif I seek to fix in a work of art— such is my motive. The work will remain, an enduring testimony to my desire to paint, to have seized the motif, here and now, now and forever.[55]

One year after *La traversée difficile*, Magritte paints a picture which delivers a powerful emotive charge and whose title is quite explicit: *Jeune fille mangeant un oiseau* (*Young Girl Eating a Bird*, 1927). This is the moment of transition from thought into action, the moment of intense emotional discharge; it cries out for symbolic interpretation, or indeed for several such readings. It is amusing to note that Magritte, a radical opponent of this method, rejecting (or should one say *disclaiming?*) every symbol, gives only one example, and that this example should be the bird:

> Questions like "what does this painting mean, what does it represent?" are only possible for people who are unable to *see a painting* in its truth, who mechanically refuse to believe that a very precise image shows precisely what it is. This means that the implicit (if there is such a thing?) is worth more than the explicit; there is nothing implicit in my art, in spite of the confusion which lends my art a symbolic meaning.

> How can people enjoy interpreting symbols? These are "substitutes" which only suit a mentality incapable of knowing the things themselves. An obsessive interpreter can never see a bird: he will only see a symbol.[56]

At this stage, however, Magritte is clearly unable to control his emotions sufficiently to paint pictures whose symbols are (or at least tend to be) emptied out, as he will in later years. This is precisely why it is so interesting to follow the evolution of the bird motif across its variations, its slow progress toward an a-symbolic state.

Young Girl Eating a Bird seems to have acquired an additional title: *Le plaisir (Pleasure)*. What is so bluntly depicted is not cruelty, then, so much as the omnipotence of desire affirming itself and giving itself free rein: the bird stands for the object of the painter's *devouring passion*. "A bird in the hand is worth two in the bush," says the proverb; but this wisdom is not shared by the painter, moved as he is by his desire to seize reality, to *get his motif down*.

In discussing his earlier experiments, Magritte makes the following suggestive remark:

> I was in the same state of innocence as the child in its crib which thinks it can catch the bird in the sky.[57]

I don't know whether this "state of innocence" has been lost here, but the artist is certainly taking a position, stating that his desire is to *seize the motif*, now; it being understood that "to seize the motif" also and especially means "to understand the reason." This, I feel, shows quite clearly to what extent the motif is the desire which drives this painter to paint, which sets him in motion and which moves him physically and emotionally, as well as the subject or object of his work. Cause and consequence at one and the same time.

If his intention was to provoke us with a startling image, he has succeeded completely, by showing us the striking picture of his own desire and pleasure: *seizing the motif*.[58] His friend Paul Nougé made no mistake about this painting, which he considered to be important:

> I can't help thinking (he writes Magritte, in April '28) that important discoveries are not to be made in that direction, but rather along the route suggested by a canvas I can never forget: the *Jeune fille mangeant un oiseau*. You'll see what I mean right away.
>
> On the whole, I feel we have everything to lose by conforming to a certain arbitrariness; it is indeed seductive, but its impact weakens continually.[59]

The pleasure and jubilation upon catching one's motif, here and now, lasts forever; this is reminiscent of the later Cézanne:

> [JOACHIM GASQUET]: So you're having a good morning?
>
> CÉZANNE: I'm at grips with my motif . . . *(He clasped his hands together.)* This is a motif, you see . . .
>
> [GASQUET]: How do you mean?
>
> CÉZANNE: All right, look at this . . . (He repeated his gesture, holding his hands apart, fingers spread wide, bringing them slowly, very slowly together

again, then squeezing and contracting them until they were interlocked.)
That's what one needs to achieve . . . [60]

In his lecture "La ligne de vie," Magritte describes the shock of discovery
which gave rise to *Les affinités électives (Elective Affinities*, 1932/33*):*

> One night in 1936 [in fact, '32 or '33], I awoke in a room where they had
> put a cage with its sleeping occupant. Thanks to a magnificent mistake, I
> saw the bird gone from the cage and replaced by an egg. In this I had a new
> and astonishing poetic secret, for the shock I felt was caused by the *affinity*
> of the two objects, the cage and the egg, whereas before this shock had been
> generated by the encounter of disparate objects. [61]

This new "poetic secret" is of course no secret for us, but a rhetorical
procedure known as *metalepsis,* i.e. the transposition of the antecedent and the
subsequent; a procedure, moreover, of which the Surrealists were fond. Thus
Éluard reworks the popular theme of the topsy-turvy world:

> The bird turned the egg upside-down; the egg turned the nest upside-down;
> the nest turned the carpet upside-down; the carpet turned the table upside-
> down . . . [62]

The rhetorical procedure may be no secret, but it still produces a poetic
image, in a strictly Jakobsonian sense. An egg is substituted for the bird by
virtue of their paradigmatic relationship on the axis of selection (where they
stand in a relation of cause and effect), an equivalence projected onto the axis
of combination.

What is important is that this rhetorical inversion allows Magritte to
free the motif from its enslavement to emotion, to detach it from the
symbolic investment which was explicit in *Jeune fille mangeant un oiseau*
and to set up a pure poetic technique which he will employ from now on.
If motif is cause and also consequence, motive *and* immobilization, a
painting's *raison d'être* as well as its subject, it is not by chance that the
metalepsis through which the painter controls this motif inverts the order
of events: the egg is substituted for the bird, and it is impossible to
determine whether this is what the bird has been or this is what the bird
has laid. It is amid such confusion over the difference between past and
future that the painter is able to paint, now. Commenting upon *Les affinités
électives,* Nougé writes:

> the promise of a bird and the engendered bird which engenders the cage the
> color of our desire. [63]

Having achieved this distance from the motif, Magritte is now able to represent it; he can also represent *himself* in it, in one of the few self-portraits we possess—certainly the only one to show him painting. Seated, the painter is at work. Turning his head, he eyes his motif—an egg on a table—while his right hand guides the brush, adding a few touches to the picture on the easel in front of him: a picture of . . . a bird. Such is *La clairvoyance* of 1936. Now all becomes clear: the painter has grasped the motive for his art, which is none other than to transform the motif—a transformation which sets it up as a "subject," and turns him into a "Surrealist."

Clairvoyance indeed: for the motif (here a bird, but others could have been chosen), when freed from its affective, emotional, erotic resonances—sublimated, if you prefer—can henceforth evolve, while also evolving Magritte's art. When the painter has finally become an artist after his struggle with the motif, the latter transforms *itself,* giving rise to numerous poetic and meta-morphic canvases, the fruits of the painter's poetic technique.

Le domaine d'Arnheim (*The Domain of Arnheim,* 1938): in the foreground, on a parapet, two eggs facing an enormous mountain, one of whose ridges looks like an eagle's beak. *L'île aux Trésors (Treasure Island):* a series of bird-feathers, chlorophyll green, with tail-stems. *Le principe d'incertitude* (*The Un-certainty Principle,* 1944): a naked woman stares toward her shadow on the wall opposite her; it is a bird with open wings. *La grande Famille* (*The Big Family,* 1963): a large bird above the sea whose body is made of clouds. *L'idole* (*The Idol,* 1965): a large stone bird, frozen in the sky above the sea . . .

THEME IN CLASSICAL MUSIC

Françoise Escal

The concept of *theme* in music has had a checkered past. Analytically overrated for a while, it suddenly suffered a setback: many considered it suspect, and some contested it strongly. For formalist purposes, its existence has been denied; it has been crossed off the list of components, in favor of the *phrase,* the *proposition,* the *motif* and the *cell.* From the time of Webern, we are told, theme vanishes from the experience of composition. I would seek to preserve this concept, to test its validity for classical music—that is, for tonal music written in Europe between the seventeenth and nineteenth centuries— if only because it is used by disciplines other than music, most notably in the metalanguage of literary criticism. I shall begin, in fact, by comparing and contrasting these two types of theme.

At first sight, it would seem that the literary and the musical theme have nothing in common. The theme in literature refers to a content (e.g. love or death), whereas music is a language without a plane of the signified (Hjelmslev: "meaning is ordered, articulated and formed in different ways by different languages"). Certainly, music is not devoid of meaning: otherwise, how could it be that intersubjective medium that we know? Music produces *discourses,* if not *signs,* and its mode of meaning, as for any language, is the *semantic* mode.[1] In this respect, Stravinsky's statement—"I consider music constitutionally incapable of expressing anything at all: a feeling, an attitude, a psychological state, a natural phenomenon . . . "—is but a paradox, a cavalier claim, or a provocation. And yet, the concept of a literary theme as a unit of content can hardly be applied to music. Literary thematics can easily constitute itself as a discipline; the same objective in music raises many more difficulties:

> the signifying function of music proves irreducible to any part of it that might be expressed or translated in verbal form. It operates below language,

and no discourse whatever, not even that of the most inspired commentator, could ever be profound enough to make it applicable.[2]

The theme in literature, at least in classical literature, is a unit of meaning. True, some forms of literature, notably modern ones, eschew psychology; they deliberately borrow their situations from popular genres (the detective novel for *Les gommes* and *Le voyeur;* soap opera adultery for *La jalousie;* the adventure novel for *Le labyrinthe;* comic-strip sex and violence for *La maison de rendez-vous*). For the function of the modern writer lies elsewhere: it is primarily in construction, in organization. For Alain Robbe-Grillet, author of these novels, form is mainly repetition. His novels are arranged thematically, constructed like a set of variations on a finite number of elements; as for these elements, these themes, they tend to be drained of content. Besides, for him, "the real writer has nothing to say":

> the novel's content . . . can actually only consist in the banality of what has always-been-said-before: a string of stereotypes lacking any originality by definition.

These "ready-made ideas" are "of no interest in themselves"; that is why they represent, for him, "the only possible material for the construction of a work of art—novel, poem, essay—empty architecture whose form is its only coherence": the writer's freedom "resides only in the infinite complexity of possible combinations."[3] Robbe-Grillet's poetics is based upon the interplay of a set of elements; theme is just a component of form. This being the case, such a poetics would be a tinkering with limits, a transgression, if one were to accept Claude Lévi-Strauss's hypothesis that music and the novel once shared the inheritance of myth:

> Music, in becoming modern with Frescobaldi and then Bach, took over its form, whereas the novel, which came into being about the same time, appropriated the deformalized residue of myth and, being henceforth released from the constraints of symmetry, found the means to develop as a free narrative. We thus arrive at a better understanding of the complementary nature of music and the novel, from the seventeenth or eighteenth centuries to the present day: the former consists of formal constructions which are always looking for meaning, and the latter of a meaning tending towards plurality, but disintegrating inwardly as it proliferates externally, because of the increasingly obvious lack of an internal framework; the New Novel tries to remedy the situation by external buttressing, but there is nothing left for the buttressing to support.[4]

However this may be, the theme in music is a signifying unit, and this is mainly why it can be heard, identified and delimited on the surface of the musical statement, whereas the literary theme presupposes an act of interpretation on the part of the reader or analyst. In music, its formal nature makes it easy to locate; in literature, theme is a conceptual construction, the product of a process of integration. In reading *L'éducation sentimentale*, for example, I derive the theme of failure and wasted opportunity from Frédéric's relationships, personal and political, with Mme. Arnoux and the other women and with humanity in general. Ultimately, when the process of integration to which I have subjected the various episodes or scenes is complete, the theme emerges as a "high-order label" (to use Shlomith Rimmon-Kenan's term), an "integrative principle," a common denominator for all or almost all of the aspects of the novel. In no case can it be directly observed: strictly speaking, it is invisible.

Literary themes are implicit: no one line can be singled out from a literary work which could be called its theme. The literary theme is not an utterance, even if it may sometimes act as the object of an explicit formulation. It is not "within," a "segment *within* the text-continuum," but a "construct put together from discontinuous elements in the text."[5] It is supralinear. And it is also transtextual. Even if it is immanent to the text, it transcends its margins: two or more texts can come across as individual instances of a single theme which transcends them. Even if the literary theme is only manifested through the work, it is not a signified whose content is exhausted by what the text has to say about it. It is both inside and outside the text. It moves, migrates and meanders through several works: it is general.

By contrast, the musical theme (as in Brahms' variations on a Haydn or Paganini theme) is specific. With few exceptions, the theme is unique to a work or to a single series of works, like the thirty-three variations by Beethoven and the fifty by other Viennese, Czech and German composers on Diabelli's only waltz. The theme, in any case, is immanent. It is a unit objectively present in the work. Its position as the *incipit* of both the variations form and the sonata form (mono- or di-thematic) endows it with a kind of superiority, a pre-eminence, the privilege of the first element to be heard. It is what is given at the outset, what is explicitly set in place at the start of the work; it vindicates its etymology: it is *that which is placed* at the start of the statement. Whatever treatment it will subsequently receive at the hands of the composer, the theme is mentioned in the title, explicitly set in place at the start of and separate from the work. The aria of Bach's Goldberg variations (BWV 988) is given and named as such at the top; the Paisiello theme which Mozart uses (K398) is likewise given at the outset, but also preceded and surmounted by the verbal notation in German, *"Thema."* The same goes for Beethoven's Diabelli variations, op. 120, except that this time the verbal notation is in Italian: *"Tema."*

In all three cases, the theme is hard to miss. All it takes to find it is a surface operation—unlike the literary theme, which must be extracted (if implicit) or suspected (if overly explicit) of being a smokescreen. The literary theme, when given as *incipit* in the fictional work, can lead to error. "Sing, goddess, the wrath of Achilles, son of Peleus": every reader of the *Iliad* is led to doubt this initial affirmation, to contest it, to discover in the course of reading that the real theme lies elsewhere, that the initially-stated theme was a red herring; at the very least, to expand on Homer's statement.[6]

In this sense, by its frequent positioning at the top, the musical theme is closer to the linguistic (phrastic) than to the literary (discursive) theme, even if, like the literary theme, it is discursive. For linguists, the theme (or "topic") designates the object in relation to which the sentence is uttered, and the rheme (or "comment") designates the information provided in connection with that object. The "Salve tu, Domine" theme is the air Mozart borrows from Paisiello, and that is what Mozart is talking about in his Variations, this is what they analyze: Mozart's Variations are a sort of commentary, a paraphrase, a gloss, an amplification, a rewriting of Paisiello's theme, or a series of perspectives upon it.

Let us now turn to the sonata form, which provides the initial movements of all instrumental genres from 1750 onwards, not only of sonatas themselves but also of symphonies, concertos and string quartets. Its first part is aptly named the *exposition,* with the first theme or group of themes in the tonic and the second theme or group of themes in the dominant. The exposition of the thematic material is followed by the *development,* with fragmentation, augmentation, diminution, inversion, combination and superposition of themes in various keys, the melodic structure being backed up by a tonal structure: beginning with the tonic and moving into the dominant, then moving into other keys and returning to the tonic.[7] Then comes the *re-exposition,* an assertive movement, re-presenting the themes of the *exposition* in an identical or similar form and bringing all re-exposed themes back to the principal tone. All things being equal, the *exposition* and *development* bear some relationship to the linguists' theme and rheme, or to the logicians' subject and predicate.

In classical music, then, what essentially guarantees the identification or pinpointing of the theme is its localization within the utterance, frequently emphasized by a verbal designation on the score: *Thema, Tema . . .* Often, the themes (or their first bars) are even given as an *incipit* in the summary at the front of the volume or collection. They serve as landmarks for the identification of works, if not of authors (a striking theme, like the melodies in Bach's chorals, can remain anonymous), in ages when generic titles (*Sonata, Symphony,* etc.) are the rule, when sonatas and symphonies are written by the tens and hundreds, and when the work of a single composer may include several sonatas all entitled *Sonata,* all written in the same key and for the same instrument, sometimes catalogued and published in the same collection. At a certain point in the history of music, the theme, synonymous with the *incipit,* becomes the very thing which attaches a work to its author. In the seventeenth and eighteenth centuries, it is rivalled by the term *invention* (classical literary rhetoric opposed *inventio* to *dispositio* and *elocutio*). If it is borrowed, it is explicitly attributed to its author in the title: *Variations on a theme by X.* If not, the borrower becomes a plagiarist, the concept of plagiarism being concurrent with that of the author as owner of a text and (if applicable) of its themes.

This concept of authorship is gradually set in place at the end of the eighteenth century. In France, it is only under the Revolution that the "privilège" (imprimatur) is transferred from the printer to the author.[8] In Vienna, when *The Magic Flute* is first performed (1791), Clementi accuses Mozart of plagiarism, of impudently stealing a theme from the first movement of one of his own sonatas. The fugue of the allegro in the Overture to *The Magic Flute* includes a main theme which Mozart supposedly heard Clementi play in a musical tournament at the Hofburg several years earlier, in December 1781 or January 1782, a tournament which pitted one against the other in the presence of the emperor. Mozart, in a letter dated 17 January 1782, mentions this encounter and writes that Clementi "played a prelude and sonata" first. In the first edition of the sonata, Clementi confirms this: "This sonata, with the toccata that follows, was played by the author before His Majesty Joseph II in 1781, Mozart being present"; in later editions he claims his theme with bitterness: "*Tulit alter honores*"...

The establishment of the concept of authorship is corroborated by the appearance of *thematic catalogues,* providing lists of works identified by their opening bars or *incipit,* at the end of the eighteenth century. From Beethoven onwards, composers give their own main works an opus number, either at time of composition or at time of publication. In the nineteenth century, a whole corpus of works is assembled from lists of pieces, giving the first bars of each. Mozart made a catalogue of his works as of 1784; Haydn drew up his own (or had them drawn up) in two incomplete volumes, one starting in 1765 and one in 1805.

Then musicologists took over from publishers, collectors (for private or public libraries) and composers, and the theme cited is henceforth accompanied by a wealth of supplementary information: full title, dedication, date and place of composition, instrumental formation, collection in which the autograph manuscript is preserved, original edition, re-printings, date and place of first performance with a note of who played it, bibliography relevant to the work, etc. This paratextual verbal inflation is linked to the establishment of the author as a living, breathing, biographic entity, exerting a "formidable paternity"[9] upon his work. From Beethoven onwards, all aspects of the creative process start to be taken into account, valorized and even fetishized: the composer's manuscripts, house, chair, bathrobe, habits, interviews . . .

So the theme in classical music, anonymous or otherwise, is original and unique. By contrast, the literary theme (such as love or death) is an entity which transcends the text, which runs right through texts and which, in direct opposition to the musical theme, is the most collective thing in the world. It is not just transtextual but transcultural. As for the linguistic theme, although—like the musical theme—it is an easily discernible, isolable segment of the statement, it is still neither original nor unique in its form, as a signifier. For it belongs to the *langue,* that social part of language which lies outside of the individual, that "treasure stored by the practice of the word [*parole*] in its subjects who belong to a single community" (Saussure). It is the *I* in "I'm coming," or the *tomorrow* in "I'm busy tomorrow."

The musical theme may be easy to spot; it is not nearly so easy to classify. If it is simple enough to know *where* it is, it is much harder to know *what* it is, to circumscribe its protean nature. In the first place—despite what I may have implied above—it is not always a signifier without a signified. It happens from time to time that instrumental music seeks to rival literature, to mean, describe or tell; in short, to give itself a content, as far as this is possible. This can be seen, for example, in the addition of a thematic element to the generic title of the work (Beethoven's *Pastoral Symphony*), showing that the work belongs to a class (Symphony) and also indicating a subject (Pastoral). Sometimes, as in Liszt's *Hunnenschlacht (Battle of the Huns),* the thematic title even replaces the generic one. In such cases, the work no longer respects the canons of form: one moves from a *deductive* type of music, in which materials are fitted into the framework of a prefabricated formal schema, to an *inductive* type whose formal structure adapts to the development of an idea.

The thematic title is sometimes reinforced by a verbal program given at the head of the score and/or distributed to the audience before the concert. Upon closer inspection, it becomes evident that the title often designates the *subject* rather than the theme, the story we are about to be 'told,' the travelog we are going to hear—Liszt's *Années de pèlerinage (Pilgrim Years): première année, Suisse; deuxième année, Italie.* Even within these new *Mémoires d'un touriste,*[10] the individual pieces have meaningful titles (like "La Chapelle de William Tell") and may be preceded by an epigraph (like Schiller's verse "Einer für Alle, Alle für Einen"), whose function it is to reveal the literary theme.

This temptation to *speak* did not wait for the nineteenth century to make itself known. Take for example what dictionaries and encyclopaedias of music call "genre pieces" or "characteristic pieces." For a long time, music has attempted to appropriate the referential, denotative function of language. Thus, in his *Wassermusik* in C major entitled *Hamburger Ebb' und Flut* (1723), Telemann addresses the theme of water for the centenary celebration of the Hamburg Admiralty. He exploits the characteristics with which *suite* dances are traditionally allotted (the suite, an alternation of calm and lively movements, is already a metaphor for ebb and flow) in order to "translate" the movements of the sea into music. These conventional characteristics are also made explicit in the titles of the various pieces—albeit accompanied by a mass of mythology, as required by classical rhetoric. After the Overture, there follows:

1. Sarabande: The Sleep of Thetis;
2. Bourrée: Thetis Awakes;
3. Loure: Neptune in Love;
4. Gavotte: The Naiads' Games;
5. Harlequinade: The Tritons' Jokes;
6. The Unleashing of Aeolus in a Storm;
7. Minuet: The Pleasant Zephyr;
8. Gigue: Ebb and Flow;
9. Canarie: The Happy Sailors . . .

Lévi-Strauss draws an opposition between "musicians concerned with a code" and "musicians concerned with a message." The first (Bach, Stravinsky and Webern) "use their messages to expound and to comment on the rules of a particular musical discourse; the second group" (Beethoven, Ravel and Schoenberg) "tell a tale."[11] But Telemann and many others had already told tales. Western music has always suffered from the temptation to rival natural language, by establishing a form of communication of the same order, based upon an exchange of signs. All descriptive and program music claims to make sense, to produce meanings by the exact and faithful depiction of referents (objects and sounds from the real world) or by the accurate expression of signifieds (moods or feelings). The entire classical and post-classical theory of imitation—of which Rousseau, among others, made himself the spokesman—is at stake here:

> Now that instruments form the most important part of music, the sonatas are extremely a-la-mode, as well as every kind of symphony; the vocal is only accessory, and the air accompanies the accompaniment . . . I dare to foretell that so unnatural a taste cannot continue. Music, purely harmonic, is trifling; to please constantly, and prevent languor, it ought to be raised to the rank of the imitative arts . . . To know what all this fracas of sonatas would mean, with which we are loaded, we must do as the ignorant painter who was obliged to write under his figures, "This is a tree." "This is a man." "And

this is a horse." I shall never forget the quip made by the celebrated Fontenelle: exasperated by these interminable symphonies, he cried aloud in a fit of impatience, "Sonata, what do you want from me?"[12]

This is the legacy of the Theory of Passions *(die Affektenlehre)*, a method which gives the characteristics of the various dances and enumerates twenty-odd feelings, along with their musical translation (Mattheson, *Der vollkommene Capellmeister*, 1739). The *affetti* are *topoi:* their content refers to something which has already been read, heard or felt; passion here only ever consists in what is said about it—a form of intertextuality. In dramatic music, opera or oratorio, the "air" functions through an *affetto* which is identified and remembered by its *incipit:* "Croce e delizia" *(La Traviata),* "Mi chiamano Mimi" *(La Bohème).* The air has a theme, in the literary sense of the term, and one may distinguish an angry air, a tender air, a brave air, and so on.

Still, the semanticization of instrumental music only becomes prevalent in the nineteenth century. It entails the transformation, if not the abandonment, of received forms, and the consequent invention of new ones, such as the symphonic poem. The symphonic poem has a subject—usually indicated by the title—and themes which function as units of content, just like literary themes. The constant, more or less discreet presence of verbal language is also evident in the form of paratext: prefaces, notes and epigraphs, titles, subtitles and intertitles, verbal notes above the musical notes of the score, like scrolls unrolling the length of the stave—truly a simultaneous "translation." How is one to interpret such a proliferation? Nineteenth-century literature certainly captures the imagination of music (cf. Liszt); but it is also perhaps a matter of music resisting the grip of meaning, at least to some extent.

Nineteenth-century music's desire to gain novelistic status may be seen in Alkan's *Grande Sonate* op. 33. It is based on the theme of the Four Ages, those periods into which world history was divided by the Greeks: Golden Age, Silver Age, Bronze Age and Iron Age. Alkan superimposes this theme onto the four ages of Man, and entitles the movements of his sonata "20," "30: Quasi-Faust," "40: A Happy Home" and "50: Prometheus Bound." In the introductory note he specifies that these movements are, respectively, a *scherzo*, an *allegro*, an *andante* and a *largo;* on the score, each is preceded by an indication of the tempo in French: "Très vite," "Assez vite," "Lentement," "Extrêmement lent." Of these four pieces he says: "Each corresponds in my mind to a given moment of existence, to a particular disposition of thought and imagination." He cites the following lines from Sophocles as an epigraph to the last movement, to serve as a program or theme for the section:

No, you could not stand my suffering!
If only fate would let me die at least!

The second piece, "30: Quasi-Faust," is a sort of musical drama. There are three main themes, whose function is to represent and characterize the three protagonists: Faust, presented from the outset as "satanic"; the "Devil," who drags him down toward Evil (an inversion of the first theme); Marguerite, or Love, a very pure melodic line to be stated "with candor." The entrance of each theme is accompanied by a verbal notation which makes its content explicit. Once the exposition—this time in the theatrical sense of the word—is complete, the action begins: the Faust and Marguerite themes fuse "passionately," musically intertwined. This *development* starts with the Faust theme and is complicated by the other two, the hero's simultaneous and contradictory tendencies[13], one toward the Devil, the other toward Love.

Four long chords in an arpeggio introduce a new theme—Faith—which is arranged, rather like Liszt's *Harmonies poétiques et religieuses,* in a fugue; it allows us at one point to hear the voice of the Lord, referred to by name, and then leads us back to the theme of love, rediscovered "with joy" and then "with delight." The theme of the Devil vainly and fleetingly attempts to assert itself one last time: the Devil is beaten in this edifying tale, and it is "with confidence" that the mingled themes of Faith and Love close the score, in a long peal of bells. Some years later, Liszt will write a *Faust Symphony in Three Psychological Portraits (Eine Faust-Symphonie in drei Charakterbildern);* this is already Alkan's aim in 1847: his themes, musically individualized and characterized, come across as literary characters.

The desire to fill music with meaning, to make it a language of communication, should doubtless be related to the new role nineteenth-century musicians were seeking to play in society. In the spirit of Beethoven's *Ode to Joy* and of his *Heiligenstadt Testament,* in which he claims to be filled with "the love of humanity and the desire to do good," they see themselves as pioneers, apostles and preachers ("Schöpfermenschen, . . . Evangelischen und Priester"); they feel charged with a civilizing mission and are only waiting to be endowed with religious and social functions ("religiöse und sociale Funktionen") just like poets and writers.[14]

Even today, the search for the theme as a unit of content haunts musicologists, if not composers themselves: the producers of the radio station France-Musique base whole series of programs on a theme which serves as a leitmotiv, collecting works whose thematic titles suggest a single signified. Under the rubric "Wars and Warriors," we are offered a variety of works such as Janequin's *Bataille de Marignan,* Beethoven's *Battle Symphony (Wellingtons Sieg oder die Schlacht bei Vittoria)* and Liszt's *Hunnenschlacht;* under the heading "Heroic and Pathetic," Beethoven's *Eroica,* Tchaikovsky's Symphony no. 6 *(Pathétique),* Strauss's *Ein Heldenleben* and Liszt's *Héroïde funèbre.* Or they decide that a certain set of works expresses, say, melancholy, even though these works also (or only) carry generic titles: Sibelius' Symphony no. 4, first movement; Bach's *Italian Concerto;* Mozart's Sonata for violin and piano in E minor, K 304; Schubert's String Quintet; Bach's *Art of the Fugue (die Kunst der Fuge)*, unfinished fugue.

The musical theme, as a unit of content, may be compared to the *leitmotiv*. Not the motif, that element of musical syntax, that component of form, but only the *leitmotiv* as defined by Wolzogen, one of Wagner's first commentators. It involves attaching a musical theme to each character, theme (love or death) and important object (Siegfried's sword), such that the *leitmotiv* appears at the same time as the object it designates. It may be modified, according to the demands of the drama. The *leitmotiv* provides information, whether about plot (it pertains to narrative analepses, anticipatory or retrospective) or about character (it may serve as a clue). At one point Ysolde is speaking to her husband, but thinking only of Tristan. Either *she* sings the theme of the one she loves, or else the orchestra sees to it, the music thus providing information as to her state of mind. If the hero is in love, the theme inflects, taking on a certain "tenderness"; if he is sad, it moves from major to minor.

For Wagner, the *leitmotiv* is only there to throw light upon the twists and turns of the drama, to clarify its meaning; it should not be considered an *a priori* element of the composition. Wagner chooses and uses his *leitmotive* "rather from the point of view of their dramatic import and effect than from that of their utility for the structure of the musical composition." Sometimes distributional, sometimes integrative units, Debussy calls them "signposts for people who can't find their way around a score." He goes on:

> In [Wagner], each person has his own "prospectus," so to speak, his "leitmotiv" which always precedes him. I must admit I find this method a little crude.[15]

Finally, the relationship between the *leitmotiv* and that which it signifies (Tristan sad, Tristan in love) is more or less analogical: its form more or less resembles its semantic content (an inflection of the theme toward greater "tenderness," a movement from major to minor) and is determined by the signified.

There is another type of musical theme with a signified as well as a signifier: this is what is sometimes misnamed a "musical anagram." It is the transposition into musical language of the letters of a word. Anglo-Saxon and Germanic countries have continued to use letters of the alphabet to refer to notes, whereas Romance areas use the initial syllables of John the Baptist's Latin hymn: the French, for example, say "do ré mi fa sol la si" rather than "A B C D E F G." In the former countries, then, a musical theme may be drawn from the sequence of letters in a name or a sentence.

The third subject of the unfinished triple fugue in *The Art of the Fugue* is the musical transcription of Bach's own name, in the German musical notation (in which B♭ is B and B is H). Some have claimed to see this as Bach's signature on his work, with all the attendant connotations of the last will and testament. Be that as it may, the musical cell B-A-C-H has undoubtedly been the single most seminal source of variations from the eighteenth century until today, and is one of the most frequently cited themes in musical literature.

These four notes contain all the wealth of melody, of chromaticism, of series in the Schoenbergian sense and of structure in the most modern sense. Firstly, they form an expressive melodic design: the double drop of a semitone has something elegiac, something plaintive about it. Next, all four notes are separated by a semitone, and one can imagine the use to which turn-of-the-century composers were able to put this characteristic chromatic interval. They can also be read as a series and subjected to permutations in keeping with serial technique. And finally, they constitute a structure: an autonomous system which maintains and sustains itself by the very play of its transformations; an abstract, "geometrical" structure, simple, self-sufficient and rich in potential. And this simple structure just happens to coincide with the name of one of the greatest Western musicians—a providential coincidence which has fed the imagination of composers from the Romantic era to the present day.

To cite a few examples at random, and in no particular order: Liszt, *Präludium und Fuge über B-A-C-H (Prelude and Fugue on B-A-C-H)*; Schumann, *Six Fugues on B-A-C-H*, op. 60; Rimsky-Korsakov, *Six Variations on B-A-C-H;* Max Reger, *Fantasia and Fugue on B-A-C-H*, op. 46; Penderecki, *The Passion According to St. Luke (Passio et mors domini nostri Jesu Christi secundum Lucam),* in which B-A-C-H plays a referential role, Bertold Hummel, *Metamorphoses on B-A-C-H for organ and wind instruments,* op. 40 (1971). Not forgetting Webern's String Quartet, op. 28, whose series is based on *B-A-C-H*. All of these works are self-conscious homages to Bach. The signified of this four-note theme is not so much a proper name as an invocation, an incantation: *Ritual* in memoriam *Johann Sebastian Bach*. Kagel's comment on the *Sankt-Bach-Passion*—"musicians may not all believe in God, but they all believe in Bach"—and the even more Kagelian "Doubt God, believe in Bach" sum the whole thing up.

The letters in Bach's name are not the only ones to have been turned into a musical theme, with all of the associations that go along with this. To celebrate the centenary of Haydn's death in 1809, composers were invited to write a piece on his name, which had been turned into H-A-D-D-G for the occasion. Vincent d'Indy, Paul Dukas, Reynaldo Hahn and Maurice Ravel all agreed to take part, as did Debussy, who called his piece *Hommage à Haydn*. In 1922, it happened again. The *Revue musicale* proposed an "alphabetical" homage to Fauré: F-A-G-D-E. Ravel took part in this collective homage, with his *Berceuse sur le nom de Gabriel Fauré*. In all these cases, the signified is clearly specified in the paratext: the title, introduction and explanatory notes.

But many works refer to names *without* stating their signified: the reference, often fleeting, remains hidden, encoded, undecipherable. These are *cryptograms,* private jokes between the composer and the happy few. For the average mortal, a cryptogram is just another musical theme in the normal definition, i.e. a formal signifying unit. In Berg's Chamber Concerto, the thematic material is drawn from the names of the three Viennese composers: Berg picks out those letters which correspond to notes in the German notation, A-D-C-H-B-E-G for Arnold Schoenberg, A-E-B-E for Anton Webern, A-B-A-B-E-G for himself, Alban Berg. The Concerto is dedicated to friendship at two levels: not only does the score bear a verbal dedication to Schoenberg on his fiftieth birthday, but it pays a more private homage, in its very texture, to him and to Webern, another of Berg's friends. As Berg confides in Schoenberg, in a letter of February 9, 1925:

> I tell you, my dear friend, that if people could know all the love and friendship, all the inner and human emotions I have put in [this work], the partisans of program music—if there were any left—would be ecstatic.

Which brings me to the musical theme in its everyday usage: a formal signifying unit. This is how it is defined in Bordas' *Science de la musique:*

> any idea, melodic, rhythmic, or more rarely harmonic, which is sufficiently distinctive and capable of development or variation.

"Capable of development or variation": a theme is never quite alone; it is always a theme-in-view-of-something. Its dimensions may vary, anywhere from four notes (the first movement of Beethoven's Fifth) to twenty-seven bars (the first movement of César Franck's Sonata for violin and piano). In any case, the term itself is a recent one: they used to say *musical idea* or *phrase.* Most importantly, the variable nature of the theme implies a diversity of functions.

The theme often undergoes transformations. But not always: the theme in Ravel's *Bolero,* consisting of two sixteen-bar phrases, is repeated nine times without any variation or modification. Ravel himself describes it as "a dance of a very moderate and constantly uniform movement, in melody and harmony as well as in rhythm." In this respect, the work is a challenge, a *tour de force:* "an extreme case of uninterrupted directionality," it develops in a single direction, by a "process of simple transformation," breaking with the oscillatory, undulatory and periodic forms so frequent in music.[16] We remain in C major for 328 bars, a modulation in E major intervening *in extremis,* fifteen bars before the end. What changes is neither pitch nor duration. Ravel includes harmony, melody and duration, those elements of language, in his theme—a veritable mini-opus with a beginning, a development and an end—and he will "freeze" them, render them invariant. The changes will result from the modulation of other parameters: intensity, timbre and orchestral mass.

The first phrase in C major, two periods of eight bars each, is carried by the first flute and immediately taken over by the clarinet. The second phrase in C minor, also of twice eight bars, is taken up by the bassoon and piccolo, and so on. Each time the motifs reappear, the orchestra is enriched by a new tone: oboe d'amore, flute, solo horn and celesta, oboe, clarinet and cor anglais, first and second violins for the successive entries of the first theme; tenor saxophone, soprano saxophone and trombone for those of the second. When its parameters reach their maximum expansion, a saturation point in fortississimo, Ravel "unfreezes" the harmonic parameter: he changes tone, renewing everything *in extremis*. The variation, then, is not on the theme, which does not change, but on the concept of orchestral color.

What was a *tour de force* in *Bolero* becomes a provocation in Satie's *Vexations:* the theme is repeated "identically" eight hundred and forty times. Satie here indulges in what classical rhetoric condemns as *perissology* or *battology:* "pointless" and "depraved" repetitions, near to stammering and pure verbiage. But this *palimphrasis,* this *palilalia* denounced by treatises as "repetition sickness," this iteration which psychiatry sees as a symptom of dementia praecox (the medievals used to cross themselves before counting to ten, for fear of the devilish automatism that might drive them to continue), is ironic in Satie, and still reminds us that in music, the old never returns without adding something new. The art of music is an art of time; even without any change in parameters or material, each repetition emits a variation, creating a difference by virtue of its position in time and the previous accumulation of music. A *reprise* is never repetition, pure and simple: in music, A is never equal to A. In other words, as limited as it may be, information content is never nil.

At least repetition ensures a return, meaning that we never have to test totally unknown waters. What threatens it is monotony. To break this monotony and prevent any boredom, classical music plays a subtle game of memory and forgetting, of reminiscence and surprise, balancing the unknown against the known. The anticipation of gratification, when briefly interrupted, is intensified. Variation, development: this is the tension that commands attention. The dialectic of theme and transformation is that of expectations and predictions on the one hand, crises and differed resolutions on the other.

As information theory teaches us, for a message to escape the noise which tends to disturb its reception, for its outline to remain essentially unaltered, it must, as it were, be encased in reiterations, in redundant distinctive traits—that is, in an overabundance of probabilities. But the clearer its meaning is, the less information it carries, since information is tied in with originality, improbability and variation. In other words, if the message is easily comprehensible, i.e. predictable, it is doomed to banality. The better the communication, the slighter the information. The richer the information, the harder it is to communicate. Somewhere in-between these two extremes, where order is not too banal nor richness too disordered, would lie those messages which are both intelligible and optimally 'full.'

In as much as its themes are recognizable throughout the range of their metamorphoses, the ethos of classical music postulates predictability, communication and security. Other, more modern forms of music tend toward irreversibility, perpetual renewal and maximal information content. Here, pleasure does not reside in the reassuring recognition of a form forever lost and rediscovered as much as in the discernment of a process of enunciation which is permanently open, based not upon the expectation of the anticipated but upon an anticipation of the unexpected. The difference between the classical and the modern text, writes Roland Barthes, is that one offers pleasure, while the other imposes a state of loss:

> Text of pleasure: the text that contents, fills, grants euphoria; the text that comes from culture and does not break with it, is linked to a *comfortable* practice of reading. Text of bliss: the text that imposes a state of loss, the text that discomforts (perhaps to the point of a certain boredom), unsettles the reader's historical, cultural, psychological assumptions, the consistency of his tastes, values, memories, brings to a crisis his relation with language.[17]

Often, then, the theme possesses a generative function, in that it is developed "further"; the score is derived from its premises and is its logical and chronological prolongation. The theme is that primary structure which allows other structures to be born. The sequence of elements which form the discourse (the score) is simply a set of correlatives on the same level as the theme, just so many complementary segments: the theme, being the matrix, is party to the rest of the utterance; the relationship which links it to its correlatives is distributional.

Here I am thinking not only of the "variations" and sonata forms, but also of the use in classical music of shorter and more concentrated motifs or cells. The first four bars of Beethoven's *Pastoral Symphony*, for example, form a matrix from which the whole first movement, the initial *allegro,* develops. Every bar, every phrase of this first movement is no more than an exploitation and elaboration of elements contained within the first four bars. In his analysis of this theme in F which starts in the tonic and ends in the dominant, Leonard Bernstein has shown that the F-C of the bass line, at a deeper level than the melody of the upper part, represents the real motif of the entire first movement and by extension of the symphony *in toto.* In short, the whole symphony is an essay on the subject of F-C.

As for the tune of the upper part—the more obvious subject of the symphony—Beethoven never ceases developing, varying and transforming it. For example, what went down—the second bar of the theme—soon goes up again, in an elementary permutation: an *inversion*. Next, it proceeds to a *deletion*. This four-bar tune ends on the dominant C; the law of symmetry would require a complementary four-bar phrase following it, ending on the tonic F, but Beethoven frustrates our expectations, eliminating this second phrase in advance, so that his initial motif may now develop freely and *press on*.

Another procedure used in this first movement is the rhetorical device of *fragmentation*. The first two bars of the theme are repeated, but shared between two instrumental voices: the second violins take the 'head' of the theme (the first bar), and the first violins answer with the rhythmical motif (second and third bars)—a motif which, as we have seen, has already been turned into an ascending figure by inversion. Another transformation: the second violins take up the head of the theme plus the first note—C—of its rhythmical ("jaunty") motif, and so the first violins play this motif *minus* its first note.

Elements of the theme become attached and detached in constant repositioning, conjoining and embedding, and this very activity of fragmentation competes with augmentation, i.e. the unfolding of the development. At first sight, the next two bars of this development merely seem to repeat what we have just observed. But two notes (B^b and G) have been added to the first violin part, and pure repetition is thus avoided. This rhetorical figure is called *auxesis*, an increase in density (in literature, an augmentative hyperbole or hyperbole of positive value: "He is faster than lightning," as opposed to *tapinosis*, or decreasing hyperbole: "He is slower than a tortoise"). The reason these two notes are added is that they form a falling third, corresponding to the rising third (B^b-D) of the head motif (the first bar of the theme). When the rising third is repeated, Beethoven adds this figure to vary it.[18]

A theme (or "cell") of similar brevity is found in Beethoven's Fifth; a theme of inexhaustible fecundity, since it contains in embryo the development of the symphony as a whole and since it cuts across all four of its movements, making them interdependent—a rare thing. Harmonically, this theme is a third: G-G-G-E^b; rhythmically, three shorts and one long, or three weak and one strong. It lends itself to "kneading" in all directions, and gives rise to all kinds of configurations: in the *andante, pianissimo* suddenly appears, first in the second violins and altos (bars 76–77), then later in the cellos (bars 88–89), a rhythmic accent which serves as a reminder of the initial organic motif. In the *scherzo*, this motif takes the form of an unfinished melody, falling in the final cell (bars 19 and onward). In the *finale*, a chain of new configurations, rising and falling, beginning with the first violins, gives the theme a freer, more lively feel (bars 45 and following). Here then is a motif which binds the entire score together.

The initial cell may thus be brief and yet still give rise to numerous developments: in this instance, five hundred bars of the first movement are generated by the G-G-G-E^b cell, whose proliferation spreads throughout the score, by a process of deepening and enrichment. Wagner writes that Mozart always presents his whole melody first, before dividing it into smaller fragments, whereas Beethoven's originality consists in starting from these fragments and using them to raise monuments, ever prouder and more imposing, before our very eyes. Wagner also points out that the development, as found in Beethoven, has a dramatic potential superseding the principle of alternation present in the *suite,* a cross between dancing and walking, with its succession of calm and lively periods.

As short as it is, the G-G-G-E^b theme still has certain distinctive features which give it its immediate and definitive tone.[19] It is a figurative reality, a trait which is indicated throughout the score by the predominance of rhythm and key over melody. Critics have spoken of the theme of Destiny, which made the piece popular in the Romantic era (Balzac mentions it twice in *César Birotteau*). The initial theme of Beethoven's Fifth Symphony has a "face" with more or less pronounced features; it is recognizable the length of its journey, through all the transformations it undergoes.

Often, however, the theme in classical music is neither hero nor character. It is a "structural field, a set of relationships with several possible incarnations, a model of behavior, pure *conditionality,*" to borrow André Boucourechliev's formula. For him, the theme of Beethoven's *Diabelli* belongs to the second type. It is a harmonic structure with a matching metrical structure, though it still possesses certain individual traits (like the anacrusis of the opening). A compensatory movement from tonic to dominant and from dominant to tonic (sixteen bars each), with harmonic shifts in the second parts of both trajectories (four bars each): this rudimentary harmonic formula is banal, spanning the history of tonal music from Vivaldi to the Beatles. It is an "abstract formula" which can be used in an infinite number of situations, a *numbering* (an operation which consists in placing, above or below the notes of a given bass line, numbers which represent chords in a given convention): a *function,* a constant, a common light source for the thirty-three strange objects which make up the *Diabelli,* whereas the theme of the "variations" or sonata form as I have described it is "a single object viewed under different lights."[20] A *generative* function gives way, perhaps, to a *generalizing* function, and the Diabelli waltz fertilizes Beethoven's imagination, rather than channeling its activity.

The generalizing function of the theme may be found in tonal music before Beethoven—in the Goldberg Variations, for example. Underneath its individual traits, the initial aria is an abstract formula, an elementary schema consisting in a harmonic series oriented from tonic to dominant and then from dominant to tonic; it is this formula which serves as the denominator common to the thirty variations which follow. The variations reduce the aria to a mere unifier, the harmonic schema that subtends it being "the only common factor" between the theme and its variations.[21] At the end, Bach inserts an *ad lib* on two popular songs, two "objets trouvés" which come from outside but which possess the same harmonic structure.

This harmonic structure common to the aria and to the thirty variations is the harmonic (and not melodic) *ground* of English composers, or the *basse fondamentale* of the French (not to be confused with the basso continuo) which is not a real bass, obtained as it is by bringing all of the chords in a piece back to their principal position and by making the resulting basses follow one another. Thus, the generalizing theme of the Goldberg or Diabelli variations is not in itself so novel, in spite of what has been claimed.[22]

In genetic terms, the theme is the initial cell of the work, its point of departure, the seed from which it grows. In structural terms, the work is more than a synopsis of its thematic genesis. The theme is inscribed within the work, only existing in and through it. The variations (or the development, in the case of the sonata) bring the theme to life, nourish, glorify and exalt it; in terms of interest or value, the subject of the work is the speculation itself, the production of the development and variations, or more specifically the way in which a composer manages to fashion a substantial piece out of very little material: for a long time, the composer's (neurotic) obsession was to produce "the same thing, in all shapes and sizes."

Still, the theme is already a structure, a schema encoded in sounds, each previous state of a structure being itself a structure, and structures engendering other structures by a relentless process of transformation. It is particularly important to note that the relationship between a theme and its development or variations is one of similitude, however blurred it may be, and whether it be an external analogy (Mozart) or an internal homology (Goldberg Variations). The theme—whether a few-note cell (Beethoven's Fifth) or a harmonic schema (Goldberg Variations)—is the connecting factor, the unifying force, the element which the different components of discourse have in common and which ties them together.[23] It is their point of reference, the minimal condition for their coherence. Between entrenchment and conditioning there is no solution of continuity, all entrenchment being a form of conditioning, however unrestrictive. In a theme with variations, just about the only element that had a meaning for Brahms was the bass; even here, the harmonic functions to which he reduces the theme are used as a foundation for the musical edifice.

A theme, that is to say, is never alone: it is always a theme-in-view-of-something. It is correlative. By definition, it is summoned up again, whatever form the development takes. It is subject to reiteration, to the law of eternal

return. Of course, it does not return unchanged: the various forms of development affect the theme and the aural impression one has of it. After thirty
Goldberg Variations, the aria we hear is no longer the same. Neither totally
identical nor totally different. In Brahms' *Variations on a Theme by J. Haydn,*
opus 56a, the Haydn theme (which, as it happens, is not by Haydn) is taken
up at the end by the whole orchestra, *fortissimo,* as if enriched by the variations it has occasioned. All the way through the Goldberg Variations, Bach
ignores the aria's particular traits, in order to retain its harmonic essence; but
he still obeys the rule of his age and gives it again at the end, creating an *effect*
of closure, of completion, of a return to the point of departure. The theme,
then, attempts to cancel the journey; it participates in a cyclical, closed conception of time.

THEME AND THEMATICS
IN CONTEMPORARY MUSIC

Jean-Yves Bosseur

If you look up the word "theme" in the *Robert,* you will find the following definition: "a melodic design which forms the subject of a musical composition and which is the object of variations."

What I would like to show throughout this paper is how trends in music have considerably expanded the concept of theme over the last three decades, proving, by the diversity of their aesthetic orientations, that melodic design is ultimately just one possibility. For this reason, my argument will be deliberately slanted toward works whose conception of the theme transcends the purely melodic.

The first point to make is that one of the main features of most contemporary musical trends has been to challenge the absolute supremacy of the harmonic dimension over other properties of sound, such as duration, timbre, intensity and interval.

As soon as he uses the word *Klangfarbenmelodie,* it is clear that Schoenberg believes in ways of expressing a melodic concept other than by a series of higher or lower notes. The concept of melody thus releases itself from its far too exclusive adherence to the phenomenon of pitch, foreshadowing multiple expansions among the various components of the acoustic phenomenon. Freeing themselves from the hegemony of harmony, composers enable themselves to grasp the concept of theme in its utmost polyvalency and to associate it with the most diverse aspects of music. In the poetics of Beethoven, it has been claimed, "everything is theme"; nowadays we may judge everything apt to become a theme, every element of the musical vocabulary capable of forming the foundation of a work.

I would like to investigate the multiple perspectives which this new interpretation of the concept, expanded to include all the elements which combine to form a musical work, has helped to create. I shall draw my first examples from the work of Mauricio Kagel, as his style is particularly representative of the tendency, so frequent in music these days, to give each work a completely individual form, to make every score a question in a specific area of musical communication, to base each project on an autonomous thematics. I choose the term "thematics" rather than "theme" as it seems to me to be more inclusive, more productive, less dependent on the melodic concept I mentioned earlier. At the start of every Kagel piece a thematics takes shape, phrased such that a problem or a question is raised, the angle of refraction changing with each new project. Taking Kagel's output as a whole, it is clear that the concept of thematics is no longer confined to the relationships between sounds; it can develop from anything pertaining to music and musicians. The practice of music abounds in themes of reflection, themes which are often caught up in the display of the work as an object and which are to be explored and made tangible with each new process of creation. The realm of music then becomes an arena for crisscrossing, interpenetrating thematics. By focusing each work upon one of them and by narrowing down their field of inquiry, sometimes to an extreme degree, composers may afford themselves the opportunity of laying bare working hypotheses which had remained concealed, partially obscured by conventions and habits.

Mauricio Kagel certainly numbers among the composers who have most thoroughly demonstrated the theatrical aspects of musical thematics—or, more generally speaking, the thematics of the acoustic act. His inquiries, systematic explorations of the world of sound, extend far beyond the framework of the concert. Even when he writes concert pieces, what he questions and analyzes with his clinical keenness are the deeper implications of the musical game.

The performers in *Match* (1964), a piece for two cellos and percussion, simulate a kind of battle between the cellists—the percussionist playing referee—and thus allow an interplay of psycho-social relationships to develop. The result of this match remains ambiguous, however, as Kagel immediately fractures its inchoate significance. On the plane of sound, the listener discerns elements of the match which do not really belong. A theatrical situation gives way to an impression of pure music; by a dialectical process, the latter ultimately derives from a situation whose origins are extra-musical. The theme of *Match* is not just competitiveness, the rivalry which arises from relationships between musicians, but also its substitution by an essentially ludic approach to instrumental activity.

Kagel's output is strewn with solo pieces, all of which share the status of a pitched battle between musician and instrument. For the musicians, in fact, it is less a question of reproducing Kagel's musical ideas than of transcending their own capacities as well as those of their instrument; not only their technique but also their function, the role assigned them within the world of music. They thus end up in a painful situation, a formidable and multi-layered tension—with the audience, who sense this attempt to transgress what they thought they knew about the instrument, as well as with the host of directions that limit the musicians' play on all sides. One might mention the bandoneon of *Pandorasbox,* an instrument rather like an accordeon used by Latin American workers and miners in the Ruhr, or again the multiple accessories of a one-man-band, that "soloist-acrobat," in *Zwei-Mann-Orchester.* The thematics which emerges from Kagel's solo works is this: a musician or singer caught in a situation in which various factors interweave in an infinitely complex fashion, involving the psychology and the physiology of instrumental play.

In his organ pieces, *Improvisation ajoutée* (1961–2) and *Phantasie* (1967), what is at stake—outside of Kagel's aesthetic conceptions and personal message, that is—is an organist's career, from apprenticeship to inclusion within the world of the Church. Thus, in the *Phantasie für Orgel mit Obbligati,* "documentary" elements in the form of recordings are allowed to intervene, in counterpoint to the notes of the organ. They sound like amplified bursts of the organist's activity between waking up and arriving at the church. Every musician who chooses to perform acquires a certain theatrical status, and Kagel makes this plain, showing music lovers what is usually hidden from their sight, whether out of modesty or from a desire to preserve, as it were, the mythical aura of artistic creation. The thematics of the work lies just as much in what may have made a musical event possible as in what is actually played; these two aspects prove to be indissociable. If the musicians in *Tactil* (1970) appear on stage half-naked, this is not to add a touch of theatre but to stress the fact that the play of their muscles and the movements of their joints—especially those of the pianist, whose warm-up exercises relate to the way he plays—form the basic conditions of their activity, and indeed of all future musical thematics.

Each work, devoted to a different type of performer—*Atem* (1970) and the *Morceau de concours* (1971) for wind instruments, *Phonophonie* (1963) for voices—thus takes the form of an inquiry based on historical documents, anecdotes or reviews; an inquiry which lies outside the privileged moment of the concert and which focuses on the musician's professional activity, her intimacy with an instrument of choice. The most private dramas, like ageing and illness, can then become *bona fide* themes in their own right.

Luciano Berio's *Sequenze,* a series of homages paid to each individual instrument through the personality of a performer, should also be mentioned here. The thematics of every *Sequenza* may be virtuosity, but Berio is dealing with multiple facets of this phenomenon, involving the most varied instrumental practices, rather than a single type of performance. In the *Sequenza* for trombone, the allusion to the art of Grock the Clown is meant to spotlight the player as well as the instrument, in the originality of the former's technique. "These days, it is only as a celebration of a special harmony between composer and performer, a testimony to a human relationship, that one may compose for a virtuoso who is worthy of the name," writes Berio.

Michel Puig, another pioneer of musical theater, claims that "when Duke Ellington composed, he did not so much use notes as the music he knew his musicians could make best. He wrote for *them*, to drive them deep into themselves." One might well infer from this that the theme of a Duke Ellington piece is not confined to the melodic motif: it is also the musician to whom he has chosen to address himself or, more generally, the type of harmony he is trying to foster between the musicians, their instruments and their partners.

Every musical domain undeniably draws on a series of presuppositions which are only apparently extrinsic. This is how Kagel tackles the reality of the fanfare in *Klangwehr* (1966–70), transforming its associated elements. Addressing the theme of the fanfare and taking a highly clichéd situation as his focal point allows him to visualize a spatialization of sound, with musicians in movement, as well as to conduct an analysis of the relationships between a given vocabulary of sound, an instrumental body and the socio-political function assigned to them. Once again, Kagel implies a dichotomy inherent in his work, by implanting a fanfare in a completely foreign context: the thematics enables him to subvert a supposedly monolithic area from within. What might be seen as a by-product of artistic activity is valorized by Kagel, explored as the potential basis of a theatro-musical drama.

As Kagel dissects the phenomenon of performance, isolating—sometimes radically—the elements of which a musical thematics is composed, he is led to emphasize the consequences of each such component. He addresses the phenomenon of lighting in *Camera Obscura* (1965), a chromatic spectacle for actors and light source, and that of "natural scenery" in *Die Himmelsmechanik* (1965), a composition with scenic images. In *Staatstheater*, it is opera—as an institution, a set of codes—which becomes the central thematics. Kagel dislocates all of its givens, removing their cultural patina and the conventions which threaten to paralyze all forms of dynamism and all critical distance. The attitudes, behavior and steps of the singers (this last aspect had already been treated in *Pas de cinq*) may form the very content of the plot. "The process become[s] the telos of the plot"; "a shake of the arm" and "a turn of the head" find themselves raised "to the level of narrative material." Viewed in context, but considered potentially autonomous, the elements of performance, inasmuch as they are interchangeable, accidental and even defective, set about taking their course, lending themselves to unexpected combinations.

In the film *Ludwig van*, the theme is Beethoven himself, along with the legend and images currently associated with him; and clues to the thematic material of *Acustica*, *Exotica* and *Musik für Renaissanceinstrumente* are, I feel, more to be found in composers' attitudes to certain types of instrument and sound-producer, such as old-fashioned or non-European instruments and miscellaneous objects, than among the sound patterns themselves.

Kagel's choice of thematics is often quite mundane, as though he were seeking to approach the origin of the musical act; it is with this in mind that he questions the material of the sound-producer, as well as its construction and mastery. In *Privat*, everyday objects, in their capacity for producing somewhat unexpected sounds, become the theme under investigation. Perception itself can be taken as a thematic center in a work like *Tremens* (1963–5) which dramatizes hallucinations brought on by the use of various drugs.

The composer's conceptual strategy is itself liable to function both as a process and as the thematics of a work. Thus *Anagrama* (1957–8) represents a meditation on serial music (the score is dedicated to Pierre Boulez) and, at the same time, one on ways to develop a thought according to the conventions of the classical syllogism:

- reaching sound conclusions based on sound premises using a sound method of reasoning, which is not necessarily fruitful in art, as the results are far too predictable;

- reaching absurd results based on sound premises, using a false method of reasoning;

- reaching absurd results based on false premises, using a sound method of reasoning.

Still, one has to wonder to what extent the theme will be understood as something explicit at the moment of the work's execution, or whether it will simply be felt to be latent. Take *Réactions* by Dieter Schnebel, another leading exponent of musical theater. Here the audience itself is taken as the driving force behind the forthcoming game. In this instance, the central thematics of the project—the reactions of the listener or viewer—must not be blatantly obvious. Only the performer may know in what way the audience's input is supposed to influence the course of her actions, to inflect her play. Otherwise, the tension between musician and audience, one of the crucial elements of the thematics, would inevitably be jeopardized.

In the works I have mentioned, thematics comes to stand for that which is designed to engage a specific process of play, to ensure the coherence of a work or project and to present it as a single immutable organism, in such a way as to make the presence of this generative theme effective for eye and ear; or at least, in the case of a latent theme, to make the whole thing work. For the composer, then, choosing a thematics comes down to setting a process in motion, deducing an inherent logic of development according to its own unique systems. Just as, in the past, each work was built on its own melodic themes (except, of course, for works based on borrowed thematic material), so today most works possess their own personal thematics which provide the most favorable form for their deployment. As each work is grounded in the choice of a specific thematics, it implicitly raises the question of its roots, the issue of its existence as an autonomous entity.

As an example, let us take the case of Karlheinz Stockhausen. Each of his compositions has at its core an element the composer proposes to explore in a privileged manner, a kind of nucleus which, to my mind, functions as a *bona fide* theme upon which the entire musical structure is built. This thematic element is usually inscribed in the title of the work, which becomes a kind of emblem for the project. Often, as if to designate the phenomenon in question with an optimal degree of concision, the titles are extremely short.

Thus the whole problematics of the "punctual" serial technique runs right beneath the surface of *Punkte; Gruppen,* a later work, places its emphasis on another phase of serialism, using the technique of groups. And in *Momente,* the thematics involves an approach—as musical as it is philosophical—to temporality, or more specifically to one of its possible forms, relatively unexploited by Western music: ephemerality, the here and now.

The choice of a title, a partial key to the thematics of a work, helps to reflect the composer's aesthetic vision: there will therefore be a desire for efficiency in this decision, for the closest approximation to the problematics at hand. While testifying to the very essence of the composer's concerns, the title also contains, in condensed form, various handles by which a thematics may be grasped, heterogeneous in nature but destined, by the existence of the work, to converge. A title may mask a multiplicity of meanings, some of which will stay more or less concealed.

Several levels thus collide in *Telemusik,* an electro-acoustic work. The Greek adverb *tele* means "far away," which makes the literal meaning of *Telemusik* "music coming from afar"; Stockhausen developed this piece in Tokyo, immersed as it were in a cultural universe different from his own. *Telemusik* could also be understood as the confrontation of musical forms which are spatio-temporally remote: these forms, which point to diverse cultural currents, are imagined—and later heard by the audience—at all kinds of distances, with electro-acoustic processes multiplying the possibilities for distancing and for camouflage. The prefix *tele-* also suggests the music's transmission through sound reproduction equipment; Telemusik could be taken to mean a mode of reception and transmission like the telephone or the television. Even relatively personal examples of this general thematics of distancing may be found within the title: the M in Musik is a sort of dedication to Mary Bauermeister (other works which start with an M, like *Mikrophonie I,*

Mikrophonie II and *Momente,* are also dedicated to her); *Telemusik* thus becomes "music composed away from Mary." So the title, which is really there to serve as the faithful reflection of a thematics, contains a whole range of meanings, from the most objective (a process of acoustic transformation, as in *Mikrophonie*) to the most subjective, autobiographical implications.

As the symbolic approach is a fundamental aspect of thematic selection, elementary geometric figures (square, circle, spiral or cross), positions (high and low), directions and the like can all be used as thematic bases for works whose titles *(Carré, Zyklus, Spiral, Kreuzspiel, Hinab-hinaus, Trans)* most powerfully encapsulate the phenomenon at hand. And from time to time a polyvalent semantic perspective opens up within the resonances of certain titles (like *Stimmung* and *Mantra*), their thematics essentially consisting in a metaphysical meditation on music seized at its source, or on the conditions for the manifestation of our consciousness.

In these thematics—and also in those which help, with deliberate precision, to describe them—there are of course elements which are as hidden as they are visible. In *Carré,* for example, the eponymous figure is formed by four orchestras and four choirs placed in the four corners of a room, but the significance of this fundamental figure goes much further than spatial configurations. Understood as the driving force behind the work, the square is to be found at all levels of the composition, turning the project into a panoramic contemplation of this basic geometric figure.

Let us now return to the *Robert:* "thema," it says, means something set up, a developed thesis, a thought or idea which forms the subject or center of (a work's) concerns, a focus of reflection or activity. Here, as in Foulquié's suggested definition of thematics as "that which poses or is posed as the object of mental activity, either implicitly, i.e. unconsciously, or explicitly, i.e. consciously," one detects a fairly large area of overlap with the aforementioned works. Although the concept of thematics may appear to be expanded, in relation to works that still depend on the prominence of the harmonic dimension, the general notion is clearly what guarantees the unity and identity of the compositional thought.

As we have seen, the thematics of most contemporary works does not necessarily appear as a motif to be followed through the piece in a more or less linear fashion. What is offered as a thematic principle may equally, or indeed additionally, be a material clue (a configuration of pitches, a set of sounds), a conceptual process. To my mind, a work may be considered essentially thematic even if the theme is not recognizable, not discernible during the performance; even if the thematic principle is destined to stay hidden within the work. As the inventors of serial music have stated repeatedly, the series is not a theme, a melodic motif that may be noticed and remembered. The logic behind the construction of a serial score is typically far from apparent. Yet to me the serial process seems powerfully thematic, in the sense that everything in the work points to a hidden unity, a principle which both centralizes and generates the piece. If I wanted to represent these considerations pictorially, I would propose the following diagrams:

- for works belonging to the tonal tradition and its related dramatic forms, I would draw one or more lines to represent the variations or developments proceeding from one or more thematic motifs;

- for serial works (though this could also apply to the above-mentioned Kagel and Stockhausen scores), I would draw a circle with a dot in the middle to represent the work's thematic core. When moving around the circumference, one does not necessarily notice this center in a conscious way, and yet everything that happens in the circle points to the omnipresence of the generating idea.

But a work which escapes all thematism, which goes beyond the bounds of any centralizing, focalizing conception of form—how are we to understand *its* underlying principle?

During the fifties and sixties, several schools of thought helped to challenge such a view of the musical work, either by radically reducing what is seen and heard—making the thematic horizon tend toward ground zero, as it were—or by using processes of indeterminacy to demolish all unifying thematic principles.

To illustrate the first point, let me mention the Fluxus group's experiments in the United States. Most of the "events" staged in the sixties by the Fluxus protagonists (La Monte Young, George Brecht and founder-member George Maciunas) situate themselves between various modes of communication; between music, drama and poetry; between art and everyday life. If anything thematic can still be detected amongst their activity, it is a thematics of ambiguity and of paradox, reduced to its simplest form and laid almost entirely bare. Thus La Monte Young's "compositions" convey a radical reduction of sensory information, as if to compress a whole situation into a single event as concisely as possible. Perched on the borders of art, the musical events of the Fluxus group are inspired, says Maciunas, by "the monostructural rather than theatrical qualities of a simple, natural event, a game or a gag. It is a mixture of Spike Jones, music hall, the gag, child's play and Duchamp." Taken as they are from daily life, these events sometimes coalesce with it: they use the most heterogeneous objects and toys, as if to prove that anything can take the place of art, so long as it catches the eye and ear and stimulates the intellect, and that the limits of art are infinitely more elastic than they seem.

George Brecht's minimalist instructions only take a few words; they read like exercises for reducing things to a single essential characteristic, to one raw and primitive element: "Switch on the radio. At the first sound, switch it off." Sometimes they isolate an action, like that of polishing a violin *(Solo for Violin)*, or emphasize an incidental aspect of an instrument's function: the vase on the piano in *Piano Piece.* The musical performance is presented as an attitude; or a social situation is foregrounded, as in La Monte Young's *Composition 6,* in which the performers watch the audience just like the audience usually watches the performers. Most of these events take the form of joint acoustic and visual phenomena; thus La Monte Young's *Fire Piece* is supposed to encourage one to "watch what one normally only listens to." As such processes are frequently permeated by the concept of play, George Brecht quite willingly uses games of chance and packs of cards. Some of these events are not intended for public performance but are meant to stay private, like the *Three Telephone Events,* "multi-sensory exercises for the listener/viewer," which stage the search for exact points of contact with reality. La Monte Young's *Compositions 60* have an obsessional side to them, the thematic element somehow becoming an *idée fixe* within which a feeling of spiritual asceticism—a feeling which will culminate in *The Dream House*—filters through. Presented as riddles, such programs are, for Dieter Schnebel, "musical thunderbolts of thought where time contracts and expands indefinitely," beyond reality. Beyond music, for that matter: the Fluxus group's multifold thematics of intervention acquires the status of a philosophical investigation, irrespective of any criteria of aesthetic appreciation, and, in broader terms, tends to establish itself as an actual art of life. All that is left is the rough outline of a few thematic clues.

The use of processes of indeterminacy to demolish the thematic principle—a method employed by John Cage—produces radically dissimilar results, notwithstanding the undeniable influence which Cage's poetics had at first on members of the Fluxus group.

In projects that correspond to the principles of indeterminacy, Cage allows a multiplicity of events to accumulate and coexist, ultimately leaving the listener or viewer immersed in a complex situation which calls for a variety of courses of action, a concoction she is supposed to *live,* like anarchy in practice.

But can we really call this "athematism"? The debate, it would seem, can not take the form of a schematic opposition between two terms, between positive and negative poles. Of course, Cage's scores (*Cartridge Music,* the *Piano Concerto* or the *Variations*) offer no controlled logical coherence in the sense of an intentional interdependence, no cause and effect relationships between events, or between the compositional structure and the resultant form: a fact which encourages a rethinking of the concept of the musical work. No longer is the work a self-contained entity: it is instead a dynamic organism. The performer's task is not just to complete it, but also to bring it to life. The concept of thematics henceforth acquires a completely different set of consequences; it is, in fact, almost the same as the work-in-progress. Cage does not so much negate the thematic principle, I feel, as distance himself from any concept of thematics which aims to make the work a homogenous whole, to produce the illusion of a coherent system, of a continuity. Take Cage's *Variations:* it seems fairly difficult to demarcate the theme of each, to define precisely what it is. The variations are not created around a theme; in a way, the two terms tend to coalesce. Cage excludes all forms of iteration, even virtual, from the variation. For him, the variation technique as envisaged by Schoenberg meant little more than repetitions of a given constant; in Cage's opinion, such a system makes the whole idea of variation cancel itself out, as it is "pointless to change one ingredient—you can always change *something*—the rest remains." He continues:

> I have a fixed object before me and at my disposal; I can vary it precisely because I know in advance that I shall still find it identical to itself. From this point of view, I am complying with Schoenberg's dictum that variation is a form, an extreme case of repetition.

For him, then, the only way to avoid the choice between repetition and variation, and even the dialectic between them, is to keep to a plane which, he says, "stays out of the conflict between these two terms and rebels against association and re-association . . . the plane of chance."

In light of the works and intellectual trends I have just been discussing, I would personally be inclined to put forward two attitudes to the concept of thematics in contemporary musical forms. One, more centripetal in its drift, involves using a new thematics for every work, betraying a will-to-power over form and material. We have seen the extent to which thematic concerns have continued to multiply and diversify for thirty-odd years; I do not, however, really see this as a re-examination of the principles of construction underpinning our classical heritage. The theme, once manifest, may well become latent; the important point is that the work still relies upon a generating principle, even if the composer makes it undergo all kinds of transformations and even transgressions.

In the other approach, more centrifugal in tendency, a thematics is what enables a hypothetical field to be opened up or a process to be set in motion, all of whose consequences the composer does not claim, *a priori,* to control. For such pieces, which could be called *open works,* the concept of thematics interferes with that of process. And if we may still speak of theme in this context, it has more to do with a mechanism of motion and interrogation than with the offer of an object.

In the first case, the theme encourages its variations to close in on themselves; in the second, the theme is only there to propel a rambling quest, with no ambition of ever reaching its goal.

Part IV

CONCLUSION

THE END OF AN ANATHEMA

Claude Bremond and Thomas Pavel

Whenever it seeks to delimit its object, thematics runs up against a series of obstacles that force it to become increasingly tolerant—at the risk, it may at first appear, of foundering in a progressive dilution of the concept of theme.

Initially it seems possible to consider thematics as the sum of a stock of ideas and images, furnished by tradition, pre-dating works of art and available for re-use and rearrangement. The problems it poses are of an inventorial or classificatory order (when seen from a synchronic perspective), and of evolution or mutation (when taken diachronically). One could, say, catalog the *topoi* and motifs of written and popular literatures; or one might trace the historical development of the Don Juan theme through the medieval *exemplum*, French and Spanish theater, opera, the symphonic poem and the novella—to name but a few genres.

But this identification of *thematics* with a material extrinsic to the work leads us to question the status of *form*. The creator who mobilizes existing material with a view to a new arrangement, or transforms this material in order to deliver a hitherto unspoken message, puts out a variant, or a variation, which enriches the thematics on which his writing is based. In his perspective, the thematic material in question is not so much the subject of the work as its medium, and the latter's telos, its *real* "aboutness" and thus its primary theme lie in the formal or semantic transformations it aims to inflict upon the existing thematics.

In this new sense of the word, the theme is the target of an ideal quest; it is a soul in search of a body. When the work is finished, the synthesis of existing material (whether adapted or incorporated as is) and the creative project presents itself as a new material, addressed to the public—including the creator, who receives no special treatment—and offered for their analysis, whether it be naïve or critical, immediate or deferred, proximate or distant. An investigation into this third phase will tend to view thematics not just as the rebirth of pre-existent material but also as the elucidation of an author's aim, or the distillation of a work's innovative elements; taking it as a whole or taking it in part, via this interpretative strategy or via that, at one level of the message or at another. For as soon as they enter the circuit of interpersonal (and even intrapersonal) exchanges, these elements are just so many themes tacked onto the existing body of material, so many *aboutnesses* capable of provoking a reusage, a reprise or a variation.

In spite of its apparent nebulousness and genuine complexity, the decision to reorient one area of literary and art-historical research back toward thematics cannot fail to bear fruit, even if only by the challenge this change of course must pose to the spectacular ascendancy of purely formal textual studies, held until very recently. This tendency found its justification in the desire to eliminate subjective interpretations from the discourse on literature; there comes a point, however, when such textualism slides into *textolatry*, pure and simple. As Daniel Dennett has argued in a different context, every time theory-builders use such terms as *sign, message* and *code* to designate events, states and structures of the system under discussion, they are hiding behind formal concepts so as to take out surreptitious loans on the account of the intelligence. And sooner or later the amounts spent must be repaid, given the fact that these signs, messages and codes presuppose senders to compose them and receivers to understand them. In the same way, each time literary theory uses such strictly formal notions as *device, discourse* and *text,* it withdraws interpretative capital, given that these texts, devices and discourses do not exist outside of the creative activity that shapes them (at one end) and the hermeneutic activity which interprets them (at the other). A structural theory of art and literature inevitably clocks up some fairly heavy debts to mental activity. The problem is not so much to eliminate subjective interpretations (the structuralists' fantasy) as to broaden the range of potential readings, and—so as to be as objective as possible—to evaluate the subjectivity of each.

Further, on discovering that structural arrangements possess a certain degree of formal autonomy from the contents they convey, textualist theory is often tempted to use this as an excuse to evade the question of the *material* in which these structures manifest themselves. There again, questions of content cannot all be dodged indefinitely: sooner or later the books must be opened for inspection. Caught between the constraints of the material and the demands of interpretation, how can a strictly autonomous structural poetics ever hope to remain solvent? And if, in spite of everything, we choose to believe that it can, would we therefore have to subscribe to Paul de Man's peremptory pronouncement that there is no common ground between poetics and hermeneutics? Can it be asserted with the same degree of assurance that there is no necessary link between poetics and *thematics*—that there is no "common ground" between these disciplines either? Doesn't such language, deeming the theme no more than the material of a work, condemn it out of hand? Something like the marble which turns into a god, a basin or a table with equal ease, depending on the hand that chisels it?

What is more, the concept of amorphous matter is in itself illusory. Matter may only be referred to in terms of a form to be brought out: at another level, that is, it will be perceived as a form. Marble has its grain and its price to distinguish it from gold or plaster; words, the materials of poetry, each have their own meanings and haloes of resonances; themes in themselves convey the echoes of a lived experience, the promise of a possible wisdom.

In the end, to raise such questions involves turning to a tripartite division of the literary work—thematic material, structural design and hermeneutic content—and accepting, as a consequence, that the theme is nothing more than its material. At variance over the relative importance of the last two factors, the proponents of structure and the supporters of interpretation would at least agree to keep the material—and thus thematics—out of the debate: it is, they would argue, but meaningless groundwork for a meaning that emerges from structure and its many interpretations.

If, however, we examine the contributions to two consecutive symposia on thematics (held in Paris in '84 and '86 respectively), we find the reality to be far more complicated: those participants who attempted to define the theme generally did so in structural terms or from an intentional point of view, seldom using the expression "thematic material" that musicologists find so useful. In fact, the only person to note this usage (Georges Leroux) did so in order to reject it, together with what he called "the extensionality of the *topos*"; as if the idea of a lexicon or inventory of themes represented a threat to the dignity of literature.[1]

Granted, a more tolerant point of view emerges from the work of Peter Cryle and Michel Collot, as they give fifties and sixties thematic criticism its due: for Gaston Bachelard, Georges Poulet and Jean-Pierre Richard, the theme, "an individual, implicit, concrete signified" which links up with other themes to contribute to the economy of the work, falls within the province of material, though this material is already mysteriously shaped by intentionality; but this point of view remains relatively isolated.[2] The implicit rejection of theme as material, and its recuperation in a formalist perspective, is found once again in Gerald Prince's piece. Theme, here understood as a conceptual framework for the text, belongs to the latter's macrostructural categories: its design, in other words.[3] The same goes for Lubomír Doležel who, in both his papers, explicitly identifies themes with the semantic constants of a text, emphasizing the impossibility of separating content from structure.[4] It should, however, be noted that Doležel, like Cesare Segre and Georges Roque, distinguishes between motifs—which are relegated to the status of material—and structural themes, whether iconographic (Panofsky), narrative (Segre) or representational (Doležel). In Marie-Laure Ryan's definition, the theme, itself determined by structure, defines the strategic choices of the tale's protagonists.

Form itself can be thematized, moreover, as an additional referent. At a performance of Marlowe's *Tamburlaine*, the spectator may notice the repetitiousness of the plot, the obsessive recurrence of challenges issued by Tamburlaine to his enemies, each one followed by a counter-challenge, a savage war, a victory for Tamburlaine and a general massacre. Form does channel thematic activity: it is these repetitions that alert the spectator to the grandeur and cruelty of the hero. But form also enjoys a certain amount of autonomy, and we could easily number "the obsessive return of the same" among this drama's themes. Conversely, themes with a precise semantic or indeed moral content, like "all things come in threes," "bad luck," "an irony of fate," "crime doesn't pay" or "every cloud has a silver lining" require certain formal plot structures—the repetition of similar events, or the addition of unexpected endings—for them to be embodied in a text.

Other authors, distinctly opposed to these structural definitions of the concept but still resistant to the idea of "thematic material," view the theme as essentially dependent upon interpretative activity. Thus, for Shlomith Rimmon-Kenan, theme functions as a label, unifying under a common denominator diverse aspects of a literary text; for Menachem Brinker, theme consists in "the principle of a possible grouping-together of texts"; while in Claude Bremond's quite similar opinion, a critic who chooses a theme is "making a wager on the structure of the text."[5] According to Philippe Hamon, the theme is "what allows us to speak about and indeed *to* the work, to summon it, to make it appear in and in front of a meta-discourse."[6] Made possible by structure but not reducible to it, theme is the smallest hermeneutic unit of a text, a vacant potential inscribed within it, offering itself to our attention, activated by the latter and by nothing else.

This position is defended at the second conference by Claude Bremond, who applies it to the reader's progressive decoding of the text; by Jean-Marie Schaeffer, who analyzes the interaction of theme, genre and text in the development of the Faust legend; and by Inge Crossman Wimmers, who situates the theme at the intersection of text and act of reading. Even modern musicologists like Françoise Escal and Jean-Yves Bosseur can, it seems, only conceive of theme as a hermeneutical nucleus: they show how the semantic approach tends to combine with, or indeed these days to replace, the musical thematics of yesteryear.

To think of theme as a function of interpretative activity means positing a variety of attention attracted to the subject matter of a text, or the representation in a painting, rather than the way in which the story is told or the picture painted; we may call this kind the *aboutness attention*—or, more simply, *referential attention*.

Theme thus finds a definition where *referential attention* meets the *aboutness* of the work. But this definition is not sufficient: it cannot hope to solve every problem in thematics, as *aboutness* is not given once and for all, independently of the attention which reveals it. Like a zoom camera, referential attention has an adjustable aperture for various levels of generality, with the disturbing consequence that the same text (say, Racine's *Phèdre*) can be seen to thematize a whole range of topics equally well: from the particular family problems of Minos' descendants, or incest in general, to the dangers inherent in any passion (as Racine implies in his preface) and even the whole predicament of our fallen nature (as described by Arnauld and the Messieurs of Port-Royal). How then are we to avoid the pitfall of logical hierarchies, contained within each and every sense impression? What is the optimal degree of concreteness to which the referential attention should be set, if we are to capture the theme or themes of a work?

Sometimes, of course, texts convey this to us by themselves: a medieval Morality play clearly demands a different thematic concreteness from that of a Ponge poem. But in other cases, the text says nothing—at least, not overtly—or contradicts itself and covers its tracks. And readers, for their part, are not forced to obey the text's suggestions or injunctions: they may reject the menu and read *à la carte*. A reader of *Le Corbeau et le Renard* decided (according to Nisard) that "the moral is in the cheese." We may laugh, but this will always be the point of view of a camembert-maker in search of a label for his little round boxes.

Less prosaically, the reader is perfectly entitled to avoid an explicit offer made by the text and find some other theme, all the more significant for being concealed. Attention is not like a searchlight, sweeping across the entire perceptual field; instead it chooses certain subjects, treasuring these at the expense of others. To concern oneself with an object, to pay attention to it, means taking an interest in that object, identifying with it. It captivates our eye, fascinating us, returning indefatigably to the heart of the visual field. The reader's interest is not permanently tethered to the general aboutness of a work, but treats itself to escapades, making for secondary aspects and marginal details. One may, for example, attempt to calculate the spatial and temporal coordinates of a text, as Victor Bérard uses the *Odyssey* to map a Mediterranean journey, as an Arabist looks for references to coffee with which to date tales from the *Arabian Nights,* or as Bernard Berenson looks at a painting's idiosyncratic treatment of details, rather than the main topic, in order to decide to whom it should be attributed. The desire to chart the diffusion of oral traditions, their circuitous journeys through space and through time, is probably what made folklorists interested in motifs in the first place; it thus—via Veselovsky, and Propp's critique of Veselovsky—informs our own reflections on the theme.

Thematics should not be viewed exclusively in terms of a work's aesthetic aims. If the criterion of "aboutness" is preserved, thematic research can just as easily lead to a symptomatology (psychoanalytical or documentary) as to a *topics*, or indeed to the study of ideologies—depending on what we are interested in, and the goals we set ourselves. If our aim is to discover themes incorporated by the artist, we will use historical evidence to support our interpretations: a reading which sees *Tamburlaine* as a reflection on absolute power finds confirmation in Machiavelli's *Prince*. If, on the other hand, our reading freely follows the themes which interest us, we are no longer constrained to be faithful to the writer or the period: like avant-garde directors manipulating texts to suit themselves, Roland Barthes highlights erotic and linguistic themes which a seventeenth-century audience can never have noticed in Racine. Barthes' readings may be lacking in historical plausibility, but—like the productions of Roger Planchon—they indicate the taste and concerns of our contemporaries.

To modernize a text means, among other things, shaking up its thematic hierarchy. The original audiences of Racine's *Bérénice* and Corneille's rival *Tite et Bérénice* must surely have thought that both tragedies dealt with the conflict between love and duty to the state. The silences of Titus in *Bérénice*, Racinian silences in marked contrast to that imperturbable Cornelian loquacity, certainly played a minor role—just symptoms of his inner turmoil and the fear of driving Bérénice to despair, or a mark of the difficulty unhappy love has in expressing itself. In Barthes, these silences take center stage: in 1963, Racine's play—following in the wake of Beckett and Ionesco, it is tempting to add—becomes a tragedy of *aphasia*, of impossible self-expression. Love disappears, along with duty: there is, says Barthes, no tangible evidence that Titus is in love with the woman he abandons. Now the reason this reading is attractive is, it might be said, precisely that it presupposes a normal interpretation, one which it overturns pleasurably. Barthes himself is hardly intent on *proving* the validity of his interpretation: he presents it as a sally, as a thrilling ride.

A thrilling ride which ends up undermining the stability of the text. At which point we may immediately challenge the criterion of *referential aboutness*, under suspicion of enslaving the work of art to goals which lie outside it, and concentrate instead on the movement of an attention with no fixed object. Rather than negating the theme, this actually generates exciting new thematic possibilities. To borrow an example from Arthur Danto (with slight modifications), let us imagine a series of paintings in an art gallery, all by the same artist, each one consisting of a square of canvas uniformly covered with red paint.[7] The title of the first is *The Crossing of the Red Sea:* the Children of Israel have all crossed over, and Pharaoh's forces have drowned. The second is *Red Square,* "a clever bit of Moscow landscape"; the third, *Nirvana,* is a metaphysical evocation; the fourth, by way of a homage to Matisse, is called *Red Table Cloth.* In an exemplary manner, thematics (in the sense of aboutness) is detached from material and structure—as well, perhaps, as aesthetic intention itself. A connoisseur might well be prepared to appreciate the rout of the Egyptians, so brilliantly rendered in the first canvas, the calm strength of the Kremlin in the second, the intensity of the third's Schopenhauerian vision and the exuberant energy of the sensible world in the last; the fact remains that none of these themes is intuitively received as the theme of the given work. What the viewer sees first and foremost is the *discrepancy* between the aboutness suggested in the title and the work that is supposed to illustrate it: not only thanks to each one's intrinsic lack of motivation, but also because the four of them cancel each other out, neither being any more or less motivated than the other three.

Of course, such a perfect elimination of aboutness from an artwork is itself bound to capture the thematic attention, as the latter casts about for an object; with the result that this series of paintings may ultimately be taken to thematize the disparity between a work and its model, very much in keeping with theories of conceptual art. Where, indeed, are we to situate material, structure and hermeneutic intention here? Should we begin by identifying the material with the biblical subject, the kind of thing that might have been set in the nineteenth century as a topic for the *prix de Rome?* If this is the material of the piece, could the square of red paint which supposedly represents the scene be called its structure? Let us assume for a moment that this is the case and that the hermeneutic intention decides to restrict its field of vision, opting for a interpretation that docilely accepts the indication in the title, reading the canvas as if it did in fact evoke the Crossing of the Red Sea. This position involves the isolation of a single painting from the group, and as such cannot be held long: the coexistence of the four images, identical in form but different in aboutness, soon dismisses it as a key to comprehension.

The hermeneutic attention has another course open to it: to switch around the "form" and the "material." Depending on the title it is given, the thematic material (a red square of paint) takes on a different form; in this new perspective, the titles become conceptual variations on the "red square of paint" theme. The square, in other words, becomes the *aboutness,* the thematic material upon which the power of a form, or of a cultural stereotype, may be tested. As for the hermeneutic attention, its task is now to extract the unifying principle from the series, the common denominator or "common place" of the four paintings in question.

This position also turns out to be unstable. If it were one of those tests in the magazines—"What, in your opinion, does this red square suggest most? 1) . . . , 2) . . . , 3) . . . or 4) . . . ?"—we could certainly accept it; the aim of the hermeneutic attention in this hypothesis is, after all, purely ludic: a test is not perceived as a work of art. But the location of these canvases—in an exhibition at an art gallery—demands that the hermeneutic attention preserve an aesthetic aim, tend toward an aboutness which rules out "The Crossing of the Red Sea" (material put into form by means of a square of red paint) just as much as it rules out "Red Square of Paint" (material put into form by means of the Crossing-of-the-Red-Sea concept). All that remains at this point to be made into a theme is the very reversibility of theme and variation. Better put, it is the hermeneutic attention itself—behind this reversibility— which becomes a third-level theme, as it oscillates between two formal variations: the *primary* attention designating the title as the theme and the painting as a formal variation upon it; the *secondary* attention designating the quadruple canvas as the theme, and the captions as its formal variations.

This example, which has much in common with some of the pieces discussed by Jean-Yves Bosseur, brings to light a striking feature of many intentional structures, namely the radical reversibility of their determinations. Elements which, under certain conditions, appear to be part of the material belong, at other times, to the structure; the converse is also true. There are thus situations in which the mind serves as a body for the body, or in which the body becomes the mind of the mind. Material and design may also, on occasion, acquire an intentional dignity; conversely, intentional configurations may be demoted to the status of design or even material, as in the face of the Mona Lisa to which the modernist added a moustache.

The fever of such reversals, at a time when all arts are practicing them, may go some way to explaining the success of so-called *self-referential* poetics, as well as the contempt evinced by recent theorists for notions of mimesis, representation and thematics—thematics, that is, in the sense of what would have to be called "hetero-referential" aboutness—any idea, in short, which misguidedly seems to stabilize this intentional effervescence. Radical reversibility, even when accepted as a permanent possibility of aesthetic practice, is not, for all that, forced to become its mandatory norm. Rather, we should preserve the priority given to those intentional structures which are traditionally seen as "well-made," a priority which is logical as well as historical, legitimate as well as effective. Only what has been stood, and understood, the right way up can then be turned on its head. For a moustache to be added to the Mona Lisa's face, da Vinci needs to have painted her; it is only because the collective imagination has been filled for so long with more sensible narratives that the impossible stories of Allais and Barthelme can today be told. Such sophisticated games may well appear to cock a snook at normality and norms, but artistic theory and artistic practice are always rooted in them. They can be subverted, but never erased; they may be ridiculed, but never ignored.

It follows from all this that poetics and aesthetics simply cannot keep feeding off intentional notions, while pretending to ignore them. We cannot, without contradiction, eliminate readerly attention *and* thematic aboutness (whether hetero- or self-referential) from the meaning of a text, in order to replace them with formal notions. These may seem fairly neutral at first; but were it not for their secret revenues, accrued from intentional-referential investments, they would literally remain insignificant. What's bred in the theme comes out in the text.

Secondly, the protean character of the theme must clearly be put up with—or better yet, put to good use. To fix it once and for all, in a definition at once universal and operational, is, it turns out, as hopeless a quest as that of defining the *object* to the philosopher's satisfaction as well as to that of the physicist. While the former is happy to work with such general but vague determinations as the "correlative of intention" or the "value of a variable," the latter manages by simply adjusting the definition as the need arises. It is therefore in our best interests to speak, as some do, of *thematic fields,* a concept which allows us to carry out detailed analyses; on condition, however, that these fields guarantee a minimum level of consistency, that the aim of each inquiry be clearly apparent, and that the elements that form the thematic base in question be compatible with both.

The idea of a dissertation on glass objects in Proust has given rise to a certain amount of hilarity; but at least this field's consistency is assured, given that nobody doubts the unity of inspiration behind that particular *opus*. Perhaps for want of a subtitle—"A Study of X"—the aim of this inquiry is less apparent, though it is possible to imagine various hypothetical issues, like the art and industry of cut glass in turn-of-the-century France. In this instance, a suitable thematic base would be formed by a list of all glass objects, classified by their position: whether decorating tables and mantlepieces, hanging from the ceiling, or whatever. Alternatively, we might decide that it is a psychoanalytic study in the Gaston Bachelard style, or a thematic piece *à la* Jean-Pierre Richard—at which point, the whole question of the thematic base needs to be reconsidered. For on the one hand, references to glass objects may, in certain contexts, seem totally insignificant; and on the other hand, objects not made of glass—even sensations, for that matter, or states of mind—may be assimilated into the category by virtue of their transparency, sharpness, sparkle, fragility and other glasslike qualities.

To thematize in this sense is neither to itemize existing themes nor to create new ones *ex nihilo*, but to go through untried possibilities one by one. That part of the work which appears, on each successive occasion, to be its aboutness is only the potential object of a thematizing attention. The contours and reliefs of thematic fields are shaped and reshaped with every movement interpretation makes; this does not, however, mean that interpretive licence knows no bounds. Every *Mont Sainte-Victoire* Cézanne painted still remains a *Mont Sainte-Victoire*, in spite of the variations in line and color.

To some extent, then, texts are like dunes, exposed to the winds of the desert; but then dunes are not designed, right from the start, to attract the attention of a reader. The aboutness of a work may have an almost infinite range of possibilities, but this is not to say that all thematizations are equal: their nature and quality are in fact determined by a number of criteria. As far as the work itself is concerned, the possibilities it contains are qualified by the constellation of "self-thematizing" components, through which the work conveys various potential themes—none of which, of course, is absolutely binding. These elements themselves run the gamut of ambiguity: explicit or implicit, suggested or secreted, discredited or denied—as are love and duty in *Bérénice*, or the thirst for temporal power in *Tamburlaine*. Thematizations are further conditioned by an indefinite number of elements—like the structure of *Tamburlaine*, or the aphasia of Titus—which appear to be semiotically neutral but which are, or can be, organized; and which anyone may turn into meaningful themes, according to their point of view.

At the other end—in terms, that is, of the attention focused on the work—thematization depends on the means and the ends of individual interpreters. This means, first of all, the nature and intensity of their interests, the interpretative systems they decide to bring to bear and the value of the methodological apparatus which is used to locate, conceptualize, formulate, order and interpret these potential themes. Finally, and most importantly—a point which should not be underestimated—there is the rigor with which these operations are carried out. Thus, depending on the interpreter's receptivity to the signals sent out by the text, as well as the value of the chosen interpretative systems and the shrewdness with which they are employed, we may divide thematizations into the abundant and the impoverished, the slapdash and the methodical, the spontaneous and the contrived, the rigid and the supple, the sensible and the daft—and even, perhaps, the realistic and the real.

Thirdly, we should not be afraid to use the concepts of norm and normality, since the supposedly subversive aesthetic theories which stress their limits, conceived as they are to justify ephemeral artistic practices, all presuppose them as the very conditions of their existence. We should doubt-

less bear in mind (in the wake of Deconstruction) that aboutness is not
imprinted in the text once and for all according to the wishes of the author,
and that representation and mimesis do not lay down the law when it comes
to interpretation. But this being said, thematic research would be well ad-
vised—if only for the sake of its methodology—to start from the primary
layers of message production: to favor, among the mass of literary and
artistic games, those referential aspects which are most brought out by the
texts themselves.

Thematics, thus construed, should place itself at the heart of interpretive
activity. It should not limit itself to defining the most profitable strategies for
inventory-making, but should try to use more general conceptual frameworks.
Thus, along the lines of the thematic field, we might consider redefining the
thematic universe, giving an aged concept a new lease on life.

The metaphor of the universe, whose advantages for the study of fiction
have already been demonstrated by Umberto Eco, Lubomír Doležel, Marie-
Laure Ryan and others, could well serve as a common horizon for various
thematic approaches. Each interpretation projects a kind of hypothetical world
in which its truth prevails, a world in which the aboutness of the text, as
summoned by the critical attention, finds its ideal habitat. We are, of course,
not referring to *the* fictional world of a given work, but to the *various* thematic universes that critical readings draw from it. Each of these thematic
universes possesses its own *index of curvature,* its own inflexion which sets it
apart from the others and which lends the thematic reading its weight and
consistency. This being so, however, the inductive method—capturing the
myriad thematic elements of a given text within the frame of the attention, so
as subsequently to derive the specific inflexions of the universe that contains
them—is neither the most efficient nor the most effective way to go about it.
It is just as legitimate to start from the other end, with an investigation into
the basic principles of the thematic universe in question, and to derive its
specific properties deductively, properties on whose distinctiveness the more
concrete thematic choices will ultimately, in large part, depend.

Never overt, the hypothetical universe hides behind a shield of anecdotic
themes, the conditions for whose existence are defined by its categories: time,
space, causality and so on. To describe these categories, to grasp their silent
singularity may, at times, appear to come down to the over-thematization of
certain scattered and indeed barely visible pieces of evidence; often, however,
when this operation is complete, a set of anecdotic themes and structural
characteristics which we once assumed we understood suddenly takes on a
range of new meanings.

Whether it proceeds deductively—starting from hypothetical universes—
or inductively (from hermeneutical or textual nuclei), thematic analysis, after

taking the credit for all transpositions of material, structure and intention, must become again on center stage what it has never stopped being behind the scenes: a privileged moment of the critical process. If we are going to engage in it, we might as well do so openly.

NOTES

What is Theme?

1. All these formulations are too superficial to capture the complex themes of *Madame Bovary*, but they are sufficient for my purpose here.

2. One should also remember that Giora does not fully explore the notion of discourse topic in this paper, because it is subordinate to her main subject, namely coherence.

3. I label 'external focalization' what Genette calls 'non-focalized récit,' for reasons I give in *Narrative Fiction* (138, n.6).

4. I am grateful to Prof. H. M. Daleski and to Drs. Moshe Ron and Yael Ziv for their help.

From Motif to Function and Back Again

1. Vladimir Propp, *Morphology of the Folktale*, tr. Laurence Scott, Austin & London: University of Texas Press, 1968, p. 20.
For the sake of consistency, I have amended the spelling of Veselóvskij's name. [Editor's note.]

2. Ibid., p. 113.
Laurence Scott carefully replaces 'subject' with 'theme'; I have restored the original confusion. [Editor's note.]

3. Ibid., p. 12.

4. Viktor Shklovsky, *Theory of Prose*, tr. Benjamin Sher, Elmwood Park, IL: Dalkey Archive Press, 1990, p. 16.

5. Boris Tomashevsky, "Thematics," *Russian Formalist Criticism: Four Essays*, tr. Lee T. Lemon and Marion J. Reis, Lincoln: University of Nebraska Press, 1965: 61–98, p. 67.

6. Ibid., p. 68.
The word 'fabula' has been added, in the interests of clarity. [Editor's note.]

7. *Grove's Dictionary of Music and Musicians,* 5th edition, ed. Eric Blom, London: Macmillan, 1954, v. 8, p. 409.

8. Ibid., v. 3, p. 90.
Once again, I have had to amend the text: here, from 'figures' to 'motifs.' [Editor's note.]

9. L. C. Knights, *Some Shakespearean Themes,* London: Chatto & Windus, 1960, p. 66.

Theme and Interpretation

1. Iurii K. Shcheglov, "Towards a Description of Detective Story Structure," *Russian Poetics in Translation* 1 (Colchester: University of Essex, 1975), 51–77.

2. L. M. O'Toole, "Analytic and Synthetic Approaches to Narrative Structure: Sherlock Holmes and 'The Sussex Vampire,'" in *Style and Structure in Literature,* ed. Roger Fowler (Ithaca: Cornell University Press, 1975), 143–176.

3. Iurii K. Shcheglov and Aleksandr K. Zholkovskii, "Towards a Theme—(Expression Devices)—Text Model of Literary Structure," *Russian Poetics in Translation* 1 (1975): 4–50.

4. Donald Fanger, *Dostoevsky and Romantic Realism* (Cambridge, Mass.: Harvard University Press, 1965).

5. Boris Tomashevsky, "Thematics," in *Russian Formalist Criticism,* ed. Lee T. Lemon and Marion J. Reis (Lincoln: University of Nebraska Press, 1965), 61–95.

6. Northrop Frye, *Anatomy of Criticism* (New York: Atheneum, 1968).

7. Monroe C. Beardsley, *Aesthetics: Problems in the Philosophy of Criticism* (New York: Harcourt, Brace and World, 1958).

8. *Fables of Aesop* (New York: Penguin Books, 1978), 12.

9. Gilbert Ryle, "About," *Analysis* 1 (1933): 10–11; Ryle, "Imaginary Objects," *Proceedings of the Aristotelian Society* (supp) 12 (1933): 18–43.

10. Nelson Goodman, "About," in *Problems and Projects* (Indianapolis: Bobbs-Merrill, 1972), 246–272.

11. John R. Searle, "The Logical Status of Fictional Discourse," in *Expression and Meaning* (Cambridge: Cambridge University Press, 1979), 58–75.

12. John Hospers, "Implied Truths in Literature," *Journal of Aesthetics and Art Criticism* 19 (1960): 37–46.

13. Nelson Goodman, "Metaphor as Moonlighting," *Critical Inquiry* 6.1 (1979): 125–130.

14. Menachem Brinker, "Verisimilitude, Conventions and Beliefs," *New Literary History* 14.2 (1983): 253–267.

15. Susan R. Suleiman, *Authoritarian Fictions: The Ideological Novel as a Literary Genre* (New York: Columbia University Press, 1983).

16. Benjamin Hrushovski, "Integrational Semantics: An Understander's Theory of Meaning in Context," in *Contemporary Perceptions of Language: Interdisciplinary Dimensions*, ed. Heidi Byrnes (Washington, D.C.: Georgetown University Press, 1982), 156–190.

17. Viacheslav Ivanov, *Freedom and the Tragic Life: A Study in Dostoyevsky* (New York: Noonday Press, 1957).

18. Nikolai A. Berdiaev, *Dostoievsky: An Interpretation*, trans. Donald Attwater (New York: Sheed and Ward, 1934).

19. Gyorgy Lukács, *Der russische Realismus in der Weltliteratur* (Berlin: Aufbau-Verlag, 1948); English trans.: Lukács, "Dostoevsky," in *Dostoevsky: A Collection of Critical Essays*, ed. Rene Wellek (Englewood Cliffs, N.J.: Prentice-Hall, 1962), 146–158.

20. Ludwig Wittgenstein, *Philosophical Investigations* (Oxford: Oxford University Press, n.d.), 193–220.

Thematic Criticism

1. My position here is, I feel, compatible with that of Thomas Kuhn (*The Structure of Scientific Revolutions*, Chicago: Univ. of Chicago Press, 1963) as well as that of Stanley Fish (*Is there a Text in this Class? The Authority of Interpretative Communities*, Cambridge MA: Harvard University Press, 1980).

2. Serge Doubrovsky's *Pourquoi la nouvelle critique? Critique et objectivité* (Paris: Mercure de France, 1963) has granted this term a certain degree of precision.

3. See for example Jean-Paul Weber, *Néo-Critique et Paléo-Critique, ou Contre Picard*, Paris: Pauvert, 1966, p. 13.

4. Raymond Picard, *Nouvelle critique ou nouvelle imposture*, Paris: Pauvert, 1965.

5. See the works cited above (notes 2 and 3).
As for Barthes' 1966 *Critique et vérité* (*Criticism and Truth*, tr. Katrine Pilcher Keuneman, Minneapolis: University of Minnesota Press, 1987), this is not a defence of thematic criticism. [Editor's note.]

6. Gaston Bachelard, *The Poetics of Space*, tr. Maria Jolas, New York: Orion Press, 1964, p. xxviii.

7. Except in Jean-Paul Weber, whose ambitious (not to say overweening) thematics didn't excite that much critical enthusiasm.
There is a playful allusion here to Giraudoux's play *La guerre de Troie n'aura pas lieu:* "The Trojan War Will Not Take Place." [Editor's note.]

8. Bachelard, *The Poetics of Space*, op. cit., p. xxiii.

9. Ibid., p. xv.

10. Ibid., p. xiv.

11. Ibid., p. xi.

12. Ibid.

13. Ibid.

14. Ibid.

15. Ibid., p. xvi.

16. Ibid., p. xv.

17. Ibid., p. xi.

18. Ibid.

19. It is at this point, according to Poulet, that Bachelard moves away from Bergson: durational time gives way to the time of the *cogito*. It is also at this point that Poulet himself "lends his full support to Bachelardian criticism." See *Les chemins actuels de la critique: Colloque de Cerisy, 1966* ("sous la direction de Georges Poulet; édition intégrale mise au point par Jean Ricardou"), Paris: Plon, p. 381.

20. *The Poetics of Space*, op. cit., p. xi.

21. Ibid., p. xii.

22. Ibid.

23. Ibid., p. xviii.

24. Ibid.

25. Georges Poulet, *La conscience critique*, Paris: Corti, 1971, p. 278.

26. Ibid.

27. Ibid., p. 281; italics his.

28. See *Les chemins actuels de la critique*, op. cit., pp. 215–6.

29. Mind you, Shoshana Feldman's *Le scandale du corps parlant* (Paris: Seuil, 1980) does discuss the problem of John Austin's wit.

30. See Roland Barthes, *Le plaisir du texte*, Paris: Seuil, 1973, *passim.*

31. Jean-Pierre Roy, *Bachelard, ou le concept contre l'image*, Montreal: Presses de l'université de Montréal, 1977.

32. See note 19.

33. *Les chemins actuels de la critique*, op. cit., p. 31.

34. Ibid., p. 32.

35. *La conscience critique*, pp. 276–7.

36. *Les chemins actuels de la critique,* op. cit., p. 372.

37. Ibid., p. 378.

38. Ibid.

39. Ibid., p. 390.

40. This term is taken up by Jean-Pierre Roy in *Bachelard,* op. cit.

41. *Les chemins actuels de la critique,* op. cit., pp. 388–9.

42. Ibid., p. 378.

43. See his *Néo-Critique et Paléo-Critique,* op. cit., p. 19: "How did we come up with the concept of theme, the idea of a single theme, this monothematism which differs so radically from the polythematism of Bachelard, Poulet, Richard and company?" Indeed, one wonders . . .

44. See Hans-Georg Gadamer, *Truth and Method,* tr. Garrett Barden & John Cumming, New York: Continuum, 1975.

45. See for example Hans-Georg Gadamer, *Philosophical Hermeneutics,* tr. David E. Linge, Berkeley: University of California Press, 1977, p. 7: "the formulation 'I and thou' already betrays an enormous alienation. There is nothing like an 'I and thou' at all—there is neither the I nor the thou as isolated, substantial realities. I may say 'thou' and I may refer to myself over against a thou, but a common understanding *[Verständigung]* always precedes these situations. We all know that to say 'thou' to someone presupposes a deep common accord *[tiefes Einverständnis]*."

46. See *Truth and Method,* op. cit., p. 355: "The understanding is entirely taken up with what is being written about." cf. also ibid., p. 236: "All correct interpretation must . . . direct its gaze on 'the things *[Sachen]* themselves' . . . It is clear that to let the object take over in this way is not a matter for the interpreter of a single decision, but is 'the first, last and constant task.'"

47. In *Truth and Method* Gadamer talks of "what is said" (*das Gesagte,* p. 333), and of what is understood, transmitted (p. 336).

48. See *Truth and Method,* op. cit., pp. 267 et seq.

A Thematics of Motivation and Action

1. Vernon characterizes Murray's themes as "patterns of press, need and action" (1969, 101).

2. Holton holds a similar view with regard to the phylogeny of scientific themes: "A scientist's thematic imagination is fashioned in the period before he becomes a professional. Some of the most fiercely held themata are evident even in childhood" (1978, 23).

3. The holistic strategy is explicitly formulated by Murray: *"By the observation of many parts one finally arrives at a conception of the whole and, then, having grasped the latter, one can reinterpret and understand the former"* (1938, 605, italics Murray's).

4. I concur with Prince (1985) that the concept of thematization should be at the very heart of thematics. However, our approaches differ in that Prince conceives of thematization as an interpretive procedure dependent pragmatically on the thematizer ("thématisateur"), while for me thematization is a semantic procedure regulated by functional pragmatics.

5. This formulation is in keeping with contemporary motivational psychology which, in contrast to the "traditional episodic view of behavior," "stresses the continuity of behavior and of its underlying motivational structure" (Atkinson and Birch 1978, 361).

6. With this modification, Vernon has no qualms about accepting 'homeostatic motivation' into the set of human motivational factors (see 1969, 36–40).

7. The conception of emotions as passions, which goes back to Descartes, has been lucidly explained by Danto: "Whatever may be the reason, the will is (which means that *we* are) impotent to *do* our feelings: we are in *their* grip (slaves of passion), and though we may dissolve them or induce them through causes, and so attain a degree of indirect mastery over them, we are, basically, impotent to have or not to have them" (1973, 151).

8. In Meursault's thematization, the killing has zero motivation: it is interpreted as a nature event.

9. Motivational thematization of action is in fact analogous and complementary to functional (Proppian) thematization. The difference lies in the nature of the "interpretant": motivational thematization relates the action to its mental conditions, whereas the Proppian links it to a higher-order (story) structure. As a function, the action of killing might be "harm caused by the villain," say, or "victory over the villain" or "a helper's assistance."

10. Incidentally, narrative theory shares this thematization procedure with psychoanalysis. Psychoanalytic themes—such as representation, transference and sublimation—are derived from conflicts of/in motivation. The parallel between the narrative and the psychoanalytic thematization of mental life is not at all surprising. At present, interpretations of Freudianism as a literary (poietic) or fictional representation abound (see, for example, Mahony 1982, Brooks 1984, Bloom 1985, Geha 1988). Some of these interpretations are marred by a radically idealistic epistemology which does not allow for a distinction between truth and falsity, reality and fiction, dreaming and waking.

11. Displacement occurs when aggression is directed "towards someone who is not its initial cause" (Vernon 1969, 67).

The Bluish Tinge in the Halfmoons

*This essay is part of a thematic study entitled *Neither Black Nor White and Yet Both*, to be published by Oxford University Press. Its presentation was inspired by the collection, *The Return of Thematic Criticism* (Cambridge, Mass.: Harvard University Press, 1993; Harvard English Studies 18), and most especially the essay by Francesco Orlando. The evidence was accumulated in reading literature "about" black-white romances and families over the years. While single instances of the telltale fingernails have caught the attention of interpreters (e.g., Pettit and Trotter), I am not aware of any secondary literature that investigates the motif comparatively. Maxine Senn-Yuen and Lauren Gwin provided very valuable and imaginative research assistance. I am grateful for questions and suggestions I received from colleagues and students at the Tudor Room, Johns Hopkins University and at the W. E. B. Du Bois Institute, Harvard University, as well as from Alide Cagidemetrio, Heather Hathaway, and Thomas Pavel.

1. Eugène Sue, *Les Mystères de Paris* (1843; repr. Paris: Marpon et Flammarion, 1879), I: 154; ch. xxi; Engl. based on anon. trans. (New York: Peter Fenelon Collier and Son, 1900), 175.

2. Dion Boucicault, *The Octoroon* (1859; repr. Upper Saddle River, N.J.: Literature House, 1970), 16–17.

3. Theodor Storm, "Von jenseit des Meeres" (1865; repr. *Gedichte, Novellen, 1848–1867*, ed. Dieter Lohmeier, Frankfurt: Deutscher Klassiker Verlag, 1987), 655.

4. Rudyard Kipling, "Kidnapped" (1887), *Plain Tales from the Hills*, ed. H. R. Woudhuysen, intr. David Trotter (Harmondsworth and New York: Penguin, 1987), 134.

5. MS. Twain, Box 37 DV 128 no. 4, "The Man with Negro Blood," cited by Arthur G. Pettit, in *Pudd'nhead Wilson and Those Extraordinary Twins*, ed. Sidney E. Berger (New York and London: W. W. Norton, 1980), 347; *Pudd'nhead Wilson*, 70.

6. Gertrude Atherton, *Senator North* (New York and London: John Lane, 1900), 94–95.

7. Dorothy Canfield, *The Bent Twig* (New York, 1915), 72.

8. William Faulkner, *Collected Stories* (New York: Random House, n.d.), 222, 218.

9. Fannie Hurst, *Imitation of Life* (New York and London: Harper, 1933), 143.

10. Frank Yerby, *The Foxes of Harrow* (New York: Dial Press, 1946), 268.

11. Menachem Brinker, "Theme and Interpretation," *The Return of Thematic Criticism* (Cambridge, Mass.: Harvard University Press, 1993, Harvard English Studies 18), 21–37. Brinker argues that "the quest for the theme or themes *of* a story is

always a quest for something that is not unique to this specific work. The theme is understood as potentially uniting different texts" (21).

12. René Wellek and Austin Warren, *Theory of Literature*, third ed. (New York: Harcourt, Brace & World, 1968), 260.

13. Barbara Herrnstein Smith, "Narrative Versions, Narrative Theories," *Critical Inquiry* 7.1 (Autumn 1980): 219.

14. See the response to this kind of question given by Francesco Orlando in his investigation of " 'Topoi' of Realism: The Metamorphosis of Colors," *The Return of Thematic Criticism*, 209–216.

15. See David Perkins, "Literary History and the Themes of Literature," *The Return of Thematic Criticism*, 115.

16. Joachim Schulze has offered some provocative thoughts on the tension in thematological work between systematic and historical approaches: he focuses on the incompatibility of studying constants and of investigating the historical unfolding of variants, concluding that the thematic school he focuses on most closely, Hellmuth Petriconi's, seems to be rather a "systematic" discipline, not a "historical one," even though it arranges its evidence chronologically and is therefore "annalistic." Schulze calls attention to some analogous difficulties in Tynyanov's concept of genre history. See "Geschichte oder Systematik? Zu einem Problem der Themen- und Motivgeschichte," *Arcadia* 10.1 (1975): 76–82.

17. Kate Chopin, "The Father of Désirée's Baby," *Vogue* (14 January 1893), 70.

18. Ross Lockridge, Jr., *Raintree County* (Boston: Houghton Mifflin, 1948), 488.

19. Claude McKay, *A Long Way From Home* (1937; repr. New York: Harcourt, Brace & World, 1970), 110–111. Perhaps it deserves mention that, with the exception of Frank Yerby, all Afro-American authors who have, to my knowledge, used the motif of the fingernails as a racial sign have done so in order to question the existence of such a mark. In addition to the texts discussed here, this is also the case in Nella Larsen's novel *Passing* (1929), in which the protagonist Irene Redfield reflects in an interior monologue:

> Did that woman, could that woman, somehow know that here before her very eyes on the roof of the Drayton sat a Negro?
>
> Absurd! Impossible! White people were so stupid about such things for all that they usually asserted that they were able to tell; and by the most ridiculous means: fingernails, palms of hands, shapes of ears, teeth, and other equally silly rot. They always took her for an Italian, a Spaniard, a Mexican, or a Gypsy. Never, when she was alone, had they even remotely seemed to suspect that she was a Negro.

Nella Larsen, *Passing* (1929), repr. in *An Intimation of Things Distant: The Collected Fiction of Nella Larsen*, ed. Charles R. Larson (New York: Doubleday, 1992), 178.

20. Frances Parkinson Keyes, *Crescent Carnival* (New York: Franklin Watts, 1942), 253.

21. Edith Pope, *Colcorton* (New York: Charles Scribner's, 1944), 151, 286, 203.

22. Chester Himes, *If He Hollers Let Him Go* (1945; repr. New York: New American Library, n.d.), 155–156.

23. Sinclair Lewis, *Kingsblood Royal* (New York: Random House, 1947), 70, 72, 73.

24. Robert Penn Warren, *Band of Angels* (New York: Random House, 1955), 78.

25. Miss M. E. Braddon, *The Octoroon* (New York: Optimus Printing. Golden Gem Library, n.d.), 6. Braddon originally serialized "The Octoroon; or, The Lily of Louisiana" in *The Halfpenny Journal* sometime between 1861 and 1865.

26. P. Bourget, *Cosmopolis* (New York: Amblard & Meyer Frères, 1895), 195, 196.

27. George Aberigh-Mackay's *Twenty-One Days in India: Being the Tour of Sir Ali Baba, K. C. B.* (1881; 6th ed. London and Calcutta: Thacker, 1898), 119; Trotter called attention to this text and to the identification of the observer in his introduction to Kipling's *Plain Tales*, 20.

28. Atherton, *Senator North*, 95.

29. This relationship of variations to a thematic formation has been reflected on by Claude Bremond, "Concept and Theme," *The Return of Thematic Criticism*, 46–59.

30. For more detailed attempts at developing such models see Marie-Laure Ryan, "In Search of the Narrative Theme," *The Return of Thematic Criticism*, 169–188.

31. Schulze, "Geschichte," 77.

32. Thomas Pavel, "Thematics and Historical Evidence," *The Return of Thematic Criticism*, 121–145. See also the Berkeley student parody issue *Misrepresentations* which argues for the availability of a certain discourse to a New Historicist professor because it appears in the student's diary.

33. When I say "little known" I mean today. Among the contemporary readers was Hans Christian Andersen in faraway Denmark who established his career with a drama based on this story, entitled *Mulatten;* his main detractor must have also read the *Revue de Paris* since he accused Andersen of lacking originality.

34. Mme Charles Reybaud, *Valdepeiras* (1839; repr. Paris: Hachette, 1864), 185.

35. Victor Hugo, *Bug-Jargal* (2nd ed. 1826; repr. ed. Roger Toumson), 307; Engl. trans. Charles Edwin Wilbour, *Jargal* (New York: Carleton, 1846), 192.

36. Ernst Bloch, "Philosophische Ansicht des Detektivromans," *Verfremdungen I* (Frankfurt: Suhrkamp, 1962), 37–63; esp. 38–39.

Sue later explains the term *sang mêlé* in a similar footnote: "Créole issue d'un blanc et d'une quarteronne esclave," *Mystères* I, 153. Probably he means "quarteronne" in the sense of Moreau de Saint-Méry's classification.

37. Médéric-Louis-Élie Moreau de St. Méry, *Description topographique, physique, civile, politique et historique de la partie française de l'Isle Saint-Domingue* (1797; repr. Paris: Société Française d'Histoire d'Outre-Mer, 1984), 73.

38. Moreau draws on, cites, and argues with Buffon, Labat, LeCat, and De Pauw; De Pauw, in turn, cites Labat, Le Cat, and Gumilla; both Buffon and Gumilla invoke the Academy report of 1702; Buffon also argues with De Pauw and cites Le Cat. Hence there is an intertextual trail of footnotes linking Hugo and Moreau to the anatomic discourse of 1702. Most of these texts also contain a genealogical nomenclature of racial mixing, though none as elaborate as Moreau's.

39. Marcello Malpighi, "Epistolae Anatomicae," *Opera Omnia* (1686; repr. Hildesheim and New York: Georg Olms, 1975).

40. "Diverses Observations Anatomiques," published in *Histoire de l'Académie Royale des Sciences* (Paris: Charles-Étienne Hochereau, 1720), 32. The report also notes specifically "que la bout du gland qui n'étoit pas couvert du prépuce étoit noir comme toute la peau, & que le reste qui étoit couvert étoit parfaitement blanc." Moreover M. Littre demonstrated to the Society that the reticular membrane that in itself is black as charcoal seemed to be only as dark as soot when seen through the epidermis. ("M. Littre fit encore voir à la Compagnie que la membrane reticulaire qui en elle-même étoit noire comme du charbon de bois, ne paroissoit noire que comme de la fuye, étant vûë au travers de l'Epiderme.")

41. Le Cat's *Traité de la Couleur de la Peau Humaine en Général, de celle des Negres en Particulier, et de la metamorphose d'une de ces Couleurs en l'autre* (Amsterdam: 1765), 91, has a slightly different version, focusing on the statement that black children (as white children) are born reddish, neither black nor white ("ni noir, ni blanc, mais d'une couleur rougeâtre"). In the case of the black child,

> only at the end of two or three days does his skin begin to darken; but starting from the time of his birth, the root of his nails and his scrotum are black.

The original text reads:

> Un Negrillon qui vient au monde, n'est ni noir, ni blanc, mais d'une couleur rougeâtre. ce n'est qu'au bout de deux ou trois jours que sa peau commence à noirçir; mais dès sa naissance la racine de ses ongles & son scrotum sont noirs. Un Européen en naissant n'est pas blanc non plus, mais rougeâtre comme le Negre. . . . Le tour de la racine des ongles est un endroit où ce

dévelopement de la couleur du Negre est précoce, parce que l'issue des ongles ouvre une espece de porte aux houpes nerveuses (91–92).

Le Cat reasons that the root of the nails opens a kind of door to the nerves ("houpes nerveuses"); again for this author there is an equivalence of fingernails and male genitalia, though he selects the scrotum as the locus of the sign.

The Academy report had pointed out that girls had *only* the fingernail mark; and several of the scholars cited implicitly or explicitly agreed. Bernard Romans, however, in *A Concise and Natural History of East and West Florida*, vol. I (New York, 1775), held that "on the moment of birth in both sexes the exterior part of generatio[n] will shew, whether the person will be black, yellow, brown, red or any other color" (111) and hence makes no mention of the fingernails.

In 1745 the Jesuit Padre Joseph Gumilla referred to the report to the French Academy in order to substantiate his own claim that children of Negroes may be born and remain white for some days but always have a black spot at the end of their nails. Padre Joseph Gumilla, S.J., *El Orinoco Ilustrado, y Defendido...* (Madrid: Manuel Fernandez, 1745), I: 82. The original reads: "Al nacer aquellos niños son blancos por algunos dias, lo que sucede tambien à los negrillos; y es digno de saberse, que assi como los hijos de los Negros nacen con su pinta negra en las extremidades de las uñas, como muestra de los que luego seràn." Gumilla also thought that newborn Indians had a similar identifying mark, a circular spot on their backs. According to Gumilla, the nails of newly born children thus served as early clues to their racial identity that was otherwise not yet clearly visible.

42. Buffon, *Natural History, General and Particular* (1749–88), Smellie transl., III: 200–201, 217. Buffon's section "On the Varieties of the Human Species" [1785] directly draws on the report to the Academy of 1702.

43. Labat, *Nouveau Voyage aux Isles de l'Amérique...* (Paris: Delespine, 1742), II: 188–189: "[la preuve] plus aisée: c'est de regarder à la naissance des ongles, cest-à-dire, à l'endroit où les ongles sortent de la chair, car si on remarque que cet endroit soit noir, c'est une marque infaillible que l'enfant sera noir; mais si cette place est blanche ou presque blanche, on peut dire avec certitude que l'enfant est Mulâtre, soit qu'il provienne d'un Blanc & d'une Négresse, ou d'une Blanche & d'un Négre." The marginal comment reads: "Comment on connoît un enfant mulâtre d'avec un noir."

44. An anonymous reviewer in the *Critical Review* 9 (1760): 82, for example, quotes the following "sensible and curious remarks":

> Here, then, it must be observed, in the first place, that the children of the Negroes come out white from their mother's womb, like ours, and have no blackness at all, except about their privities, and a small black circle about their nails, next to the flesh; that of the rest of their bodies being contracted gradually after the birth, in twenty-four hours by some, and by others in a week, more or less.

The reference to this review appears in Winthrop D. Jordan, *White over Black: American Attitudes Toward the Negro, 1550–1812* (1968; repr. Baltimore: Penguin, 1969), 248–249. Jordan also writes: "The concept of degeneration from primitive whiteness was seemingly confirmed by a curious phenomenon: Negro babies are born considerably lighter than they shortly become, a fact which many eighteenth-century writers noted with almost gleeful interest" (Jordan 248–249). He cites the following texts as evidence: Sloane, *Voyage to the Islands* (1707–25) I, liii; Smith, *Natural History of Leeward Islands*, 231; Le Cat, *Traité de la Couleur de la Peau*, 91; Romans, *Florida*, 111; John Hunter, *An Inaugural Dissertation . . .* (Edinburgh, 1775), trans. Bendyshe, in his *Treatises of Blumenbach*, 372; Blumenbach, *Natural Variety* (1795), in *ibid.*, 211; Buffon, *Natural History*, trans. [Smellie], III, 200; Jansen, ed., *Oeuvres de Pierre Camper*, II, 469–70; Stedman, *Narrative of Expedition*, II, 253. Jordan comments: "These assertions placed the newborns' color at anything from absolutely white to darkish grey or brown; several mentioned that the genitals and/or cuticles of the nails were dark from the beginning. One writer reversed colors by saying Negroes were born black except for their 'privities' and a small circle about the nails, an assertion still current today" (Jordan 249n). There are probably many other instances.

For example, Cornelis de Pauw, drawing on Gumilla and Labat, both of whom he also cites elsewhere in his works, writes in the section "De la couleur des Américains" ("Of the color of Americans") in his *Recherches Philosophiques sur les Américains* (1770) that, at birth, Negro children "are only black at the nails and sometimes at the genitals." See de Pauw, *Recherches Philosophiques sur les Américains . . .* , I (London, 1770), 183. Again, only the former mark of those two is universally and unfailingly present. De Pauw gives a more precise description and explanation than his precursors of the supposed racial sign on the nails:

> c'est un filet noir que les Négrittes & les Négrillons ont à la racine des ongles, dès l'instant de leur naissance. Comme la substance cornée des ongles se durcit dans l'enfant, bien plutôt que la glu de la membrane réticulaire, les ongles peuvent, dans l'endroit où ils compriment le plus l'extrémité du doigt, intercepter quelques atomes noirâtres qui dècoulent du corps interne.

> (There is a black band which, from the moment of their birth, male and female Negro children have at the roots of their nails. Since, in the infant, the horny substance of the nails hardens more quickly than the reticular membrane, the nails can, in the area where they press upon the extremity of the finger, absorb certain blackish atoms which come loose from the inner body.)

The reference to the "reticular membrane" may be echoing the Academy report. De Pauw continues:

> Les Physiciens ont gardé jusqu'à présent un profond silence sur ces deux signes qui caractérisent les enfants des Nègres, soit qu'ils ayent craint de se tromper, en voulant dévoiler les causes encore inconnues de ces phénomènes surprenants, soit qu'ils ayent négligé ces particularités comme indignes d'exercer leurs méditations réservées pour de plus grands objets.

(Doctors have, up to the present, kept a deep silence about these two signs which characterize the children of Negroes, whether because they believe that they might be wrong in wanting to unveil the yet unknown causes of these surprising phenomena, or because they have neglected these peculiarities as unworthy of their reflections, reserved for greater subjects.) (I:183)

45. Friedrich Alexander von Humboldt, *Versuch über den politischen Zustand des Königreichs Neu-Spanien*, vol. 1 (Tübingen: Cotta, 1809), 193, observed the aristocratic sense among whites as a constitutive feature of the American continent when he wrote: "In einem, von Weißen beherrschten, Lande sind die Familien, von welchen man annimmt, daß sie am wenigsten mit Negern- oder Mulatten-Blut vermischt seien, am geehrtesten; so wie as auch in Spanien für eine Art von Adel gilt, weder von Juden noch von Mauren abzustammen" ("In a country dominated by whites families of whom it is assumed that they are least intermingled with Negro or Mulatto blood are those most highly honored; just as it is considered a kind of nobility in Spain to be descended neither from Jews nor Moors"). Humboldt adds that a barefoot white man who mounts a horse believes he belongs to the aristocracy of the land, and that color even generates a sense of equality among whites: thus a common man may address one high above him with the phrase, "do you believe that you are any whiter than I am?" Humboldt also gives a terminological essay on racial crossing.

46. Francis Galton notes in the introduction to *Finger Prints* (London and New York: Macmillan, 1892), 17–18, that his "great expectations" that fingerprints could be used "in indicating Race and Temperament" had been "falsified." Instead he discovered that "English, Welsh, Jews, Negroes, and Basques, may all be spoken of as identical in the character of their finger prints; the same familiar patterns appearing in all of them with much the same degrees of frequency, the differences between groups of different races being not larger than those that occasionally occur between groups of the same race." In the more detailed discussion in chapter 12, however, Galton still battles with his own belief that the marks ought to work as a racial sign; he adds the following qualification to his finding that Negro prints are not different from those of others:

> Still, whether it be from pure fancy on my part, or from the way in which they were printed, the general aspect of the Negro print strikes me as characteristic. The width of the ridges seems more uniform, their intervals more regular, and their courses more parallel than with us. In short, they give an idea of greater simplicity, due to causes that I have not yet succeeded in submitting to the test of measurement. (196)

See also the discussions by Michael Rogin, "Francis Galton and Mark Twain" and Susan Gilman, "Sure Identifiers," both in *Mark Twain's Pudd'nhead Wilson*, eds. Susan Gilman and Forrest G. Robinson (Durham and London: Duke University Press, 1990), esp. 78–80 and 97–100. Earnest Albert Hooton, *Up From the Ape* (New York: Macmillan, 1947), 523–30, relates research suggesting that finger prints may possibly reveal racial affinities but considers the results inconclusive and contradictory; he does not mention nails.

47. Elizabeth Madox Roberts, *My Heart and My Flesh* (1927), 50; this is written as if alluding to the fingernail motif without being specific about its signs while amplifying its associations with the psychology of disgust. Earlier, Theodosia had been "fascinated by her shame" (38) when encountering the black children at Aunt Deesie's house, experiencing a sense of "superiority and loathing, in a delicate nausea experienced when she knelt near the baby's quilt. . . . She knew the half-pleasant disgust felt for the young of another kind, a remote species. Their acts sent little stabs of joy over her, sickly stabs of pleasant contempt and pride" (39).

48. Gustave Flaubert, *Madame Bovary,* édition nouvelle établie par la Société des Études littéraires françaises (Paris: Club de l'Honnête homme, 1971), 62 (i.e. part 1, ch. 2); Engl transl. from *Best-Known Works of Gustave Flaubert* (New York: Blue Ribbon Books, 1904), 9. Twelve other instances of "ongle" and "ongles" are listed in Charles Carlut, Pierre H. Dubé, and J. Raymond Dugan, *A Concordance to Flaubert's Madame Bovary* (New York and London: Garland, 1978), 157.

49. Newbell Niles Puckett, *The Magic and Folk Beliefs of the Southern Negro* (1926; repr. New York: Dover Press, 1969), 457–458. In André Schwarz-Bart's novel *La mulâtresse solitude* (1972, transl. Ralph Mannheim 1973) the fingernails are used to make a sign that signals color: "the old man put down his fingernail on the black skin of his forearm in a gesture that she had seen dozens of times in the course of her short life. It was the *color sign,* which for the whites, blacks, and mulattoes of the du Parc plantation summed up all things here below" (57).

50. Riccardo Di Segni reports the *Acharè Moth*'s interpretation (II 79 a, b) according to which the growth of nails (and hair) is a residue of the impurity the snake introduced following Eve's sin; he also develops an interesting connection between the motif of the fingernail and the veil (as in Exodus 33: 23). See Riccardo Di Segni, *Le unghie di Adama: Studi di antropologia ebraica* (Napoli: Guida editori, 1981), 154, 159.

51. Samuel Monash, "Normal Pigmentation in the Nails of the Negro," *Archives of Dermatology and Syphilology* 25 (1932): 876–881; here 877, 881. Charles B. Davenport, *Heredity of Skin Color in Negro-White Crosses* (Washington, D.C.: Carnegie Institute Publication £ 188, 1913) and Caroline Bond Day, *A Study of Some Negro-White Families in the United States* (Cambridge, Mass.: Peabody Museum of Harvard University, 1932; Harvard African Studies £ 10) do not discuss fingernails in their sections on physiological signs in racially mixed families; Julian Herman Lewis, "Pigmentation of the Nails," *The Biology of the Negro* (Chicago: University of Chicago Press, 1942), 55–57, draws on Monash.

52. Cited in Norman L. Willey, "Exotic Elements in Storm and Sealsfield," *Germanic Review* 13 (1939): 31. This reply puts the fingernail motif into a special category, pretending to refer to "nature" (in the human body that, by the reference to the "moons," seems related to a cosmic order), but in fact referring to cultural beliefs expressed in certain texts for two and a half centuries.

A Semantics for Thematics

1. In a somewhat disparaging manner, Bremond designates this identification of the theme as "journalistic" (Bremond 1982, 138).

2. In both Weisstein (1973) and Jost (1974), Thompson's work is mentioned only in passing.

3. It should be noted that for both authors "internationalism" does not extend beyond the Elbe.

4. As far as thematic criticism is concerned, Bremond's objections should be supplemented with Todorov's earlier critical remarks (Todorov 1970, 102–106).

5. This dichotomy pervades a thematologist's thinking down to the most minute details, as can be seen from the following symptomatic differentiation: "As a literary category, the situation [unlike the 'motif' or the 'action'] is . . . more closely linked to structure than to content and carries relatively little thematological weight" (Weisstein, op. cit., 147).

6. There is no clearer symptom of the immense gap existing between selective and structural thematics than the fact that the proponents of the former are totally unaware of the accomplishments of the latter. Even in the most recent discussions of the theoretical issues of selective thematics (Weisstein 1973 and Jost 1974) the work of Propp is unknown. Trousson ventured into the antechamber of structural thematics, but returned with the reassurance that "le thème ne trouve sa dimension que dans l'histoire, où s'enracine ses incarnations, et dans cette palingénésie que constitue son être même" (Trousson 1980, 8).

7. In order for Emma Bovary and Ivan Karamazov to become compossible, a new fictional world has to be constructed (as in Woody Allen's experiments).

8. The Amphytrion theme has been studied by Perrot (1979) and Dimić (1979). A related medieval theme of two close friends (Amicus-Amelius) has been analyzed in Dimić 1975. Jauss (1979) transfers the theme from *Stoffgeschichte* into *Rezeptionsgeschichte*, thus making explicit the obvious continuity between them.

9. In this respect (and not only in this respect), fictional semantics transcends the standard restrictions of logical semantics. While it has been acknowledged that the logical concept of possibility must be broader than causal or natural possibility (Plantinga 1977, 245), the logical semantics of possible worlds preserves a mild form of essentialism. Thus, for example, Linsky claims that in no possible world could a person become a wiener (Linsky 1977, 148); such alterations can easily affect a fictional individual.

10. The transformation of a human individual into an unspecified *Ungeziefer* occurs in one kind of world, a *hybrid* world, where such events are possible by the very nature of its modal conditions (for a detailed study of Kafka's hybrid world, see Doležel 1984).

11. A theory of authentication is presented in Doležel 1980.

12. In its ambiguous variant, the theme of the double leaves the domain of the fantastic and enters the realm of psychological fiction. It is interesting to note that as a purely psychopathological symptom, the theme returns in the last works of Dostojevski, especially in *The Raw Youth* (1875) and in *The Brothers Karamazov* (1879–1880) (cf. Fischer 1929, 197; Chizhevsky 1962, 117ff.).

13. This position is explicitly defended by Trousson: "La comparaison esthétique des divers traitements du thème fait que les auteurs cessent d'être de simples agents de transmission; l'attention se porte sur leur apport personnel et s'impose ainsi l'analyse étroite de l'oeuvre elle-même pour tenter d'éclairer le processus créateur" (Trousson, op. cit., 4).

Variations on the Theme of Faust

1. *Paul Valéry: Plays*, tr. David Paul & Robert Fitzgerald, New York: Pantheon, 1960, p. 14. For a survey of Faustian literature, see Charles Dedeyan, *Le thème de Faust dans la littérature européenne*, Paris: Lettres Modernes, 1956–61, André Dabezies, *Visages de Faust au XXe siècle*, Paris: PUF, 1967 and *idem, Le mythe de Faust*, Paris: Armand Colin, 1972.

2. This theme is inextricably bound up with Protestant theology, in which the ultimate mortal sin is despair, as this amounts to doubting in the omnipotence of Grace. In Marlowe, despair and defiance form an indivisible whole; it is interesting to note that Kierkegaard, in *The Sickness unto Death*, also sees them as interdependent.

3. See Pedro Calderón de la Barca, *The Prodigious Magician*, tr. Bruce W. Wardropper, Madrid: José Porrúa Turanzas, 1982, ll. 2664–2758.

4. The bet is in any case won in advance: Faust's salvation lies in the simple fact that he is a man and can only act in accordance with his nature, which is nothing other than the thirst for the absolute. Whence, in Goethe, the "Prologue in Heaven," which determines the outcome of the play before it has even started.

5. Disregarding the various difficulties posed by the multiple versions of the text, I quote from the Reclam edition, Stuttgart: Reclam Verlag, 1964.

6. See André Jolles, *Formes simples*, Paris: Seuil, 1972, pp. 46–49.

7. Op. cit., title page.

8. Ibid., p. 152.
I have used the Jerusalem Bible's translation of Peter I, 5: 8–9. [Editor's note.]

9. "The Lament of Doctor Faustus." [Editor's note.]

10. Marlowe knew the German text through an English translation which I have not been able to locate. As to the author of the comic scenes in *Doctor Faustus*, I take no position. I use the name "Marlowe" to designate the author or authors to whom we owe the canonical form of the drama, Version B of 1616.

11. Op. cit., p. 15; translated in 1592 as "studie and speculate the course and order of the elements." *The History of the Damnable Life and the Deserved Death of Doctor John Faustus,* Hildesheim: Georg Olms Verlag, 1985, p. 7.

12. Cf. *Marlowe's Plays and Poems,* London: J. M. Dent and Sons, 1955, p. 122.

13. In the *Historia,* the anti-papal polemic ran counter to the functionality of the anti-legend: in attacking the Pope, Faust was merely acting as a good Lutheran. By making Faustus the accomplice of an anti-pope, Marlowe appears to attenuate this centrifugal effect: Faustus' anti-papal action, now that it is made for the benefit of an anti-pope, seems to remain inscribed within a Catholic strategy and thus be reprehensible from a Protestant point of view. This reading overlooks the fact that the anti-pope really represents clerical submission to royal power—in this instance, the emperor—and thus fits in with the position of English Protestantism on dealings between clerical and lay powers.

14. Numerous ambiguities in Marlowe's text seem to result from this state of affairs; it is therefore superfluous to ascribe a specifically ironic intention to Marlowe (as Robert Ornstein does in "The Comic Synthesis in *Doctor Faustus,*" *Marlowe: "Doctor Faustus," A Casebook,* ed. John D. Jump, London: Macmillan, 1969, pp. 165–172) in order to explain them.

15. See, for example, Harry Levin, "Science Without Conscience," *Marlowe: "Doctor Faustus," A Casebook,* op. cit., 134–164, p. 137; and Nicholas Brooke, "The Moral Tragedy of Doctor Faustus," ibid., 101–133, p. 105.

16. See Gérard Genette, *Palimpsestes,* Paris: Seuil, 1982, p. 35.

17. Ibid., pp. 428–429.

18. Käte Hamburger, "Anachronistische Symbolik: Fragen an Thomas Manns Faustus-Roman," *Fritz Martini zum 60. Geburtstag,* Stuttgart: Metzler Verlag, 1969, pp. 529–553.

19. One should of course distinguish between the hermeneutical function fulfilled by "Faustus" and the modelizing function which characterizes Nietzsche's career. By way of this connection, Nietzsche himself ends up within the Faustian thematics.

20. More commonly known as "wood grouse." [Editor's note.]

Racinian Spaces

1. Claude Bremond and Thomas G. Pavel, "The End of an Anathema," in this volume.

2. Roland Barthes, *On Racine,* tr. Richard Howard, New York: Performing Arts Journal Publications, 1983; see especially pp. 3–8.

3. "Sortons, Paulin: je ne lui puis rien dire." (*Bérénice* II:4.) Jean Racine, *Andromache and Other Plays*, tr. John Cairncross, London: Penguin, 1967, p. 251.

4. "Par un chemin obscur une esclave me guide . . ." (*Bajazet* I:1.) *Bajazet*, tr. Alan Hollinghurst, London: Chatto & Windus, 1991, p. 8.

5. "Sortez. Que le Sérail soit désormais fermé,/Et que tout rentre ici dans l'ordre accoutumé." *Bajazet* II:2, ibid., p. 22.

6. "Où suis-je? Qu'ai-je fait? Que dois-je faire encore?/Quel transport me saisit? Quel chagrin me dévore?/Errante, et sans dessein, je cours dans ce palais." *Andromaque* V:1, *Andromache*, op. cit., p. 102.

"Madame, où courez-vous? Quels aveugles transports/Vous font tenter sur vous de criminels efforts?" *Mithridate* V:1, *Mithridates*, tr. Howard David Spoerl, Tufts College, MA: Tufts College Press, 1926, p. 74.

"Je volais toute entière au secours de son fils;/Et m'arrachant des bras d'Œnone épouvantée . . ." *Phèdre* IV:5, *Phaedra and Other Plays*, tr. John Cairncross, London: Penguin, 1970, p. 197.

7. "Mais qu'est-ce que je voi?/Dieux! Achille?" *Iphigénie* V:1, *Phaedra*, op. cit., p. 115.

8. "Elle me fuit! Veillé-je? ou n'est-ce point un songe?" *Iphigénie* II:7, ibid., p. 83.
"Le Roi vient. Fuyez, Prince, et partez promptement." *Phèdre* V:1, ibid., p. 205.
"Quoi! Prince, vous partiez? Quelle raison subite/Presse votre départ, ou plutôt votre fuite?" *Bérénice* III:1, *Andromache*, op. cit., p. 253.

9. "Venez, venez, ma fille, on n'attend plus que vous . . ." *Iphigénie* IV:4, *Phaedra*, op. cit., p. 101.

10. "N'allons point plus avant. Demeurons, chère Œnone./Je ne me soutiens plus, ma force m'abandonne." *Phèdre* I:3, ibid., p. 155.

11. "Déjà, sur un vaisseau dans le port préparé/Chargeant de mon débris les reliques plus chères,/Je méditais ma fuite aux terres étrangères." *Bajazet* III:3, *Bajazet*, op. cit., p. 36.
"Nos vaisseaux sont tout prêts, et le vent nous appelle." *Andromaque* III:1, *Andromache*, op. cit., p. 77.
"Si vous voulez partir, la voile est préparée." *Phèdre* II:6, *Phaedra*, op. cit., p. 178.

12. Subligny, *La folle querelle* [1668]: *Les contemporains de Molière* III, ed. Victor Tournel, Paris: Firmin-Didot, 1875, p. 515.

13. Alfred de Musset, "Tragedy (In Connection with Mademoiselle Rachel's First Appearance)," *The Complete Writings of Alfred de Musset* IX, tr. Mary W. Artois, New York: Hill, 1905, pp. 308–9.

14. Ibid., pp. 309–310.

15. This metaphor is, of course, taken from modern production techniques: these lighting effects did not exist in the seventeenth century. See S. Wilma Holsbœr, *L'histoire de la mise en scène dans le théâtre français de 1600 à 1657*, Paris: Droz, 1933.

16. "Dans un mois, dans un an, comment souffrirons-nous,/Seigneur, que tant de mers me séparent de vous?" *Bérénice* IV:5, *Andromaque*, op. cit., p. 270.

17. "Oui, puisque je retrouve un ami si fidèle . . ." *Andromaque* I:1, ibid., p. 47.

18. "Tu vis mon désespoir; et tu m'as vu depuis/Traîner de mers en mers ma chaîne et mes ennuis." *Andromaque* I:1, ibid., p. 48.

19. "Captive, toujours triste, importune à moi-même . . ." *Andromaque* I:4, ibid., p. 57;
"Vaincu, chargé de fers, de regrets consumé,/Brûlé de plus de feux que je n'en allumai . . ." *Andromaque* I:4, ibid., p. 58;
"Tout m'afflige et me nuit, et conspire à me nuire." *Phèdre* I:3, *Phaedra*, op. cit., p. 155.

20. "Mes soldats presque nus, dans l'ombre intimidés,/Les rangs de toutes parts mal pris et mal gardés,/Le désordre partout redoublant les alarmes,/Nous-mêmes contre nous tournant nos propres armes,/Les cris que les rochers renvoyaient plus affreux,/Enfin toute l'horreur d'un combat ténébreux . . ." *Mithridate* II:3, *Mithridates*, op. cit., p. 30.

21. "Je n'ai point du silence affecté le mystère . . . /Je n'ai pour lui parler consulté que mon coeur." *Andromaque* II:1, *Andromache*, op. cit., p. 63.

22. "Mon repos, mon bonheur semblait être affermi,/Athènes me montra mon superbe ennemi./Je le vis, je rougis, je pâlis à sa vue;/Un trouble s'éleva dans mon âme éperdue . . ." *Phèdre* I:3, *Phaedra*, op. cit., p. 161.

23. "Un songe (me devrais-je inquiéter d'un songe?)" *Athalie* II:5, ibid., p. 258.

24. "Contre moi-même enfin j'osai me révolter:/J'excitai mon courage à le persécuter." *Phèdre* I:3, ibid., p. 161.
"Tu sais de quel courroux mon coeur alors épris/Voulut en l'oubliant punir tous ses mépris." *Andromaque* I:1, *Andromache*, op. cit., p. 48.

25. "De mes feux mal éteints je reconnus la trace;/Je sentis que ma haine allait finir son cours,/Ou plutôt je sentis que je l'aimais toujours." *Andromaque* I:1, ibid., p. 49;
"Vaines précautions! Cruelle destinée!/Par mon époux lui-même à Trézène amenée,/J'ai revu l'ennemi que j'avais éloigné:/Ma blessure trop vive aussitôt a saigné." *Phèdre* I:3, *Phaedra*, op. cit., p. 161.

26. "C'est Vénus tout entière à sa proie attachée." *Phèdre* I:3, ibid., p. 161.

27. "Puisqu'après tant d'efforts ma résistance est vaine,/Je me livre en aveugle au destin qui m'entraîne./J'aime; je viens chercher Hermione en ces lieux,/La fléchir, l'enlever, ou mourir à ses yeux." *Andromaque* I:1, *Andromache*, op. cit., p. 50;
"Je voulais en mourant prendre soin de ma gloire,/Et dérober au jour une flamme si noire . . ." *Phèdre* I:3, *Phaedra*, op. cit., p. 162.

28. "J'ai déclaré ma honte aux yeux de mon vainqueur,/Et l'espoir, malgré moi, s'est glissé dans mon coeur . . ." *Phèdre* III:1, ibid., p. 181.

29. This is Jacques Scherer's formulation. In *his* explanation, the Abbé d'Aubignac relates this practice to contemporary enthusiasm for on-stage deliberations: "open your Stage, as near, as tis possible, to the Catastrophe, that you may employ less time in the negotiation part, and have more Liberty in extending the Passions and Discourses which may please" (François Hedelin, Abbé d'Aubignac, *The Whole Art of the Stage [La pratique du théâtre]*, London: W. Cadman, 1684, p. 118).

30. Preface to *La Sylvanire, Théâtre du XVIIe siècle* I, ed. Jacques Scherer, Paris: Gallimard, 1986, p. 486.

31. Not without fluctuations, however: after a "classical" phase, Corneille returned to more complicated plots in 1645. And as has often been noted, authors of the years 1646–1666 had something of a predilection for the peripeteia.

32. "Quand il faut que l'un meure et par les mains de l'autre,/C'est un raisonnement bien mauvais que le vôtre." *Horace* III:4, *Pierre Corneille: Seven Plays*, tr. Samuel Solomon, New York: Random House, 1969, p. 157.

33. "On m'attend, Madame, il faut partir." *Britannicus* V:1, *Andromache*, op. cit., p. 201.

34. "A peine du Palais il sortait dans la rue,/Qu'une flèche a parti d'une main inconnue . . . " *Suréna* V:5, *Seven Plays*, op. cit., p. 650.

35. Jean Laporte, "Les verités de la grâce," *La doctrine de Port-Royal* II, Paris: PUF, 1923, pp. 74–94.

Painters and their Motifs

1. Cf. Alain Schnapp, "Des vases, des images et de quelques-uns de leurs usages sociaux," *Dialoghi di Archeologia* 3:1 (1985), pp. 69–75.

2. Concerning the ICONCLASS classification system perfected by Henri van de Waal at the University of Leyden for Western art of the sixteenth to eighteenth centuries, see Roelof van Straten's introduction, *Een Inleiding in de Iconografie* (Muiderberg: Coutinho, 1985).

3. Erwin Panofsky, *Studies in Iconology: Humanistic Themes in the Art of the Renaissance*, New York: Harper & Row, 1939, p. 5.

4. Ibid., p. 18.

5. Erwin Panofsky, *Renaissance and Renascences in Western Art*, New York: Harper & Row, 1972, pp. 84 et seq.; it is here that the "principle of disjunction" makes its first appearance.

6. Erwin Panofsky, *Studies in Iconology*, op. cit., p. 28.

7. Ibid., p. 30.

8. Erwin & Dora Panofsky, *Pandora's Box*, Princeton: Princeton University Press, 1962.

9. Cf. George Kubler, *The Shape of Time: Remarks on the History of Things*, New Haven & London: Yale University Press, 1976 [1962], p. 27.

10. Cf. Hubert Damisch, "Sémiologie et iconographie," *La sociologie de l'art et sa vocation interdisciplinaire: L'oeuvre et l'influence de Pierre Francastel*, Paris: Denoël/Gonthier, 1976, pp. 29–39.

11. "It is not always possible to establish a nonequivocal correspondence between a figurative work and its 'subject.' Consider, for instance, a painting of the 1880s representing the corner of a room, a man in an armchair reading the Journal des Débats, a mantlepiece with a Louis XV clock and a vase of flowers, a mirror on the wall, part of a window, and so on. Of all these objects, which is the 'true subject' of the picture?" (Robert Klein, *Form and Meaning: Essays on the Renaissance and Modern Art*, tr. Madeline Jay & Leon Wieseltier, New York: Viking, 1974, p. 143.)

12. Ad Reinhardt, "Art-as-Art," *Art International* (December 1962), qtd. in *American Artists on Art from 1940 to 1980*, ed. Ellen H. Johnson, New York: Harper & Row, 1982, p. 31.

13. Andrei Nakov's introduction to Viktor Shklovsky's *Résurrection du mot*, Paris: Gérard Lebovici, 1985, p. 33.

14. Ibid., p. 40.

15. Boris Tomachevsky, "Thématique," *Théorie de la littérature*, ed. & tr. Tzvetan Todorov, Paris: Seuil, 1965, p. 263.

16. Carlo Ginzburg, "De Aby Warburg à E. H. Gombrich: Notes sur un problème de méthode," *Le promeneur* XXXI (1984), p. 4.

17. Ernst Robert Curtius, "Antike Pathosformeln in der Literatur des Mittelalters," *Estudios dedicados a Menendez Pidal (I)*, Madrid: Consejo Superior de Investigaziones Cientificas, 1950: 257–263, p. 257.

18. Cf. Fritz Saxl, "Die Ausdrucksgebärden der bildenden Kunst" (1932), reprinted in Aby M. Warburg, *Ausegewählte Schriften und Würdigungen*, ed. Dieter Wuttke, Baden-Baden: Valentin Koerner, 1980, pp. 419–431.

19. Cf. Gertrud Bing's preface to the Italian translation of Warburg's *Collected Writings*, reprinted in German in A. M. Warburg, *Ausegewählte Schriften und Würdigungen*, op. cit.: 437–452, p. 444.

20. E. R. Curtius, "Antike Pathosformeln in der Literatur des Mittelalters," op. cit., p. 257.

21. E. R. Curtius, *European Literature and the Latin Middle Ages*, New York & Evanston: Harper & Row, 1953, p. 382. Warburg's famous phrase, *"Der liebe Gott*

steckt im Detail," which the erudite suspect him to have lifted from Flaubert, has already caused a lot of ink-shed. On November 21, 1949, Panofsky wrote to Gombrich, mentioning a conversation he'd had with Curtius (then at Princeton), and asking if he could identify the alleged quotation from Flaubert; Gombrich's reply is not known. (Panofsky's letter is cited by Dieter Wuttke in Aby M. Warburg, *Ausegewählte Schriften und Würdigungen,* op. cit., pp. 623–4.)

Still on the subject of Warburg's "little phrase," see William S. Heckscher's brilliant notes in *"Petites Perceptions:* an Account of *Sortes Warburgianae," Journal of Medieval and Renaissance Studies* 4 (1974), pp. 101–132.

22. William S. Heckscher, "The Genesis of Iconology," *Stil und Überlieferung in der Kunst des Abendlandes: Akten des 21. Internationalen Kongresses für Kunstgeschichte* in Bonn 1964, v. 3, Berlin: Gebr. Mann, 1967, pp. 239–61.

23. Guillaume Apollinaire, *The Cubist Painters: Aesthetic Mediations, 1913,* tr. Lionel Abel, New York: Wittenborn & Schultz, 1949, p. 12.

24. Shlomith Rimmon-Kenan, "What Is Theme and How Do We Get At It?", in this volume.

25. Cf. William Chapin Seitz's catalogue of the 'Art of Assemblage' exhibition. New York: Museum of Modern Art, 1961, p. 17.

26. André Chastel points out that the famous page of Gide's *Diary* is "ultimately too schematic and even confused" (*Fables, Formes, Figures* II, Paris: Flammarion, 1978, p. 73).

27. Cf. especially the catalogue of the 'Références' exhibition. Charleroi: Palais des Beaux-Arts, 1984.

28. Jean Dubuffet, *L'homme du commun à l'ouvrage,* Paris: Gallimard, 1973, p. 25.

29. Dora Vallier, "Mark Rothko ou l'absence de thème devenue thème," *XXᵉ siècle* 21 (May 1963), pp. 53–56.

30. Henri Matisse, "Henri Matisse on Modernism and Tradition," *The Studio* 109 (1935): 236–9, p. 238. For this problem in Pollock, see also Hubert Damisch, "La figure et l'entrelacs," *Fenêtre jaune cadmium,* Paris: Seuil, 1984, pp. 74–91.

31. Cf. the catalogue for the 'Journal de véloscopie' exhibition, Le Creusot: Crapac, 1975; the motif of the bicycle in art was chiefly explored at the Knokke-le-Zoute exhibition in 1976.

32. Cf. the catalogue for the 'Machine as Seen at the End of the Mechanical Age' exhibition. New York: Museum of Modern Art, 1968.

33. For the grid motif, see for example Rosalind Krauss' preface to the catalogue of the 'Grids, Format and Image in 20th Century Art' exhibition. New York: Pace Gallery, 1979.

34. *Littré* recognizes the musical motif (second definition: "a melodic phrase") and the architectural motif (third definition: "used of certain subjects for sculpture") but ignores the visual motif. For the *Petit Robert*, painting takes first place among the arts (second definition: "subject of a painting. *To work on the motif,* with a model"); then comes a subdivision of this second definition, "an isolated or repeated ornament, serving as a decorative theme"; and only then music, in a second subdivision: "a phrase or passage remarkable for its (melodic or rhythmic) *design*" (my emphasis).

Finally, as if to confirm the importance of the motif in the visual sense, the thesaurus index of the *Encyclopaedia Universalis* devotes a whole article to it, consigning the musical motif to the "musical composition" and "leitmotiv" entries.

35. John Rewald, "Les derniers motifs à Aix," in the catalogue of the 'Cézanne, les dernières années (1895–1906)' exhibition, Paris: Grand Palais, 1978, pp. 25–40.

36. In Meyer Schapiro, "The Apples of Cézanne: An Essay on the Meaning of Still-Life," *Modern Art, 19th and 20th Centuries: Selected Papers,* New York: George Braziller, 1978: 1–38, p. 16.

37. Ibid., p. 15.

38. Erwin Panofsky, *Studies in Iconology,* op. cit., p. 8.

39. Hubert Damisch, *Théorie du nuage: Pour une histoire de la peinture,* Paris: Seuil, 1972.

40. Cf. Pierre Georgel & Anne-Marie Lecoq, "Le motif de la fenêtre d'Alberti à Cézanne," in the catalogue of the 'D'un espace à l'autre: la fenêtre' exhibition. Saint-Tropez: Musée de l'Annonciade, 1978, p. 21.

41. See, for example, Daniel Arasse, "Les miroirs de la peinture," in *L'imitation, aliénation ou source de liberté?,* Paris: La Documentation française, "Rencontres de l'école du Louvre," 1985, p. 65. Cf. also Joachim Schickel, "Narziß oder die Erfindung der Malerei: Das Bild des Malers und das Bild des Spiegels," in the catalogue of the 'Spiegelbilder' exhibition, Kunstverein Hanover, 1982: *"Das Spiegelbild als Bild 'des Spiegels' und das Malerbild als Bild 'des Malers' sollen einander 'ähnlich' sein"* ("The mirror-picture, as a picture 'of the mirror,' and the painter-picture, as a picture 'of the painter,' should be 'similar' to one another"—p. 16).

42. Cf. André Chastel, "Le tableau dans le tableau," *Fables, Formes, Figures* II, op. cit., p. 77.

43. Jean Starobinski, *Portrait de l'artiste en saltimbanque* (1970), Paris: Flammarion, 1983, p. 7.

44. The two meanings of *this* motif, on which Masson is punning, are of course "élan" and "eland." [Editor's note.]

See my paper, "Chasseur d'images: Iconologie et cynégétique," which I gave at the *Imaginaires et réalités de la chasse aujourd'hui* colloquium in Chalon-sur-Saône (January 1986). Proceedings are due to appear.

In the same vein, Claude Gandelman has shown how the motif of the flayed body has come to stand for the artist herself as a human being flayed alive ("L'art comme *mortificatio carnis:* le thème de l'écorché vif, de Vésale à Kafka," chapter 3 of his book *Le regard dans le texte,* Paris: Klincksieck/Méridiens, 1986.)

45. For some of the questions raised by self-reflexivity, see Daniel Bougnoux, "Vices et vertus des cercles (pour introduire aux problèmes de l'auto-réference)," *Recherches sur la philosophie et le langage* 3 (1983): 7–33.

46. *Beyond Good and Evil,* tr. R. Hollingdale, London: Penguin, 1990, p. 221.

47. René Magritte, *Écrits complets,* ed. André Blavier, Paris: Flammarion, 1979: interview with Carl Waï, p. 663.

48. For the resistance of Magritte's work to iconological interpretation, see my article "L'iconologie chez Magritte" in *Cahiers pour un temps: Erwin Panofsky,* Paris: Centre Georges-Pompidou & Aix: Pandora Editions, 1983, pp. 167–183.

49. René Magritte, *Écrits complets,* op. cit., p. 367.

50. Cf. Magritte's letter to J. T. Soby of May 20, 1965, reprinted in the catalogue of the 'René Magritte' exhibition, New York: Museum of Modern Art, 1965, p. 8.

51. Cf. A. M. Hammacher, *René Magritte,* Paris: Cercle d'art, 1974, p. 43.

52. In *Nocturne* (1925), an important picture, being his first work—after an advertisement for the fashion house Norine called *Robe "Musette"*—to contain the motif of the painting-within-a-painting, the bird also occupies a similar structural position, on the borders of representation. Escaping from the painting-within-a-painting (a house on fire), it is portrayed on the very boundary, still belonging to the space of the painting-within-the-painting but already in the space of the painting it is flying to, aiming toward a skittle.

53. Xavière Gauthier, *Surréalisme et sexualité,* Paris: Gallimard, 1971, p. 343.

54. This drawing, along with three others, was only published in February 1940, in the first issue of *L'invention collective* (reprinted in Marcel Mariën, *L'activité surréaliste en Belgique,* Brussels: Lebeer-Hossman, 1979, p. 312). In all probability, however, its inspiration predates it. In a letter to Paul Nougé of May 1930(?), Magritte explicitly mentions two of the other three drawings: "When I have time, I'll make some drawings with a title in clear print beneath the figures. It will be as follows: if the figure represents a female torso, the title will be 'Secret Drawing'; for a drawing depicting a bored schoolboy doing his homework, the title would be: 'The Disagreeable Sound'; and so on." "Lettres surréalistes (1924–1940)," *Le fait accompli* 81–95 (May–August 1973), letter 187, p. 100.

55. Michel Serres formulated this idea at a colloquium on the concept of time, in the course of discussion. See "Maintenant est ce que je tiens avec la main," *Sur l'aménagement du temps: Essais de chronogénie,* Paris: Denoël/Gonthier, 1981, p. 244.

56. René Magritte, letter to Chavée (13 September 1960), *Écrits complets,* op. cit., p. 597.

57. René Magritte, *La ligne de vie,* ibid., p. 106. Ever since Freud's "Three Essays," we have known how things stand with the child as far as "innocence" is concerned. But I shall not dwell on this, except to mention—as Shklovsky does—that "in French erotic vocabulary, a certain sexual act performed in haste is called 'catching a sparrow.'" Interestingly, Shklovsky refers to this in the context of a discussion on the relationships between literature and film, citing it as a case of specific "subjects" whose "form resembles that of the 'image' and the pun" and which can therefore not be transferred onto the screen. *Littérature et cinématographe,* reprinted in an appendix to *Résurrection du mot,* op. cit., pp. 124–5.

It should be also noted—to change the tone completely—that in Richardson's *Iconology* (1779), a young girl holding a bird in her hand symbolizes the sense of touch.

58. In 1927, the same year as *La jeune fille mangeant un oiseau,* Magritte also paints *Le ciel meurtrier.* Four slaughtered birds hang in the air above a cliff; "the slaughtered birds have lost all their blood,/they fly without mercy and sing at random" writes Camille Goemans in *L'adieu a Marie* (1927), reprinted in Marcel Mariën, *L'activite surréaliste en Belgique,* op. cit., p. 143.

For the pleasure of killing birds, cf. also André Breton: "An illustrated history of France, probably the first that I ever saw, around the age of four, showed a very young King Louis XV massacring some birds in an aviary in that way, *just for his pleasure.* I do not know whether I had already discovered cruelty then, but there is no doubt that I retain, in relation to that image, a certain ambivalence in feeling." (*Mad Love,* tr. Mary Ann Caws, Lincoln & London: Univ. of Nebraska Press, 1987, p. 109).

And, on a different level, this text by Yves Klein in which the figure/ground relationship is inverted, the motif here being the sky, the bird being the disturbance which interrupts the narrator's contemplation of the background: "That day, as I lay stretched out on the beach at Nice, I started to feel hatred for the birds flying here and there in my beautiful cloudless blue sky, because they were trying to make holes in the greatest and most beautiful of my works. The birds must be destroyed, down to the last one." (qtd. in the Catalogue of the 'Nouveaux Réalistes' exhibition, Nice: Galerie des Ponchettes & Galerie d'art contemporain des musées de Nice, 1982, p. 60).

It would of course also be useful to mention the ancient belief that by eating the hearts of omen birds, one acquires their prophetic gifts; cf. the "Homoeopathic Magic of a Flesh Diet" chapter in J. G. Frazer, *Aftermath: A Supplement to the Golden Bough,* London: Macmillan, 1936.

59. Paul Nougé, letter to Magritte (April 1928), "Lettres surréalistes," op. cit., letter 144, p. 77.

60. Joachim Gasquet, *Joachim Gasquet's Cézanne,* tr. Christopher Pemberton, London: Thames & Hudson, 1991, p. 148.

61. René Magritte, *Écrits complets,* op. cit., p. 110.

62. Paul Eluard, *Les sentiers et les routes de la poésie*, qtd. in Frederick Tristan, *Le monde à l'envers*, Paris: Atelier Hachette/Massin, 1980, p. 82.

63. Paul Nougé, *Histoire de ne pas rire* (1956), Lausanne: L'âge de l'Homme, 1980, p. 259.
Some years earlier, Magritte wrote to Nougé: "I am becoming more aware that the objects in my painting have no cause (there is more effect than cause)" (Feb-Mar. 1928, "Lettres surréalistes," op. cit., letter 131, p. 69).

Theme in Classical Music

1. Cf. Émile Benveniste, "Sémiologie de la langue," *Semiotica* 1,1 (1969) and 1, 2 (1969).

2. Claude Lévi-Strauss, *The Naked Man,* tr. John & Doreen Weightman, London: Jonathan Cape, 1981, p. 649.

3. Alain Robbe-Grillet, *Ghosts in the Mirror,* tr. Jo Levy, London: Calder, 1988, pp. 154–5.

4. Lévi-Strauss, op. cit., p. 653.

5. Shlomith Rimmon-Kenan, "What Is Theme and How Do We Get At It?", in this volume.

6. Claude Bremond, "Concept et thème," *Poétique* 64 (1985), 415–423, p. 421.

7. Haydn and Beethoven often begin to "develop" right from the exposition. Conversely, it is quite common for a new theme to appear during the development. The two main themes of Liszt's *Sonata in B minor* are only stated in an *allegro energico* after an initial *lento*, etc. If we are to believe Thomas Mann's character Wendell Kretschmar, Beethoven put an end to the sonata as a traditional art form from opus 111 onward (*Doctor Faustus,* tr. H. T. Lowe-Porter, New York: Vintage, 1948, p. 55).

8. Texts dating from January 1791 and July/September 1793 concerning composers', artists' and designers' rights of ownership to writings in all genres (cf. Michel Gautreau, *La musique et les musiciens en droit français,* Paris: PUF, 1970, p. 4).

9. A reference to Barthes' *The Pleasure of the Text* (tr. Richard Miller, New York: Hill & Wang, 1975, p. 27). [Editor's note.]

10. By Stendhal (1838). [Editor's note.]

11. Claude Lévi-Strauss, *The Raw and the Cooked,* tr. John & Doreen Weightman, New York & Evanston: Harper & Row, 1969, p. 30.

12. Jean-Jacques Rousseau's article "Sonate" in the *Dictionnaire de musique* (1768). *A Complete Dictionary of Music: Consisting of a copious Explanation of all Words necessary*

to a true Knowledge and Understanding of Music, tr. William Waring, London: J. Murray, 1779, p. 369.

Punctuation has been amended slightly and the last sentence added. [Editor's note.]

13. An allusion to Baudelaire's *postulations simultanées:* "il y a dans tout homme, à toute heure, deux postulations simultanées, l'une vers Dieu, l'autre vers Satan." ("In every man, and at all times, there are two simultaneous yearnings—the one towards God, the other towards Satan." *My Heart Laid Bare and other prose-writings,* tr. Norman Cameron, London: Weidenfeld & Nicholson, 1950, p. 181.) [Editor's note.]

14. Franz Lizst, *Gesammelte Schriften* II, Hildesheim & New York: Georg Olms Verlag, 1978, pp. 5 & 26.

15. Claude Debussy, *Monsieur Croche et autres écrits,* Paris: Gallimard, 1971, p. 271.

16. Henri Pousseur, *Fragments théoriques sur la musique expérimentale,* Brussels: Editions de l'institut de sociologie, Université libre de Bruxelles, 1970, p. 246.

17. Roland Barthes, *The Pleasure of the Text,* op. cit., p. 14.

18. Leonard Bernstein, *The Unanswered Question: Six Talks at Harvard,* Cambridge, Mass.: Harvard Univ. Press, 1976; see especially pp. 159–167.

19. Still, its features are not so distinct as to preclude diverse interpretations. During World War II, the theme in its original form provided the signature tune for Nazi news bulletins; in inverted form, reduced to a structure without specific pitch, it served as an emblem of free France on radio London. It is true that the percussion part (four clashes of cymbals, " . . . —") means "V" (for "victory") in Morse code.

20. André Boucourechliev, "Transmutations," *L'arc* 40 (1970), pp. 49–56.

21. Henri Pousseur, *Musique, Sémantique, Société,* Paris & Tournai: Casterman, 1972, p. 84.

22. Cf. Alberto Basso on the Goldberg aria: "This aria is characterized by its bass line, eight descending quarter notes in the first four bars, reintroducing a figure extremely common in the literature of the period and which lasted until Beethoven, undaunted in the midst of so many musical revolutions: a *fundamentum* (*ground* to the English, *bass* for the French) known as the Italian galliard" (*Jean-Sebastien Bach,* Paris: Fayard, 1985, vol. II, p. 763).

According to Bach's first biographer, Forkel, Bach himself was well aware of working on a traditional harmonic *ground* in the Goldberg variations: "These pieces were to be of a calm, rather joyous nature, to restore him during his nights of rest. Bach felt that this aim would be achieved by means of variations; up to then he had considered this type of work, in which harmony periodically takes similar turns, a highly thankless task" (Gilles Cantagrel, *Bach en son temps,* Paris: Hachette, 1982, pp. 421–22).

23. For Boris de Schloezer, the harmonic schema of the aria—a formal element—admittedly intervenes in the harmonic structure of the thirty variations which follow: but by delimiting, down to the last detail, the nature of the complex field in which variations are to be produced, it determines the work in its melodic and rhythmic structure. (*Introduction à J. S. Bach* [1947], Paris: Gallimard, 1979, p. 296).

The End of an Anathema

1. Georges Leroux, "Du topos au thème," *Poétique* 64 (1985), pp. 445–454.

2. Peter Cryle, "Thematic Criticism," in this volume.

3. Gerald Prince, "Thématiser," *Poétique* 64 (1985), pp. 425–433. An English version may be found in *Narrative as Theme: Studies in French Fiction*, Lincoln: University of Nebraska Press, 1992.

4. Lubomír Doležel, "A Semantics for Thematics: The Case of the Double," in this volume.

5. Menachem Brinker, "Theme and Interprétation," in this volume.
Shlomith Rimmon-Kenan, "What is Theme and How Do We Get At It?," in this volume.

6. Philippe Hamon, "Thème et effet de réel," *Poétique* 64 (1985), pp. 495–503.

7. Arthur Danto, *The Transfiguration of the Commonplace*, Cambridge, MA: Harvard University Press, 1981. See especially pp. 1–6.

CONTRIBUTORS

Jean-Yves Bosseur, composer and theoretician at the Centre national de la recherche scientifique (CNRS) in Paris, has writen *Music: Passion for an Art* (New York: Rizzoli, 1991), *Vocabulaire de la musique contemporaine* (Paris: Minerve, 1992) and, with Dominique Bosseur, *Révolutions musicales: la musique contemporaine depuis 1945* (Paris: Le Sycomore, 1979).

Claude Bremond, professor of the Ecole des hautes études en sciences sociales in Paris, is the author of *Logique du récit* (Paris: Seuil, 1973), co-author of *L'«Exemplum»* (Turnhout, Belgium: Brepols, 1982) and *Mille et un contes de la nuit* (Paris: Gallimard, 1991), and co-editor of *Formes médiévales du conte merveilleux* (Paris: Stock, 1989). He has also written extensively on narratology, film studies, folklore, the exemplum and the *Arabian Nights*.

Menachem Brinker has published numerous studies in Hebrew, among them *Through the Imaginary: Meaning and Presentation in the Fictive Enterprise* (Tel Aviv: Porter Institute for Poetry and Semiotics, 1980), *Aesthetics as Criticism: Issues and Points in its Development* (Tel Aviv: Department of Defence, 1982), *The Singularity of Brenner* (Jerusalem: Israeli National Institute for Sciences, 1987), *Is Literary Study Possible? Essays on the Boundaries between Philosophy and Literature* (Tel Aviv: Workers' Library, 1989) and *Up to the Tiberian Path: an Essay on Storytelling and Thought in the Work of Brenner* (Tel Aviv: 'Am Oved, 1990). He currently holds a joint position in Philosophy and Comparative Literature at the Hebrew University of Jerusalem.

Peter Cryle has written *L'exil et le royaume d'Albert Camus: essai d'analyse* (Paris: Minard, 1973), *Roger Martin du Gard, ou, De l'intégrité de l'être à l'intégrité du roman* (Paris: Minard, 1984) and *The Thematics of Commitment: the Tower and the Plain* (Princeton: Princeton University Press, 1985). He teaches French literature at the University of Queensland, Australia.

Lubomír Dolezel now teaches at the University of Toronto in Canada. While in Czechoslovakia, he wrote *O stylu moderni ceske prozy* (Prague: Nakl. Ceskoslovenske Akademie Ved, 1960) and *Knizka o jazyce a stylu soudobe ceske literatury* (Prague: Orbis, 1962); his publications since then include *Narrative*

Modes in Czech literature (Toronto: University of Toronto Press, 1973) and *Occidental poetics: tradition and progress* (Lincoln: University of Nebraska Press, 1990). He has also co-authored a *Dictionary of the Czech Literary Language* (University, AL: University of Alabama Press, 1966) and co-edited *An annotated bibliography of statistical stylistics* (Ann Arbor: University of Michigan Press, 1968).

Françoise Escal, a professor at the Ecole des hautes études en sciences sociales, has written *Espaces sociaux, espaces musicaux* (Paris: Payot, 1979), *Le compositeur et ses modèles* (Paris: Presses universitaires de France, 1984) and *Contrepoints: musique et littérature* (Paris: Klincksieck, 1990).

Thomas Pavel, author of *Infléxions de voix* (Montreal: Presses de l'Université de Montréal, 1976), *La Syntaxe narrative des tragédies de Corneille* (Paris: Klincksieck, 1976), *The Poetics of Plot: The Case of English Renaissance Drama* (Mineapolis: University of Minnesota Press, 1985), *Fictional Worlds* (Cambridge, MA: Harvard University Press, 1986) and *The Feud of Language* (Oxford: Blackwell, 1989; originally published in French), is professor of French and Comparative Literature at Princeton University.

Shlomith Rimmon-Kenan has published *The Concept of Ambiguity: the Example of James* (Chicago: University of Chicago Press, 1977) and *Narrative Fiction: Contemporary Poetics* (London: Methuen, 1983), as well as editing the *Discourse in Psychoanalysis and Literature* collection (London: Methuen, 1987). She teaches English at the Hebrew University of Jerusalem.

Georges Roque, a historian of contemporary art at the CNRS, is the author of *Ceci n'est pas un Magritte: essai sur Magritte et la publicité* (Paris: Flammarion, 1983).

Jean-Marie Schaeffer, also a research associate at the CNRS, has published the following texts on literary and visual aesthetics: *La naissance de la littérature: la théorie esthétique du romantisme allemand* (Paris: Presses de l'Ecole Normale Supérieure, 1983); *L'image précaire: du dispositif photographique* (Paris: Seuil, 1987); *Qu'est-ce qu'un genre littéraire?* (Paris: Seuil, 1989); and *L'art de l'âge moderne: l'esthétique et la philosophie de l'art du XVIIIe siècle à nos jours* (Paris: Gallimard, 1992).

Cesare Segre teaches at the University of Pavia in Italy. His publications include *I segni e la critica* (Torino: Einaudi, 1969), translated as *Semiotics and Literary Criticism* by John Meddemmen (The Hague: Mouton, 1973); *Le strutture e il tempo* (Torino: Einaudi, 1974), translated—also by John

Meddemmen—as *Structures and Time: Narration, Poetry, Models* (Chicago: University of Chicago Press, 1979); *Lingua, stile e società* (Milano: Feltrinelli, 1974); *Semiotica, Storia e cultura* (Padova: Liviana, 1977); *Semiotica filologica: testo e modelli culturali* (Torino: Einaudi, 1979); *Avviamento all'analisi del testo letterario* (Torino: Einaudi, 1985), translated as *Introduction to the Analysis of the Literary Text*, (tr. John Meddemmen, Bloomington: Indiana University Press, 1988); and *Fuori del mondo: i modelli nella fellia e nelle immagini dell'aldila* (Torino: Einaudi, 1990).

Werner Sollors, professor of American Studies and Comparative Literature at Harvard, is the author of *Amiri Baraka/LeRoi Jones: the Quest for a "Populist Modernism"* (New York: Columbia University Press, 1978), *Beyond Ethnicity: Consent and Descent in American Culture* (New York: Columbia University Press, 1986) and *The Invention of Ethnicity* (New York: Oxford University Press, 1989); he has also edited *Blacks at Harvard: a Documentary History of African-American Experience at Harvard and Radcliffe* (New York: New York University Press, 1993) and *The Return of Thematic Criticism* (Cambridge, MA: Harvard University Press, 1993).

NAME INDEX

SUBJECT INDEX

aboutness, 4, 9, 117, 126, 132, 181–2, 185–9; as potential object of a thematizing attention, 190; not reducible to intention, 191; mobile, 113; eliminated by certain works, 142, 187; different types: referential, linguistic, rhetorical, fictional, 37–8, 43, 53; semantic and pragmatic, 12; absolute and relative, 40, 43

action, modes, theories and thematics of, 57–8, 60, 62–3

art, visual. *See* theme.

artist: situation and position of, 5, 140, 153, 157, 182, 186, 216; selecting themes and/or motifs, 139, 140–7, 171–3, 191; privileging theme over form, 142–3

attention (referential, thematic), 2, 4, 184–91; flexibility of, 34, 36, 113, 185–6; as theme, 188

author. *See* artist.

catalogue. *See* inventory.

content. *See* form.

critique, nouvelle, 45–6, 52

Don Juan theme, 105–6, 108, 181

double, theme of the, 93–100, 207; simultaneous type, valorized over exclusive type, 96, 98–9; 'Amphytrion,' 'Orlando' and eponymous types, 95–6; genesis (by fusion, scission or metamorphosis), 97–8

exemplification (of a theme, by textual segments), 3, 103–5, 107–8, 110–2; possibility of borrowing a specific exemplification, 108; cases of exemplification without instantiation, 110; cases of neither, 104

Faust subject and its two themes, 3, 103–4, 110–1, 156–7, 184

folklore studies, 22–3, 26, 57, 90, 186

form and content, dichotomy of, 15–17; in music, 150; precedence in creation (inductive and deductive approaches), 142–3, 154; difficulty of describing either in purely formal terms, 120, 126, 138; constant crossover between the categories, 91, 184, 188; limited autonomy of form, 182, 184; form functioning as theme, 1, 54, 184; form essential to content, 91–2, 133, 150, 183–4; form and content changing places, 187

formalism, 1, 6, 21–4, 45, 48–52, 54–5, 132–3, 149,182–3. *See also* Propp, Tomashevsky, Veselovsky

function, 24, 27–8, 92, 100, 120, 164

generic factors: conflicting with a theme's own hypertextual logic, 2–3, 26, 36, 97, 103–112; multiplicity of, leading to internal conflict, 3, 106, 112, 118, 120–1

generic specialization, 3, 118, 120–1

Geneva school, 45. *See also* Poulet.

genre: anti-legend, 104, 106–9, 111–2; collage, 134–5; drama, 36, 39–40, 104–9, 113–26, 186; epic, 3, 35, 118, 120–2; morality play, 108–9, 185; musical theater, 169–71; program music, 154, 156, 160; serial music, 159, 171–4; sonata, 151–2, 155, 157, 160–2, 164–6; tragedy, 36, 39, 113–26; variations form, 151, 162, 164–5. *See also* generic factors.

hermeneutics, 6, 41, 49, 51, 54–5, 106–7, 111–2, 142, 182–3. *See also* interpretation.